easy BIKING
in NORTHERN CALIFORNIA

More Than 100 Places
Anyone Can Ride This Weekend

ANN MARIE BROWN

1-57354-061-7

Easy Biking in Northern California:
More Than 100 Places Anyone Can Ride This Weekend
Second EDITION

Ann Marie Brown

Published by
Avalon Travel Publishing
5855 Beaudry St.
Emeryville, CA 94608, USA

Please send all comments, corrections, additions, amendments, and critiques to:
Foghorn Press
AVALON TRAVEL PUBLISHING
5855 BEAUDRY ST.
EMERYVILLE, CA 94608, USA
email: atpfeedback@avalonpub.com
www.travelmatters.com

2nd edition— June 1999
5 4 3 2

ISBN: 1-57354-061-7
ISSN: 1086-7848

Distributed by Publishers Group West

Printed in the United States by Quest Print

Editor in Chief	Kyle Morgan
Maps	Kirk McInroy
Photo Credits	Ann Marie Brown
Cover Photo	Mark Gibson, Mount Shasta

INTRODUCTION

When I was a kid, I loved riding my bike more than just about anything. I rode it all around the rural area where my family lived, explored back roads, pedaled around the edges of our local lake, and cruised over to my friends' houses. I thought that the bicycle was the perfect means of transportation.

As I got older, things changed. I attended college, then graduate school, then entered the working world. I lived in big cities—Los Angeles and later San Francisco. I was in a hurry most of the time, and bicycling didn't seem like much of an option any more. My 10-speed sat in storage for years; eventually I sold it at a garage sale. When mountain bikes became popular in the early 1980s, I bought one and tried it out, but quickly learned that mountain biking can be a far cry from a relaxing outdoor experience. That first day's ride consisted of too much grunting, sweating, and climbing rocky, steep hills—only to fly down the other side fearing for my life.

I thought about it some more and realized what I really wanted was just to get on a bike and pedal around, somewhere where I didn't have to worry about car traffic, rocks, or steep hills. Somewhere where I could feel the wind in my hair, stop and take in a pretty view, then glide along some more. I wanted paths where I'd find cool, shady forests, maybe a lake or a stream, or even some wildlife. I wanted trails that required no herculean effort, rides with no worries. And so the idea for this book was born.

I made it my mission to seek out paved and dirt bike paths in Northern California where you could ride virtually free of car traffic; where you could take your kids and not fear for their safety; where there were no painfully steep hills to climb; and where you could just pedal, glide, and let your thoughts flow freely.

In the process of writing this book, I put more than 1,000 miles on my bicycle and more than 5,000 miles on my car. To choose these 110 bike rides, I rode every trail in this book, some of them many times over. I rode many other trails that never made it into these pages, often because they were too difficult or too dull to ensure that everybody would have fun. What I found in researching this book is that there are plenty of bike trails out there for ordinary people, not just for hardcore cyclists. And when people ride them, they feel pretty happy.

Hope to see you on the trail—

Ann Marie Brown

CONTENTS

Answers to Questions—p. 10

How to Use This Book—p. 16

Best Bike Rides List—p. 17

North Coast & The Redwoods—p. 19

1. Lake Earl & Yontocket Indian Village Trail, *Lake Earl State Park*... 20
2. Howland Hill Road, *Jedediah Smith Redwoods State Park* 22
3. Coastal Trail, *Prairie Creek Redwoods State Park* 24
4. Jogging Trail/Davison Trail, *Prairie Creek Redwoods State Park* 26
5. Lost Man Creek Trail, *Redwood National Park* 28
6. Hammond Trail, *Humboldt County Parks* 30
7. Arcata Marsh & Wildlife Sanctuary Trail, *City of Arcata* 32
8. Bull Creek Road to Gould Barn, *Humboldt Redwoods State Park* ... 33

Redding & Shasta—p. 35

9. Siskiyou Lake North Shore, *Shasta-Trinity National Forest* 36
10. Waters Gulch & Fish Loop Trails, *Shasta-Trinity National Forest* .. 37
11. Clikapudi Creek Trail to Jones Valley Camp,
    Shasta-Trinity National Forest 39
12. Tower House Historic District & Mill Creek Trails,
    Whiskeytown National Recreation Area 41
13. Water Ditch Trail, *Whiskeytown National Recreation Area* 43
14. Sacramento River Trail, *City of Redding* 45

Napa, Sonoma, & Mendocino—p. 47

15. Old Haul Road, *MacKerricher State Park* 48
16. Fern Canyon & Falls Loop Trails, *Russian Gulch State Park* 50
17. Fern Canyon Trail, *Van Damme State Park* 52
18. Pygmy Forest Trail Loop, *Salt Point State Park* 53
19. Gerstle Cove to Stump Beach Cove Trail, *Salt Point State Park* 56
20. Sebastopol-Santa Rosa Multi-Use Trail,
    Sonoma County Regional Parks 58
21. Howarth Park & Spring Lake Park Trails,
    Sonoma County Regional Parks 59
22. Lake Ilsanjo Trail Loop, *Annadel State Park* 61
23. Meadow & Hillside Trail Loop, *Sugarloaf Ridge State Park* 63
24. Lake Trail, *Jack London State Historic Park* 65

Sierra Foothills & Central Valley—p. 67

25. Bidwell Park Ride, *City of Chico* 68
26. Chico to Durham Bike Path, *Butte County* 70
27. Hardrock Trail, *Empire Mine State Historic Park* 71
28. Quarry Road Trail, *Auburn State Recreation Area* 73
29. American River Parkway: Beal's Point to Negro Bar,
      Folsom Lake State Recreation Area 75

Tahoe—p. 77

30. Carr, Feely, & Island Lakes Trail, *Tahoe National Forest* 78
31. Watson Lake & Fibreboard Freeway Loop, *Northstar at Tahoe* 80
32. Burton Creek State Park Trails, *Burton Creek State Park* 83
33. Truckee River Recreation Trail, *Tahoe City Parks and Recreation* 85
34. Ward Creek Trail, *Tahoe National Forest* 87
35. Blackwood Canyon, *Tahoe National Forest* 88
36. General Creek Loop, *Sugar Pine Point State Park* 90
37. Pope-Baldwin Bike Path, *Lake Tahoe Basin Management Unit* 92
38. Fallen Leaf Lake Trails, *Tahoe National Forest* 94
39. Angora Lakes Trail, *Tahoe National Forest* 96

North San Francisco Bay Area—p. 99

40. Marshall Beach Trail, *Point Reyes National Seashore* 100
41. Abbott's Lagoon Trail, *Point Reyes National Seashore* 101
42. Bull Point Trail, *Point Reyes National Seashore* 103
43. Estero Trail to Sunset Beach, *Point Reyes National Seashore* 105
44. Estero Trail to Drake's Head, *Point Reyes National Seashore* 108
45. Muddy Hollow Trail, *Point Reyes National Seashore* 110
46. Coast Trail, *Point Reyes National Seashore* 112
47. Bear Valley Trail to Arch Rock, *Point Reyes National Seashore* 114
48. Olema Valley Trail, *Golden Gate National Recreation Area* 116
49. Tomales Bay Trail, *Golden Gate National Recreation Area* 117
50. Bolinas Ridge Trail, *Golden Gate National Recreation Area* 119
51. Cross Marin Trail & Sir Francis Drake Bikeway, *Golden Gate
      National Recreation Area & Samuel P. Taylor State Park* 121
52. Devil's Gulch Trail, *Samuel P. Taylor State Park* 124
53. Kent Pump Road, *Marin Municipal Water District* 126
54. Lake Lagunitas Loop, *Marin Municipal Water District* 128
55. Phoenix Lake to Bolinas-Fairfax Road,
      Marin Municipal Water District 130
56. Las Gallinas Wildlife Ponds, *Las Gallinas Valley Sanitary District* .. 132
57. Shoreline Trail, *China Camp State Park* 134

58. Tiburon Bike Path, *City of Tiburon* 136
59. Perimeter Trail, *Angel Island State Park* 138
60. Laurel Dell Fire Road, *Marin Municipal Water District* 140
61. Old Stage Road: Pantoll to West Point Inn,
    Mount Tamalpais State Park 142
62. Old Railroad Grade: East Peak to West Point Inn,
    Mount Tamalpais State Park 144
63. Tennessee Valley Trail, *Golden Gate National Recreation Area* 146
64. Mill Valley & Sausalito Bike Path, *Marin County Parks* 148

East San Francisco Bay Area—p. 151

65. Point Pinole Road & Bay View Trail,
    Point Pinole Regional Shoreline 152
66. Wildcat Creek Trail, *Wildcat Canyon Regional Park* 154
67. Nimitz Way Bike Trail, *Tilden Regional Park* 156
68. Lafayette Reservoir Trail, *East Bay Municipal Utility District* 158
69. Lafayette-Moraga Regional Trail, *East Bay Regional Park District* .. 161
70. Iron Horse Regional Trail to Danville,
    East Bay Regional Park District 163
71. Eastern Contra Costa Regional Trails,
    East Bay Regional Park District 164
72. Round Valley Regional Preserve, *East Bay Regional Park District* ... 166
73. Morgan Territory Regional Preserve,
    East Bay Regional Park District 168
74. Lake Chabot West & East Shore Trails,
    Anthony Chabot Regional Park 171
75. Bay View Trail, *Coyote Hills Regional Park* 173
76. Tidelands Loop & Newark Slough Trail,
    San Francisco Bay National Wildlife Refuge 175

San Francisco & South Bay Area—p. 177

77. Coastal Trail & Great Highway Bike Path,
    Golden Gate National Recreation Area 178
78. Lake Merced Bike Path, *San Francisco Parks & Recreation* 180
79. Saddle & Old Guadalupe Trails,
    San Bruno Mountain State & County Park 182
80. Sweeney Ridge Paved Trail,
    Golden Gate National Recreation Area 184
81. Sawyer Camp Recreation Trail, *San Mateo County Parks* 186
82. Cañada Road Bicycle Sundays, *San Mateo County Parks* 188
83. Ranch Trail, *Burleigh Murray Ranch State Park* 190

84. Half Moon Bay Bike Path, *Half Moon Bay State Beach* 192
85. Corte Madera Trail, *Arastradero Preserve* 193
86. Dumbarton Bridge Ride,
     San Francisco Bay National Wildlife Refuge 195
87. Mountain View to Palo Alto Baylands,
     Mountain View Shoreline Park 196
88. Alviso Slough Trail, *San Francisco Bay National Wildlife Refuge* 199
89. Penitencia Creek Trail, *Alum Rock Park* 200
90. Los Gatos Creek Trail, *Vasona Lake County Park* 202
91. Coyote Creek Trail, *Coyote Hellyer County Park* 204
92. Russian Ridge Loop, *Russian Ridge Open Space Preserve* 206
93. Old Haul Road, *Pescadero Creek County Park* 208
94. Skyline-to-the-Sea Trail, *Big Basin Redwoods State Park* 209
95. Wilder Ridge & Zane Gray Loop, *Wilder Ranch State Park* ....,,,, 212
96. Old Landing Cove Trail, *Wilder Ranch State Park* 214
97. Pipeline Road, *Henry Cowell Redwoods State Park* 216
98. Aptos Creek Fire Road, *Forest of Nisene Marks State Park* 219
99. Monterey Peninsula Recreational Trail, *Monterey & Pacific Grove* . 220

Yosemite & Mammoth Lakes—p. 223

100. Merced River Railroad Grade, *BLM Folsom Resource Area* 224
101. Yosemite Valley Bike Path, *Yosemite National Park* 226
102. Bodie Ghost Town Ride, *Bodie State Historic Park* 229
103. Mono Lake South Tufa Area Trails,
      Mono Lake Tufa State Reserve 230
104. Inyo Craters Loop, *Inyo National Forest* 233
105. Shady Rest Trail, *Shady Rest Town Park* 235
106. Paper Route & Juniper Trails, *Mammoth Mountain Bike Park* 236
107. Beach Cruiser Trail, *Mammoth Mountain Bike Park* 239
108. Horseshoe Lake Loop, *Inyo National Forest* 240
109. Twin Lakes Route, *Inyo National Forest* 243
110. Hot Creek Fish Hatchery & Geothermal Area,
      Inyo National Forest 245

Index—p. 248

Appendix—p. 261

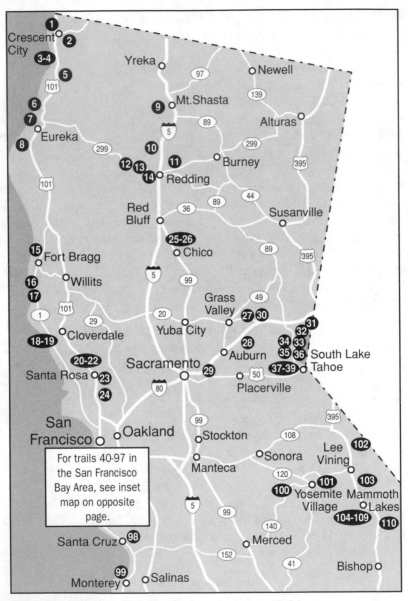

For trails 40-97 in the San Francisco Bay Area, see inset map on opposite page.

Rides 1-8, North Coast & The Redwoods, pages 19-34
Rides 9-14, Redding & Shasta, pages 35-46
Rides 15-24, Napa, Sonoma, & Mendocino, pages 47-66
Rides 25-29, Sierra Foothills & Central Valley, pages 67-76
Rides 30-39, Tahoe, pages 77-98
Rides 40-99 San Francisco Bay Area (see inset map opposite)
Rides 100-110, Yosemite & Mammoth Lakes, pages 223-247

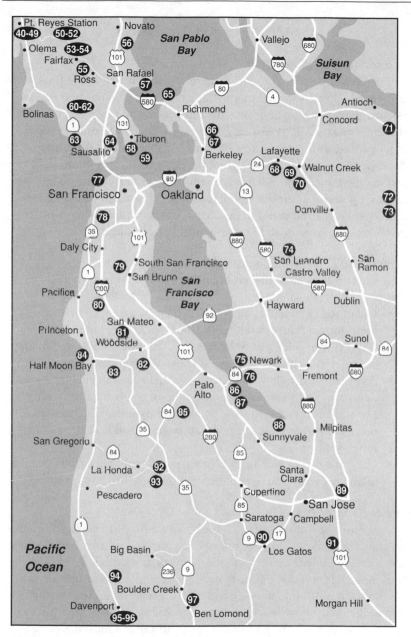

San Francisco Bay Area (inset)

Rides 40-64, North San Francisco Bay Area, pages 99-150
Rides 65-76, East San Francisco Bay Area, pages 151-176
Rides 77-99, San Francisco & South Bay Area, pages 177-222

ANSWERS TO QUESTIONS

What's an Easy Bike Ride?

An easy ride is one in which there are no thousand-foot hill climbs, and your legs aren't shaved by the hot exhaust of passing cars. An easy ride can be on pavement or on dirt, but it must be rideable and enjoyable by almost anybody. An easy bike ride is fun for families, or for older people, or for young and fit people who are tired of pushing all the time. An easy ride offers a good payoff, a reason for going besides just for the exercise, whether it is a stunning view, a chance to see wildlife, or a peaceful jaunt through a fern-filled forest. An easy bike ride takes you away from cars and exhaust fumes to a place where you can pedal without worries and focus on your surroundings.

How Were These Trails Selected?

These rules were followed in choosing the 110 bike trails in this book:

- The paved rides had to be less than 15 miles long and rideable in under 2.5 hours. Some are as short as 5 miles long.
- The dirt trail rides had to be less than 10 miles long and rideable in under 2.5 hours. Some are as short as 2.5 miles long.
- Every ride had to have something special about it, such as a great destination or a reason for doing it besides just for the exercise.
- The trails had to be rideable by almost anybody, which meant no trails with terribly steep elevation gains and no extremely rough trail surfaces.
- The trails had to be completely separated from auto traffic, or in an area where cars are the exception rather than the rule.

What Kind of Bike Do I Need?

Seventy-one of the rides in this book are on dirt trails and suitable for mountain bikes ("fat tire" bikes) only, and the other 39 are on pavement and suitable for either mountain bikes or road bikes ("skinny tire" bikes). If you don't already own a bike and are planning to buy one, keep in mind that a mountain bike is generally more versatile and well-suited for various types of trails. Many adults who return to bicycling after years away from the sport find that a mountain bike, with its upright handlebar positioning and wider tires, is more comfortable to ride. Also, the huge range of gears now available on mountain bikes (usually somewhere around 21 speeds) makes hill climbing a lot easier.

Take a trip to your local bike store and test ride a few bikes. Make sure a friendly, knowledgeable salesperson helps you get the right "fit" in a bike. If you test ride a few different models, you'll see the wide variance in the way a bike can fit your torso, arms, and legs. A good fit is far more important than what brand you buy or how many speeds your bike has.

If you're riding with children who are too young to be on their own bikes, you can choose between child seats, which are positioned directly behind your saddle, or child trailers, which are separate units with wheels. The trailer hooks on to your bike, and the child rides behind you in his or her own little vehicle. Trailers are great, but they are only useful on paved trails. A child seat is more versatile and can be used on varied terrain.

What Should I Bring on the Trail?

• *A helmet for your head.* Put it on and strap it securely. Don't get on your bike without one. Many parks are now requiring riders to wear helmets, and the ones that don't, should. Just as you wear your seat belt when you drive, wear your helmet when you ride. It's not optional equipment because your head is not optional equipment.

• *Cycling gloves and cycling shorts.* These *are* optional equipment, but many riders say that cycling gloves and shorts make their trip a lot more comfortable. Cycling gloves come with padded palms, so the nerves in your hands are protected from extensive pressure when you lean your upper body weight on the handlebars. Cycling shorts come with padding in the butt, and you can guess what that does.

• *Food and water.* There's nothing like being hungry or thirsty to spoil a good time, or make you anxious about getting back to the car. Even if you aren't the least bit hungry or thirsty when you start, you may feel completely different after an hour of riding. Always carry a water bottle on your bike, and make sure it is full of fresh, clean water when you head out. A small daypack or fannysack filled with snacks and extra water can keep you happily supplied for the day.

• *A map of the park or area you're visiting.* Sometimes trails are well-signed, sometimes they're not. Signs get knocked down or disappear with alarming frequency, due to rain, wind, or park visitors looking for souvenirs. Don't rely on trail signs to keep you from getting lost.

Get a map from the managing agency of the park you're visiting. All their names and phone numbers are in this book. At state parks and national parks you can often just pick up a map when you drive into the park entrance. If it costs a buck, pay it. City and county parks usually have maps that are available for free if you write or phone for them, and maps are often posted at trailheads in the park. Trails located in national forest lands are the only ones that may require a little advance planning. For these, send $4 per map to USDA Forest Service, Office of Information, 1323 Club Drive, Vallejo, CA 94592 and ask for a map of the national forest you'll be visiting. For more information, their phone number is (707) 562-8737.

We've drawn some trail maps in this book to help you find your way on more complicated loop trips and connecting trails, but they are no substitute for the real thing. Get an updated trail map from the park you are visiting whenever possible.

• *A small bike repair kit.* Nothing major is required here, but if you're going to be more than a mile or two from your car, you better have what you'll need to fix a flat tire. You can travel great distances quickly on a bike. This is never more apparent than when you get a flat tire after 30 minutes of riding and it takes you two hours to walk back. So why walk? Carry a spare tube, a patch kit, tire levers, and a bike pump attached to your bike frame. Learn how to use them—your local bike shop can show you how. Here's a critical tip: Make sure your bike pump fits the valves on your bike (yes, they make two different kinds). This will save you a great deal of potential swearing.

It's also a good idea to carry a set of allen wrenches and a crescent wrench. These are good for adjusting the angle on your bike seat, making minor repairs, and fidgeting with brake and gear cables. If you're riding on dirt trails, carry extra chain lubricant with you, or at least keep some in your car. You'll use it.

Finally, remember to check your tire pressure, seat height, brakes, and shifters before you begin each ride. Lubricate your chain. Make sure all is well before you set out on the trail.

• *A bike lock.* This, too, is optional equipment, but it comes in handy when you want to stop for a latte. Some of the trails in this book combine a bike ride with a short hike, in which case a bike lock is a necessity. Never leave your bike unlocked and unattended.

• *Extra clothing.* On the trail, weather and temperature conditions can change at any time. It may get windy or start to rain, or you can get too warm as you ride uphill in the sun and then too cold as you ride downhill in the shade. Wear layers. Bring a lightweight jacket and a rain poncho with you. Tie your extra clothes around your waist or put them in your daypack.

• *Sunglasses and sunscreen.* Of course you know the dangers of the sun. Wear both sunglasses and sunscreen. Put on your sunscreen 30 minutes before you go outdoors so it has time to take effect.

• *First aid kit.* While first-aid items are probably not essential if you're riding on paved bike trails near urban areas, they're more than a good idea when riding on dirt trails in rural areas. Mountain bikers, take note: A few large and small band-aids, moleskin for blisters, and an ace bandage for minor emergencies can be valuable tools. Also, if anyone in your party is allergic to bee stings or anything else in the outdoors, carry their medication. I also like to carry a Swiss army knife, one with several blades, a can opener, and a scissors on it. I've never used it to perform first aid, but it does come in handy for picnics. Finally, it's a good idea to carry matches in a waterproof container and a candle, just in case you ever need to build a fire in a serious emergency.

What If Somebody Gets Lost?

If you're riding with a family or group, make sure everyone knows to stay together. Because riders come in all different ability levels, it's very easy for one rider to get way ahead or way behind the others. One hill can quickly turn a group ride into a solo journey. Keep your eyes on each other as you ride. If you're a strong rider, be prepared to stop and wait for others.

If anyone decides to split off from the group for any reason, make sure they have a trail map with them and know how to read it. Also, ensure that everyone in your group knows the key rules regarding what to do if they get lost:

• Whistle or shout loudly at regular intervals.

• "Hug" a tree. Or a big rock or a bush. That means find a noticeable landmark, sit down next to it, and don't move. Continue to whistle or shout loudly. A lost person is easier to find if they stay in one place.

About Mountain Biking

Mountain bikes are great. They give you an alternative to pavement, a way out of the concrete jungle. They guarantee your freedom from auto traffic. They take you into the woods and the wild, to places of natural beauty.

On the other hand, mountain bikes are the cause of a lot of controversy. In the past decade, mountain bikers have started to show up on trails that were once the exclusive domain of hikers and horseback riders. Some say the peace and quiet has been shattered. Some say that trail surfaces are being ruined by the weight and force of bicycles. Some say that bikes are too fast, and too clumsy, to share the trail with other types of users.

Much of the debate can be resolved if bikers follow a few simple rules, and if non-bikers practice a little tolerance. The following are a list of rules for low-impact, "soft cycling." If you obey them, you'll help to give mountain biking the good name it deserves:

- Make sure you ride only on trails where bikes are permitted.
- Yield to equestrians. Horses can be badly spooked by bicyclists, so give them plenty of room. If horses are approaching you, stop alongside the trail until they pass. If horses are traveling in your direction and you need to pass them, call out politely to the rider and ask permission. Don't just speed past, and never shout.
- Yield to hikers. Bikers travel much faster than hikers. You must understand that you have the potential to scare the heck out of pedestrians as you speed downhill around a curve and overtake them from behind. Make sure you give other trail users plenty of room, and keep your speed down around them.
- Be as friendly and polite as possible. Potential ill will can be eliminated by friendly greetings as you ride by: "Hello, how are you, beautiful day today..." Always say thank you to other trail users for allowing you to pass.
- Avoid riding on wet trails. Bike tires leave ruts in wet soil that accelerate erosion.
- Riders going downhill should always yield to riders going uphill on narrow trails. Get out of their way so they can keep their momentum as they climb.

Mountain Biking for the First Time?

- If you've never mountain biked before, you may be surprised at how much time you spend walking instead of riding. You may walk your bike up steep grades, down steep grades, and in flat places where the terrain is too rugged. Mountain bikers constantly have to deal with rocks, boulders, tree roots, sand traps, holes in the ground, stream crossings, eroded trails, and so on, which force them to find some way to ride through or walk their bikes. If you are used to riding on pavement, free of all obstacles, this is a strange concept. Get used to it, though, and use it to your advantage. If you are unsure of your ability to stay in control while heading downhill, or your capacity to keep your balance on a rocky surface, get off and walk your bike. It can save you plenty of band-aids.

- Learn to shift gears *before* you need to. This takes some practice, but you'll soon find that it's easier to shift before you're halfway up the hill and the pedals and chain are under pressure. When you see a hill coming up ahead, downshift.
- Play around with the height of your seat. When the seat is properly adjusted, you will have a slight bend in your knee while your leg is fully extended on the lower of the two pedals.
- Take it easy on the handlebar grips. Many beginners squeeze the daylights out of their handlebars, which leads to hand, arm, shoulder, and upper back discomfort. Grip the handlebars loosely and keep a little bend in your elbows.
- Learn to read the trail ahead of you, especially on downhills. Keep your eyes open for rocks or ruts which can take you by surprise and upset your balance.
- Go slow. As long as you never exceed the speed at which you feel comfortable and in control, you'll be fine.

Paved Trails for Road Bikers

If it's smooth pavement that you seek, check out the appendix on pages 261-262, which lists all the paved trails in this book.

Protecting the Outdoors

Take good care of this beautiful land you're riding on. The primary rules are to leave no trace of your visit, to pack out all your trash, and to try not to disturb animal or plant life. But you can go the extra mile, if you want, and pick up any litter that you see on the trail. Teach your children to do this as well. Carry an extra bag to hold picked-up litter until you get to a trash receptacle, or just keep an empty pocket for that purpose in your day pack or fanny sack.

If you have the extra time or energy, you can join a trail organization in your area or spend some time volunteering in your local park. Anything you do to help this beautiful planet will be repaid to you, many times over.

HOW TO USE THIS BOOK

This book is organized geographically, with each ride numbered from 1 to 110. Use the maps on pages 8 and 9 to locate trails in the areas of Northern California where you want to ride your bike. Then find the trails' stories by using the table of contents or just thumbing through the book. (The trails are arranged in numerical order.)

Or you can simply turn to the chapter covering the region where you'd like to ride and read all of the stories in that chapter.

Each of the 110 bike rides in this book is rated for trail distance and time required for riding. While the mileages are as accurate as possible, the time required is more subjective and you may find that you take a longer or shorter time. Don't consider the listed mileages to be your only options. Since many of the rides are out-and-back trips rather than loops, you can easily shorten or extend the length of your ride.

Each ride also has a short description of the trail surface and the notation "**MB**" or "**RB or MB**," meaning the trail is suitable for mountain bikes only, or for road bikes and/or mountain bikes. Finally, each ride has two sets of "wheel ratings" listed with it, which rate the trail for steepness and skill level required.

The steepness rating is as follows:

⊛ The trail is completely flat, or nearly so.

⊛ ⊛ The trail is somewhat hilly.

⊛ ⊛ ⊛ The trail is steep in places, with a moderate elevation gain. Beginners may have to walk some sections of the route.

The skill level rating is as follows:

⊛ The trail is paved or very smooth dirt. Anyone who can balance on a bike can ride it.

⊛ ⊛ The trail is dirt and has a surface that is somewhat eroded or rough.

⊛ ⊛ ⊛ The trail is dirt and has some technical sections, including mud, rocks, or other obstacles, and requires some mountain biking experience to ride. Beginners may have to walk some sections of the route.

At the end of each trail listing you'll find the feature "Make it easier" or "Make it more challenging." This feature gives you some options for customizing your ride.

BEST BIKE RIDES LIST

5 Best Paved Bike Trails:
Fern Canyon & Falls Loop Trails, *Russian Gulch State Park,* p. 50
Cross Marin Trail & Sir Francis Drake Bikeway, *Golden Gate National Recreation Area & Samuel P. Taylor State Park,* p. 121
Nimitz Way Bike Trail, *Tilden Regional Park,* p. 156
Sawyer Camp Recreation Trail, *San Mateo County Parks,* p. 186
Pipeline Road, *Henry Cowell Redwoods State Park,* p. 216

5 Toughest Climbs:
Pygmy Forest Trail Loop, *Salt Point State Park,* p. 53
Lake Ilsanjo Trail Loop, *Annadel State Park,* p. 61
Lake Trail, *Jack London State Historic Park,* p. 65
Carr, Feely, & Island Lakes Trail, *Tahoe National Forest,* p. 78
Wilder Ridge & Zane Gray Loop, *Wilder Ranch State Park,* p. 212

5 Best Rides for Tricycles/Training Wheels:
Howarth Park & Spring Lake Park Trails, *Sonoma County Parks,* p. 59
Tiburon Bike Path, *City of Tiburon,* p. 136
Lafayette-Moraga Regional Trail, *East Bay Regional Park District,* p. 161
Half Moon Bay Bike Path, *Half Moon Bay State Beach,* p. 192
Los Gatos Creek Trail, *Vasona Lake County Park,* p. 202

5 Easiest Mountain Bike Rides:
Bull Creek Road to Gould Barn, *Humboldt Redwoods State Park,* p. 33
Bear Valley Trail to Arch Rock, *Point Reyes National Seashore,* p. 114
Kent Pump Road, *Marin Municipal Water District,* p. 126
Lake Lagunitas Loop, *Marin Municipal Water District,* p. 128
Tennessee Valley Trail, *Golden Gate National Recreation Area,* p. 146

5 Best Rides to See Waterfalls:
Coastal Trail, *Prairie Creek Redwoods State Park,* p. 24
Fern Canyon & Falls Loop Trails, *Russian Gulch State Park,* p. 50
Skyline-to-the-Sea Trail, *Big Basin Redwoods State Park,* p. 209
Yosemite Valley Bike Path, *Yosemite National Park,* p. 226
Twin Lakes Route, *Inyo National Forest,* p. 243

5 Best Rides for Scenic Views:
Perimeter Trail, *Angel Island State Park,* p. 138
Old Stage Road, *Mount Tamalpais State Park,* p. 142
Nimitz Way Bike Trail, *Tilden Regional Park,* p. 156
Saddle & Old Guadalupe Trails, *San Bruno Mountain State Park,* p. 182
Sweeney Ridge Paved Trail, *Golden Gate National Recreation Area,* p. 184

5 Best Rides to See Wildlife:
Coastal Trail, *Prairie Creek Redwoods State Park,* p. 24
Estero Trail to Drake's Head, *Point Reyes National Seashore,* p. 108
Shoreline Trail, *China Camp State Park,* p. 134
Wildcat Creek Trail, *Wildcat Canyon Regional Park,* p. 154
Old Landing Cove Trail, *Wilder Ranch State Park,* p. 214

5 Best Rides to See Birds:
Arcata Marsh & Wildlife Sanctuary Trail, *City of Arcata,* p. 32
Abbott's Lagoon Trail, *Point Reyes National Seashore,* p. 101
Las Gallinas Wildlife Ponds, *Las Gallinas Sanitary District,* p. 132
Tidelands Loop & Newark Slough Trail, *San Francisco Bay National
    Wildlife Refuge,* p. 175
Alviso Slough Trail, *San Francisco Bay National Wildlife Refuge,* p. 199

5 Best Coastal Rides:
Coastal Trail, *Prairie Creek Redwoods State Park,* p. 24
Old Haul Road, *MacKerricher State Park,* p. 48
Gerstle Cove to Stump Beach Cove Trail, *Salt Point State Park,* p. 56
Coastal Trail & Great Highway Bike Path, *Golden Gate National
    Recreation Area,* p. 178
Old Landing Cove Trail, *Wilder Ranch State Park,* p. 214

5 Best Riverside/Streamside Rides:
Fern Canyon & Falls Loop Trails, *Russian Gulch State Park,* p. 50
Quarry Road Trail, *Auburn State Recreation Area,* p. 73
Truckee River Recreation Trail, *Tahoe City Parks and Recreation,* p. 85
Merced River Railroad Grade, *BLM Folsom Resource Area,* p. 224
Skyline-to-the-Sea Trail, *Big Basin Redwoods State Park,* p. 209

5 Best Lakeside Rides:
Water Ditch Trail, *Whiskeytown National Recreation Area,* p. 43
Fallen Leaf Lake Trails, *Tahoe National Forest,* p. 94
Lake Lagunitas Loop, *Marin Municipal Water District,* p. 128
Mono Lake South Tufa Area Trails, *Mono Lake Tufa State Reserve,* p. 230
Twin Lakes Route, *Inyo National Forest,* p. 243

5 Most Unusual Rides:
Hardrock Trail, *Empire Mine State Historic Park,* p. 71
Perimeter Trail, *Angel Island State Park,* p. 138
Bodie Ghost Town Ride, *Bodie State Historic Park,* p. 229
Mono Lake South Tufa Area Trails, *Mono Lake Tufa State Reserve,* p. 230
Hot Creek Fish Hatchery & Geothermal Area Trail,
    Inyo National Forest, p. 245

North Coast &
The Redwoods

1—Lake Earl & Yontocket Indian Village Trail, *Lake Earl State Park* 20
2—Howland Hill Road, *Jedediah Smith Redwoods State Park* 22
3—Coastal Trail, *Prairie Creek Redwoods State Park* 24
4—Jogging Trail/Davison Trail, *Prairie Creek Redwoods State Park* 26
5— Loot Man Creek Trail, *Redwood National Park* 28
6—Hammond Trail, *Humboldt County Parks* 30
7—Arcata Marsh & Wildlife Sanctuary Trail, *City of Arcata* 32
8—Bull Creek Road to Gould Barn, *Humboldt Redwoods State Park* 33

For locations of trails, see map on page 8.

1. LAKE EARL & YONTOCKET INDIAN VILLAGE TRAIL
Lake Earl State Park

Off U.S. 101 near Crescent City
7 miles/1.5 hours — dirt and gravel double-track/MB
steepness: ◉   skill level: ◉

Riding your bike at Lake Earl State Park is filled with the pleasures of discovering new country, finding untrammeled territory where you're guaranteed precious solitude and natural beauty. Lake Earl is so far north it's almost out of California, a few miles and a few turns off U.S. 101. The lake doesn't get a whole lot of recreation traffic, except from locals-in-the-know in nearby Crescent City. It's set smack on the coast, surrounded by miles of lowlands that roll gently to the sea. That makes it just about perfect for an easy bicycling trip.

Lake Earl State Park and Lake Earl Wildlife Area encompass 5,000 acres of land and water, including lakes Earl and Talawa, oceanfront beaches and sand dunes, and a huge coastal wetland. Although much of the park is undeveloped, and some of it has been taken over by off-road-vehicle users, the area north of the lakes and just south of the Smith River is crossed by a little-used biker/hiker/horse trail. It leads through coastal meadows to a Yontocket Indian cemetery and a view of the Smith River.

One year, I rode my mountain bike on this trail on the day before

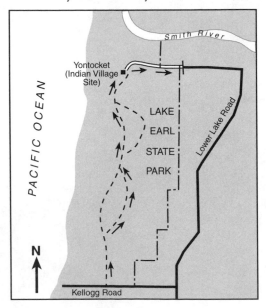

Thanksgiving. The marshy landscape with its gray and wintery sky was resplendent with harvest color; the foliage reflected every possible shade of green, gold and orange. Ferns growing along the trail were a deep, bold red, vibrant in their last days of life before going dormant for the winter. The dark greens and golds of the meadow grasses were set against the steel blue of the ponds and wetlands. My memories of this colorful day have long remained.

The trailhead is a little tricky to spot (follow the directions exactly), but once you find it, the rest of the trip is a breeze. The trail is a gravel roadbed, composed of very fine stones that are as smooth as glass to ride on. You glide up and down a series of small hills, passing some environmental campsites at the start of the trail, then cruise all the way to the park's northeastern boundary near where the Smith River reaches the ocean.

The only direction you need to follow is to

Lake Earl/Yontocket Indian Village Trail

stay on the wide, main trail. There are two possible loops you can take that lead off the main route and then reconnect further on. Ignore the several single-track cutoffs for horseback riders; if you follow any of them you will quickly become mired in sand up to your saddle. This will necessitate walking your bike, which will slow down your progress considerably. Guess how I know?

At the first intersection, which is signed for the marsh to your left and the ponds to your right, head right, staying on the main trail. At the next trail split, take the left fork, which is again the main trail, and you'll wind up at the Yontocket Indian Memorial Cemetery, which was once the site of a thriving Native American village. If you climb the small hill to the cemetery, you'll get a good view of the Smith River and surrounding marshes.

You are now almost three miles from the trailhead. From here, you can ride only another half-mile further, veering to the right past the cemetery to the gated park boundary. There's no way to make a loop out of this trail; just turn around at the boundary sign. The ride back is pure fun and mostly downhill, like sailing on a gentle rollercoaster. It feels like you are always coasting, but you never go fast enough to get out of control.

One possible minus at Lake Earl is that the place is popular with hunters, so you may hear the occasional sounds of shooting in the distance, particularly in the autumn months. We saw a few pheasant hunters just beyond the park boundary, although none were in the park. A sign at the trailhead announces that waterfowl hunting is permitted on Saturdays, Sundays, and Wednesdays only. If hunting offends your sensibilities, plan your trip for the other days of the week.

Make it easier: Just cut your trip short and turn around sooner.

Trip notes: There is no fee. For more information and a map, contact Lake Earl State Park, 1375 Elk Valley Road, Crescent City, CA 95531; (707) 445-6547 or (707) 464-6101.

Directions: From U.S. 101 in northern Crescent City, drive northwest on Northcrest Drive, which later becomes Lake Earl Drive, for 5.8 miles. Turn left on Lower Lake Road and drive 2.4 miles. Turn left on Kellogg Road and drive six-tenths of a mile (following the signs for Kellogg Beach/Coastal Access) to the marked trailhead. The trailhead is difficult to spot, as the sign is set back from the road. Look for the dirt and gravel trail on the right side of Kellogg Road. There is a small pullout area for a few cars.

---

2. HOWLAND HILL ROAD
Jedediah Smith Redwoods State Park
Off U.S. 101 near Crescent City
4 miles/1 hour — dirt and gravel road/MB
steepness: ◉ ◉   skill level: ◉ ◉

Howland Hill Road has one of the most incredible fern displays on the face of this planet, and for that reason alone you should come here and ride. If the ferns aren't enough to motivate you, consider that the road passes through one of the finest old-growth redwood groves in northwestern California. Come here. Be wowed.

There is one problem, however. You'll have to deal with some car traffic on Howland Hill Road, which is a dirt road that is open to passenger vehicles but closed to trailers and motor homes. In summer, the region gets the heaviest traffic, so for the least amount of cars and the greatest chance of seeing the majestic redwoods in peace, visit in fall or winter. Those who are completely opposed to riding alongside occasional automobiles should see the alternate trail listed under "Make it easier." But at the very least, *drive* this road. It's that good.

You can avoid a lot of the car traffic, and a big hill, by riding only a portion of Howland Hill Road. The quietest section is the end that is farthest from the Stout Grove, where most park visitors head to see the Stout Tree, the largest

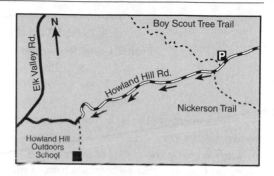

redwood in the park. You may miss out on the Stout Tree on this trip, but don't worry, you'll see plenty other big, magnificent redwoods. Plus you'll leave your car at the hiker's trailhead for the Boy Scout Tree Trail, so when you're finished riding, you have the option of hiking a mile or two among the big trees.

For now, the ride: From the Boy Scout Tree Trailhead, head west (toward Crescent City) on your bike, following Howland Hill Road. You can travel for almost two miles in this direction before the road starts to climb toward Howland Summit; turn around when you don't want to climb any more. This gives you about a four-mile round-trip, but if you want more time and mileage in the big trees, you can ride east from the Boy Scout Tree Trailhead for a mile or two as well.

The trail directions are simple, so you can just focus on your surroundings, which are an untempered dose of redwoods, ferns, and as much greenery per square foot as the earth can deliver. Ride and be humbled by this magnificent forest.

Make it easier: If you want complete freedom from cars, drive to where Howland Hill Road turns from pavement to dirt, on the Crescent City side of Howland Summit. A gate on the right side of the road is signed for the Mill Creek horse trail. Bikes are allowed to ride up the dirt road (but not on the horse trail cutoff), through second- and third-growth redwoods, to the Howland Hill Outdoors School. Check out the huge redwood stumps along the road, which remind us that this forest used to look as spectacular as the one on Howland Hill Road.

Trip notes: There is no fee. For more information and a map, contact Jedediah Smith Redwoods State Park, 1375 Elk Valley Road, Crescent City, CA 95531; (707) 464-6101 or (707) 445-6547.

Directions: In Crescent City, head south on U.S. 101 and turn east on Elk Valley Road. Drive 1.1 miles and turn right on Howland Hill Road. Drive 1.5 miles till the pavement turns to dirt at Howland Summit. Continue 2.5 miles further to the Boy Scout Tree Trailhead on the left.

3. COASTAL TRAIL
Prairie Creek Redwoods State Park
Off U.S. 101 near Orick
6 miles/1.5 hours — dirt single-track/MB
steepness: ◉   skill level: ◉ ◉

Imagine a single-track trail that runs parallel to the ocean, framed by coastal bluffs and a mossy spruce forest. Imagine there is plenty of wildlife along the trail, fearless enough to stand still and let you take pictures. Imagine three waterfalls tucked into the forest, one after another as you pass by, like secret treasures you discover.

Okay, now imagine that this trail is open to bikes. Sound impossible? Of course it sounds impossible. Few bike trails, especially few easy bike trails, are this good. What the heck, few *hiking* trails are this good. But the Coastal Trail in Prairie Creek Redwoods State Park, from Fern Canyon to the start of the Ossagon Trail, is spectacular. I rate this as one of the top easy mountain bike trails in all of California. Go there, ride it and see for yourself.

Getting there, however, requires some effort. The route to the trailhead is a seven-mile stint on unpaved Davison Road, which may or may not be graded, depending on recent weather. Once when I drove here the road was full of potholes; another time it was as smooth as asphalt. At the trailhead, there will probably be several other cars, but

Roosevelt elk along the Coastal Trail

North Coast & The Redwoods

most visitors are making the short hike through neighboring Fern Canyon. With your bike, you'll head due north (straight) on the Coastal Trail from the parking area. The trickiest part of the whole trip is in the first two-tenths of a mile from the trailhead, where you have to cross a few streams and plow through a very wet, muddy, and narrow section in the forest. Depending on how wet it is, the trail can be almost impossible to negotiate on a bike, so just walk the first stretch until you reach a wide coastal bluff. Once you're out of the forest, the Coastal Trail is drier and more hard-packed, making the riding easy.

Although you can't always see the ocean, its nonstop roar accompanies you. You ride along the inland perimeter of flat grassland bluffs, just before they intersect with the steep cliffs on your right. In between the cliffs and the grasslands is a narrow strip of forest—mostly alders and mossy Sitka spruce—where the waterfalls are hidden.

At about one mile you come to the first waterfall, but you can barely hear or see it through the trees. You'll need to be tipped off by its sound, then peek into the forest canopy to see it. If you are riding too fast, you'll miss it, but even if you do, there are two more waterfalls to come. Each one is a tall, narrow plume of water cascading down the hillside.

What you can't miss are the huge Roosevelt elk that roam this coastal prairie, munching on grasses all day long to feed their 700- to 1,000-pound bulk. A quarter-mile beyond the first waterfall, I rode past four of them, each with big antlers, who refused to leave the trail. They're gentle animals, but give them plenty of room. They're bigger than you are, and you're in their home.

The second waterfall is more easily spotted; it has a little clearing in front of it and a wooden viewing bench. The third waterfall is only about 100 yards beyond the second and is the easiest of all to find. A little spur trail leads right to it. Walk your bike into the forest and take a minute to appreciate these watery wonders.

In the final mile of the bikes-allowed section of the Coastal Trail, you move inland, away from the oceanside bluffs, and enter into a narrow strip of forest. Shortly you arrive at the hiker/biker camp at Butler Creek, where there is a little stream crossing. Then head back into the meadow again for the last half-mile to Coastal Trail's junction with Ossagon Trail. Ossagon is also open to bikes, but the trail climbs right away and returns to the highway in 1.8 miles, so turn around and head back on the Coastal Trail, experiencing the magic all over again.

You may ask yourself: Can a trail open to mountain bikes really be this good? Yes, yes.

Make it easier: Just cut your trip short by riding to one of the waterfalls and then turning around.

Trip notes: A $5 day-use fee is charged per vehicle. A park map is available at the entrance kiosk for 50 cents. For more information, contact Prairie Creek Redwoods State Park, Orick, CA 95555; (707) 464-6101 or (707) 445-6547.

Directions: From Eureka, drive north on U.S. 101 for 41 miles to Orick. Continue north for 2.5 more miles to Davison Road, then turn left (west) and drive eight miles to the Fern Canyon Trailhead. (You will pass the entrance kiosk where you pay your day-use fee about halfway in). No trailers or motor homes are permitted on unpaved Davison Road.

4. JOGGING TRAIL/DAVISON TRAIL
Prairie Creek Redwoods State Park
Off U.S. 101 near Orick
8 miles/2 hours — paved, gravel double-track & dirt single-track/MB
steepness: ✹   skill level: ✹ ✹

In my best daydreams, mountain biking is like this: I picture myself riding through a fern-filled canyon with towering redwood trees on one side and a deep, lush ravine on the other. The foliage is so thick it makes a tunnel just high and wide enough for me to ride through. Nobody is around, except for the animals and birds in the forest, who welcome me with their calls. The trail is smooth and hard, and I glide along in perfect rhythm...

One day, I woke up from my daydream and realized it's all for real at Prairie Creek Redwoods State Park.

No kidding. The Jogging Trail (also called Davison Trail) at Prairie Creek is a slice of bicycling heaven. It's easy enough for beginners to ride (on a combination double-track and single-track trail), but so much fun that even experienced mountain bikers will delight in it.

You won't need a map—the trail is well-marked the whole way. The first few hundred yards border a huge meadow, aptly named Elk Prairie, where a herd of Roosevelt elk like to hang out and entertain the tourists driving on the Scenic Parkway. (For more on the elk, see the previous story.) Beyond the meadow, the trail is briefly disrupted by its intersection with a gated park access road, but you jog right and then left, following the signs, and you're back on the trail again.

The trail moves away from the Scenic Parkway, slowly shedding all vestiges of civilization. At the one-mile mark, it heads deep into the forest, into a veritable tunnel of vegetation. A sign at the two-mile mark states "turn around here," but it's not for you. It's for joggers completing a four-mile circuit. Continue as the trail narrows from double-track to single-track and disintegrates from an old paved road, to a gravel roadbed, to plain old dirt and mud.

As you ride, the canyon drops off steeply on your left. It's filled with big redwood trees—they're second growth, but big nonetheless. You're surrounded by a lush treasury of ferns, azaleas, salmonberry, red alders and other shade- and water-loving plants and trees. Water-loving? That's right, it rains a lot

Jogging Trail, Prairie Creek Redwoods State Park

here, but don't let that stop you from riding. I rode this trail on a day when even my glamorous plastic green poncho couldn't keep me dry, but I was smiling the whole time. Just make sure you have some dry clothes to change into back in your car.

Speaking of rain, this is a good trail for getting a lesson in how to ride in mud, if you haven't done much of it. After the two-mile mark the trail gets a little technical, with some puddles and wet spots in addition to the occasional fallen tree branch, but it's never difficult, just fun. Remember to make as little trail impact as possible, which means ride slowly and gently, especially on wet soil. (No careening around corners or racing to finish.)

At nearly three miles, you reach a gate across the trail, which is only 50 yards from the edge of Davison Road, a graded dirt road with some car traffic. You can turn around here if you wish, or take one of two possible loop routes. Ambitious mountain bikers make a 19-mile loop by turning right on Davison Road, then following Coastal Trail (see the previous story), and returning on Ossagon Trail and the paved

Newton B. Drury Scenic Parkway.

A loop that's better suited for easy bikers is to turn left on Davison Road, ride two miles, then turn left on a newly built section of the Jogging Trail/Davison Trail that parallels the Scenic Parkway. This will bring you back to your starting point for an eight-mile round-trip.

Make it easier: Just ride the first two miles of trail, to where the jogger's sign says "turn around here," then ride back. The trail gets slightly more technical after this point.

Trip notes: A $5 day-use fee is charged per vehicle. A park map is available at the entrance kiosk for 50 cents. For more information, contact Prairie Creek Redwoods State Park, Orick, CA 95555; (707) 464-6101 or (707) 445-6547.

Directions: From Eureka, drive north on U.S. 101 for 41 miles to Orick. Continue north for approximately five more miles, taking the Newton B. Drury Scenic Parkway exit and turning left, following the signs for one mile toward the Visitors Center. Turn left at the sign for Elk Prairie Campground/Visitors Center, pay the day-use fee at the entrance kiosk, and drive straight past the kiosk to the three day-use parking areas just before the camping area. Park there, then ride your bike on the camp access road for two-tenths of a mile, staying to the left when the road forks, and pick up the jogging/bicycle trail that leads from the hike/bike camp (near the trailer dump station).

---

5. LOST MAN CREEK TRAIL
Redwood National Park
Off U.S. 101 near Orick
3 miles/1 hour — dirt road/MB
steepness: ⊙   skill level: ⊙

Is there anybody on the planet who can visit the Redwood Empire and not fall completely in love with the giant redwood trees and the deep, lasting green of the forests? Take the ride on (and the drive in to) the Lost Man Creek Trail, for example. No matter what the weather is like, the scenery is absolutely phenomenal. Trees that are hundreds of years old are everywhere you look, moss hangs from the alders, ferns grow to huge sizes. These sights are the essence of a trip to the redwoods, the reason that bikers and hikers flock here every year to be awed and humbled by the majestic forests.

Now a little surveying on a map will tell you that the Lost Man Creek Trail is much longer than the mileage I suggest above. After the first four miles, it reaches Holter Ridge and continues along it for six more miles. However, the operative word in Holter Ridge is "ridge," meaning you have to gain about 1,400 feet in elevation to get to it, most of it in the space of only two miles. I gave it a try and said, "No, thank you," but the option remains, if you're up for a steep and challenging climb. The key is that the first mile-and-a-half of the Lost Man Creek Trail are almost perfectly flat, paralleling gurgling Lost Man Creek. Those who want a gorgeous and easy ride through first- and second-growth redwoods can go out and back almost effortlessly, turning around when the trail starts to climb like a son-of-a-gun, then have a picnic at the trailhead and sit around gawking at the trees. This is a perfect trip for families with small kids. Stronger riders can tackle the hill, heading as far as they darn well please.

Want to add some mileage to your ride without having to go up? The paved portion of Lost Man Road, which you drove in on to get to the trailhead, is another riding option. You have to be ready for a possible encounter with auto traffic, but the only cars on the road will be those heading to the trailhead, since the road dead-ends there. That keeps the number of vehicles low. If you ride out-and-back from the trailhead to Lost Man Road's intersection with U.S. 101, you can add 1.8 miles to your trip.

Lost Man Creek Trail, Redwood National Park

The trail itself is an old gravel roadbed, smooth as silk and very easy to ride on, with plenty of fallen leaves and soft pine and fir needles. The only obstacles are bright yellow and green banana slugs—you'll expend great energy trying to avoid squashing them as they slowly slug across the road.

For the first mile, you ride along the creek, where a couple of wide bridge crossings offer eye-opening peeks into the beautiful creek canyon. The bridges can be slippery when wet, which they often are, since it rains frequently on this stretch of coast. One bridge is curiously signed "Weight Limit 19 Tons," a little odd for a road that is no longer open to vehicles.

The big attraction is the trees, of course, and luckily they provide some cover if it rains. In addition to the huge redwoods are thick stands of alders along the creek, providing a bit of color in the fall. In winter, after they lose their leaves, you can see how heavy moss has completely covered every inch of their trunks and branches like a thick fur coat.

Make it more challenging: Just ride further, either on the flat paved section of Lost Man Road, or higher up the dirt road toward Holter Ridge.

Trip notes: There is no fee. For more information and a free map, contact Redwood National Park Headquarters at 1111 Second Street, Crescent City, CA 95531; (707) 464-6101.

Directions: From Eureka, drive north on U.S. 101 for 41 miles to Orick, then continue north for three more miles to the well-signed turnoff for Lost Man Road (on the right). Drive nine-tenths of a mile to the end of the paved portion of the road, where the trailhead is located. Ride your bike straight through the picnic area.

6. HAMMOND TRAIL
Humboldt County Parks
Off U.S. 101 in Arcata
6 miles/1 hour — paved bike trail and gravel single-track/RB or MB
steepness: ◉ ◉   skill level: ◉

On the Hammond Trail, you learn your lesson: All rail trails are not created equal. The Hammond Trail is just plain superior.

The movement to convert abandoned railroad lines to multi-use trails for bicyclists, walkers, wheelchair-users, equestrians, and anyone else under non-motorized power has gained a lot of momentum in the United States, particularly in California, with its thousands of miles of unused railroad track. The trend has resulted in trails of varying quality, some of which are downright pedestrian—completely straight, flat, in barren surroundings and going nowhere interesting. But the Hammond Trail makes all rail-trail proponents proud and all trail users happy, because it offers so much more than just an easy route from Arcata to McKinleyville (or vice versa). It also provides stellar views of the coast and rural farmlands, beach access, and an unusual ride through an old steel railroad bridge that is closed to all motorized traffic.

Once used to transport lumber, this rail route is now paved for its first two miles, then turns to gravel for the next mile as it parallels the ocean near McKinleyville. In between, it passes through the farmlands of Arcata Bottoms, which look a lot like the English countryside with their green, pastoral fields and grazing cows and horses. It also adjoins Mad River County Park and crosses over the Mad River, which in summer and fall provides good perch fishing where it meets the sea.

The trail starts out with a bang as you begin by riding over the old railroad bridge across the Mad River. Since the bridge is raised higher than the surrounding lands, it offers great views to the east and west, but also requires a short, steep climb up to it, followed by a quick coast down the other side. The trail connects to Fisher Road, which has some houses on it and local traffic, then crosses over School Road and continues north (straight) on Fisher Avenue. At the end of Fisher Avenue the trail picks up again on the right, separate from any streets. Your total stint on roads is under a half mile, and auto traffic is close to nil.

The Hammond Trail then crosses Hiller Road and heads along the edge of Hiller Park, a small community park. The best part comes next as you ride into a thick tunnel of coastal forest, with trees, vines and bushes so dense that it can seem dark inside. When you exit this stretch of flora, you are at Murray Road, where there is a neighborhood consisting of large, odd-looking houses, all built to resemble castles. Why? We never figured it out.

The trail becomes gravel here and heads along the beach, so mountain bikers can continue to ride while road bikers will have to walk their bikes. (Humboldt County Parks has plans to extend the paved portion of the trail, but at present the pavement ends at Murray Road.) In several places, old rails are still embedded in the coastal bluff alongside the gravel and dirt trail. The coastal views through the trees here are spectacular, particularly at sunset. Several offshoot trails lead down to the beach, where you can beachcomb or picnic.

Make it more challenging: All of the country roads in the Arcata Bottoms area and around Mad River County Park are suitable for easy biking, as they are flat and have very little auto traffic.

Trip notes: There is no fee. For more information, contact Humboldt County Parks, 1106 Second Street, Eureka, CA 95501; (707) 445-7651.

Directions: From U.S. 101 in Eureka, drive north about 10 miles to the north end of Arcata, then take the Giuntoli Lane exit and head west (left). Cross over the freeway, then turn right on to Heindon Road and drive three-tenths of a mile. Turn left on Miller Lane and drive eight-tenths of a mile. Turn right on Mad River Road and drive 1.6 miles to an old railroad bridge and the start of the bike trail. Park in the dirt pullouts by the bridge.

7. ARCATA MARSH & WILDLIFE SANCTUARY TRAIL
City of Arcata
Off U.S. 101 in Arcata
2 miles/1 hour — dirt and gravel single-track/MB
steepness: ⦿   skill level: ⦿

Few wildlife refuges have policies friendly toward bicyclists; most of them forbid riders for fear of scaring off the wildlife they are trying to protect. Arcata Marsh is an exception to the rule, a small sanctuary built near a wastewater treatment facility that allows bike riders, as well as walkers and anglers, to tread on its gravel levees. What you get when you ride here is the opportunity to see birds—tons of them—and lots of pretty views of marsh, water and shoreline.

Arcata Marsh is not a huge place, and there are only a couple of miles of trails, so don't come here expecting a major workout. You're better off showing up with your binoculars, your camera, your fishing pole or maybe just a good book in your bike bag. This is a bike ride for nature lovers, not speed demons on two wheels. Here's your chance to see ospreys, peregrine falcons, kingfishers, egrets, herons, and even some plain old seagulls and mud hens.

The history of the place is a good recycling story: The Arcata Marsh and Wildlife Sanctuary was formerly a sanitary landfill, but thanks to some forward thinking on the part of city officials, it was

Arcata Marsh and Wildlife Sanctuary Trail

converted to 154 acres of fish and wildlife habitat in four marshes and one small lake, all set right along Humboldt Bay. The variety of salt-water and freshwater habitat is what attracts the huge diversity of birds.

What surprised me most about Arcata Marsh is its popularity. On a Monday afternoon in November, the parking lot was nearly half full. Most of the visitors were local people looking for a quiet, scenic spot to eat their lunch; some came to feed the seagulls, who were clearly accustomed to the routine. Others were there to fish on the bay side of the marsh, casting from the levee that separates the Franklin R. Klopp Recreation Lake from Arcata Bay.

We rode the trail that tops the levee and goes all the way around the lake, plus the connecting trail that runs parallel to the access road (I Street) and is routed inland, toward the wind sock at the waste treatment center. We probably did more stopping than riding, taking plenty of time to enjoy the views, watch the fishermen, identify the birds, and take photographs. It's not a place where you'll want to hurry.

Make it easier: Just ride the short loop around the lake, then have a picnic along the marsh or the shore of the bay,

Trip notes: There is no fee. For more information and a free map, contact the City of Arcata Environmental Services Department, 736 F Street, Arcata, CA 95521; (707) 822-5953.

Directions: From U.S. 101 in Eureka, drive north about 10 miles to Arcata, take the Samoa Boulevard exit west and drive for six-tenths of a mile to I Street, where you turn left (south). Drive for one mile to where I Street ends at the parking area for Arcata Marsh. Start riding on the trail between the parking lot and the lake.

8. BULL CREEK ROAD to GOULD BARN
Humboldt Redwoods State Park
Off U.S. 101 near Garberville
7 miles/1.5 hours — dirt road/MB
steepness: ⊛ ⊛   skill level: ⊛

I admit it—hill climbing is not my strong suit. If it takes a lot of grunting and panting to get to the top, I'm not too interested. When I phoned Humboldt Redwoods State Park to ask them which trails were open for bike riding, and they rattled off a whole list but added that they all climbed halfway to heaven, I almost canceled my trip. Hey, if I want to climb, I'll head for the Himalayas. But then a ranger tipped me off to Bull Creek Road, just past the Rockefeller Forest section of Humboldt Redwoods. It's a four-mile-long fire road that never gains more than 250 feet. So I packed up my helmet and wheels and headed for Humboldt.

Bull Creek Road is really fun to ride, and the fun begins before you even reach the trailhead. That's because accessing the trail requires a drive on Mattole Road (also called Bull Creek Flats Road) through the Rockefeller Forest, one of the greatest redwood forests in the entire Redwood Empire. It has huge trees and a lush fern understory, and you drive right through the best of it. From your car window, the big trees are often close enough to touch. On my trip, a mother bear and her cub crossed the road right in front of my car.

Get your fill of the huge old trees on the way in, because once you start riding on Bull Creek Road, you'll be in a second-growth forest, where the trees are merely large in size, not gargantuan. The second growth is no disappointment, however. Mixed in with Douglas firs, oaks, willows, and alders, the trees provide shade that alternates with open, grassy sections along the trail. Due to its more southern, inland location and lack of a dense forest canopy, this is one of the few trails in the Redwood Empire where you can actually get too hot in the summer. Be sure to pack along some water, or fill up your water bottle at the spring across the road from Bull Creek Trail Camp, 3.2 miles in.

The road is old pavement at the start, but soon turns to gravel. It's very smooth and tightly compacted, making the riding easy. There is only one noticeable hill on the way out; the rest of the trip is a very gradual ascent of less than 300 feet and then almost all downhill cruising on the way back. For your entire trip, you are accompanied by Bull Creek, which you cross and recross a few times on wooden bridges.

This trail intersects with several others after Bull Creek Trail Camp, including Kemp Road and Preacher Gulch Road, both of which climb almost immediately. Avoid them and stay on Bull Creek Road till it intersects with Gould Road. There, turn right and ride 50 yards to Lower Gould Barn, an old barn left by early settlers. It has a nice picnic spot behind it, by the creek.

Make it easier: Cut your trip short at any point and turn around.

Trip notes: There is no fee. For more information and a $1 map, contact Humboldt Redwoods State Park, P.O. Box 100, Weott, CA 95571; (707) 946-2409 or (707) 445-6547.

Directions: From Garberville, drive north on U.S. 101 for approximately 20 miles. Take the Founder's Grove/Rockefeller Forest exit and drive 7.5 miles on Mattole Road/Bull Creek Flats Road to the Bull Creek Road trailhead on the left side of the road. (It is located just before the Pioneer Cemetery, which is on the right side of the road.) Park alongside the gated dirt road, being careful not to block the gate.

Redding & Shasta

9—Siskiyou Lake North Shore, *Shasta-Trinity National Forest* 36
10—Waters Gulch & Fish Loop Trails, *Shasta-Trinity National Forest* ... 37
11—Clikapudi Creek Trail to Jones Valley Camp, *Shasta-Trinity National Forest* 39
12—Tower House Historic District & Mill Creek Trails, *Whiskeytown National Recreation Area* 41
13—Water Ditch Trail, *Whiskeytown National Recreation Area* 43
14—Sacramento River Trail, *City of Redding* 45

For locations of trails, see map on page 8.

9. SISKIYOU LAKE NORTH SHORE
Shasta-Trinity National Forest
Off Interstate 5 near Mount Shasta
4 miles/1 hour — dirt roads/MB
steepness: ⦿   skill level: ⦿

If you're vacationing at Lake Shasta and all the jet-skiers, water-skiers and houseboaters are starting to wear you down, a trip to Lake Siskiyou could be just the antidote you need. Lake Siskiyou is one of the few lakes in California that was built specifically for recreation, but the quiet kind, not the loud kind. That means two things: One—water managers leave the lake level alone, even when other lakes in the area are drawn down in drought years, so Siskiyou is full and pretty year-round, and two—you won't be bugged by the roar of jet boats as you ride, because the lake speed limit is 10 miles per hour.

Key to your trip is the fact that you'll ride on the north shore of the lake, not the busier south shore where the marina and campground are located. Your route is on Forest Service dirt roads, which only rarely get car traffic because the main attractions are on the other side of the lake, reachable by pavement.

Start riding from where you parked your car, near the start of North Shore Road. The first two-thirds of a mile give no indication that you are about to come to beautiful Lake Siskiyou, so when you get your first view through the trees, it's a great surprise. Deep blue and always full to the brim, Siskiyou is a lake for scenery-lovers, surrounded by a thick conifer forest and with Mount Shasta in the background.

You'll pass several turnoffs on your left leading to dirt parking areas and shoreline access, any of which you can take to get an unobstructed lake view, drop in a fishing line, or just sit by the water. You may notice a single-track trail leading along the shoreline of the lake; it looks tempting to ride but leave it for the anglers who have built it. (Trout fishing is popular here in spring, bass fishing in summer.)

The dirt road you're on gets rougher as you ride to the west end of Lake Siskiyou, where the reservoir gets narrower and narrower until it melds with the Sacramento River. We rode to a major intersection of dirt roads at two miles (past the point where we could see the lake any more). The trail got too rocky to make continuing enjoyable, so we turned back for a four-mile round-trip. The condition of the road will vary greatly according to what time of year you ride; it is smoothest and most tightly compacted in late summer and fall. Fall is probably the best season to ride here anyway, as the thick pine forest gets lit up by occasional splashes of color from deciduous oak trees.

On your way out or upon your return, make a stop at the first dirt parking lot on the northeast edge of the lake (the first left turnoff you'll see on your ride out), for a terrific view of Mount Shasta on clear days.

Make it easier: Shorten your trip by parking at the first dirt parking lot on the northeast side of the lake, by the water's edge. Ride back up the parking lot access road and then turn left to ride along the lakeshore.

Trip notes: There is no fee. For more information and a map, contact Shasta-Trinity National Forest, Mt. Shasta Ranger District, 204 West Alma Street, Mt. Shasta, CA 96067; (530) 926-4511.

Directions: From Redding, drive north on Interstate 5 for 65 miles to the town of Mt. Shasta, then take the central Mt. Shasta exit and turn left at the stop sign. Go over the overpass and travel one-half mile to South Old Stage Road. Turn left on South Old Stage Road and travel two-tenths of a mile until you come to a Y in the road. Veer right on to W.A. Barr Road and travel seven-tenths of a mile to North Shore Road, where you turn right. Park your car in the pullout where the pavement turns to dirt. Begin riding west on the dirt road.

---

10. WATERS GULCH & FISH LOOP TRAILS
Shasta-Trinity National Forest
Off Interstate 5 on Shasta Lake
4.5 miles/1.5 hours — dirt single-track/MB
steepness: ⊕ ⊕   skill level: ⊕ ⊕ ⊕

When you're ready for an easy mountain biking challenge, you're ready to ride on the Forest Service trails at Lake Shasta. They'll challenge you not because they have steep uphills that climb forever—in fact, the Waters Gulch and Fish Loop trails roll along with only short ups and downs—but because they are lessons in technical riding, with plenty of bridges to cross, rocks strewn along your path, tree roots that sneak up on you, and some sections with steep dropoffs into Lake Shasta. Whoops—better keep your eyes on the road.

If all that doesn't scare you off, even novices can have a good time on the Waters Gulch/Fish Loop trails, provided they take their time and walk their bikes on some of the trickier parts. The views of Lake Shasta are great, the trails cut through a thick mixed forest of pines and oaks, and there are nice smooth sections of trail in between the technical parts. The only riders who probably shouldn't attempt this trail are kids under 12 or so, because their balance may not be developed enough for the narrow path. Not only that, but watching them ride may give their parents conniption fits.

Waters Gulch & Fish Loop Trails, overlooking Lake Shasta

For beginning mountain bike riders, the best advice is to slow down and not attempt anything that looks too tricky. If you find yourself wondering if you can negotiate a tight curve or make it across a narrow bridge, don't try it. Stop and walk your bike. Also, keep your speed down at all times, staying prepared for surprise tight turns and the trail's steep dropoffs.

All disclaimers aside, this ride is pure fun. The most experienced rider should ride first (setting a slow, safe pace) and warn those behind of upcoming obstacles. These obstacles can include occasional hikers on the trail, although they are rare except on peak summer weekends. If you see anybody walking on the narrow trail, get off your bike immediately and let them pass safely. These trails were built years ago, when the sport of mountain biking was a mere twinkle in somebody's eye, and they were built for hikers. It's only by the good grace of the Forest Service that bikes are allowed here at all, so we must behave as decorously as possible.

Start riding on Fish Loop, a short, half-mile loop around the perimeter of Packers Bay on Shasta Lake. The trail gets narrower and narrower as manzanita bushes crowd in and brush your ankles as you ride by. The leaves of black oaks and white oaks sometimes get caught in your spokes, making a great shuffling sound as they spin around.

Almost at its end, the loop connects to Waters Gulch Trail. Go left on Waters Gulch until the trail gets too treacherous, which was about two miles in for me, where the trail moves away from the lake. Much of the upper part of Waters Gulch Trail is suitable for hiking boots only, as it has been heavily eroded and the trail is too rocky and narrow for bikes. When you're ready, turn around and retrace your tire treads on Waters Gulch. You can either stay on Waters Gulch or get back on Fish Loop—both trails return you to the parking area.

Make it easier: Beginners can just ride the Fish Loop Trail and return to the parking lot, instead of connecting to Waters Gulch. Or they can ride out-and-back on Waters Gulch, ignoring the cutoff for Fish Loop. Both Waters Gulch and Fish Loop trailheads are about 20 yards apart at the parking area.

Trip notes: There is a $2 fee per vehicle for parking at the boat ramp. For more information and a map, contact Shasta-Trinity National Forest, Shasta Lake Ranger District, 14225 Holiday Road, Redding, CA 96003; (530) 275-1587.

Directions: From Interstate 5 at Redding, drive north for 15 miles to Lake Shasta and take the Packers Bay exit. Drive southwest on Packers Bay Road for 1.5 miles to the boat ramp and parking area at the end of the road. The trailhead for the Fish Loop Trail is on the right side of the parking lot, 20 yards below a separate trailhead for the Waters Gulch Trail.

---

11. CLIKAPUDI CREEK TRAIL to JONES VALLEY CAMP
Shasta-Trinity National Forest
Off Interstate 5 on Shasta Lake
3 miles/1 hour — dirt single-track/MB
steepness: ⊛ ⊛   skill level: ⊛ ⊛

Compared to many trails along Shasta Lake, the Clikapudi Creek Trail is way out there, near the far southeast Pit River arm of the lake, with no direct access from Interstate 5. That's good news for bikers, though, because it means fewer folks to share the trail with.

Although they are both Shasta lakeside trails, the big difference between riding this trail and riding Waters Gulch (see story on page 37), is that this trail is a little further from the water's edge, with fewer steep dropoffs, making it better for less skilled riders. Also, the single-track here is almost completely free of obstacles.

The critical element with bike riding at Shasta Lake is timing. Show up in the late summer or fall, and you'll hit hard-packed trails. Show up in the spring, and you'll slide all over the place. I'd recommend riding here in the fall, when the forest is most colorful. The black and white oaks turn yellow and orange, contrasting with the crimson bark of madrones and manzanita. If you like conifers in your forest, plenty of Douglas fir and pines provide shade and color year-round. Another advantage to an autumn trip is that the place is usually deserted; even the nearby Jones Valley Campground is often empty.

The fall colors are sometimes more of a draw than the views of Shasta Lake from this trail. By the end of summer, the lake's water level is often drawn down, if not to send water to Central Valley farmers, then to make room for snowmelt. Unfortunately, that leaves the shoreline looking pretty barren, so it's good there are other attractions.

The entire Clikapudi Creek Trail is an eight-mile loop, with a more difficult, steeper section on the north side of Jones Valley Road, but you don't need to ride all of it to have a great trip. The mileage listed above assumes that you ride only on the south (lake) side of Jones Valley Road, making an out-and-back trip rather than a loop. That keeps you near the water's edge the entire time.

Start at the boat ramp's western Clikapudi trailhead (there's another one on the east side), then ride south and west to the Lower Jones Valley Campground.

Clikapudi Creek Trail

You'll pass an intersection with a sharp left turn about one mile in; this is the route for those who are crossing to the north side of Jones Valley Road to ride the entire Clikapudi loop. You want to continue straight for another half-mile to the campground, then when the trail ends near the picnic area, turn around and ride back.

For many, this three-mile out-and-back ride will be enough, but those who wish to continue can pick up the trail at the other Clikapudi trailhead on the east side of the boat ramp parking lot, and ride for another three miles, heading up the Clikapudi cove of Shasta Lake. The trail stays relatively flat all along the lake; it is only when it leaves the water that it begins to climb and get more technical.

Make it more challenging: Add on the section of trail from the east side of the boat ramp, turning around when you leave the lakeshore, for a total nine-mile round-trip with almost no climbing.

Trip notes: There is a $2 fee per vehicle for parking at the boat ramp. For more information and a map, contact Shasta-Trinity National Forest, Shasta Lake Ranger District, 14225 Holiday Road, Redding, CA 96003; (530) 275-1587.

Directions: From Interstate 5 in Redding, take Highway 299 east for 5.5 miles to Bella Vista. At Bella Vista, turn left on Dry Creek Road and drive seven miles to a fork in the road. At the fork, go straight (slightly to the right, now on Jones Valley Road). Continue past the turnoff for Jones Valley Marina, following the signs for the Jones Valley campgrounds and then going past them until Jones Valley Road ends at the Forest Service boat launching facility and parking area. This trailhead for the Clikapudi Creek Trail is on the left (west) side of the parking lot. (There is another Clikapudi Trailhead on the east/right side of the parking lot.)

12. TOWER HOUSE HISTORIC DISTRICT & MILL CREEK TRAILS
Whiskeytown National Recreation Area
Off Highway 299 west of Redding
2 miles/1 hour — dirt double-track and single-track/MB
steepness: ● skill level: ●

If you're looking for an easy trail at Whiskeytown Lake, and you're not ready for the single-track technicality of the Water Ditch Trail (see story on page 43), the double-track at Tower House Historic District gives you a short flat loop to ride on, with a couple of options for extending your trip. You can also get a little history lesson in the process as you pass by the El Dorado Mine, plus the homestead of Charles Camden and gravesite of Levi Tower, two early entrepreneurs who settled here and made good on the area's gold riches in the late 1800s.

Start your tour by walking your bike down the paved trail from the parking lot, then over a wooden bridge. It was once a covered bridge and a part of the toll road that Camden built and operated in order to take money from anyone who wanted to pass through. Turn left immediately after the bridge, mount your bike and ride through the white picket gate. Cross a second bridge and start on the wide dirt trail that heads straight, past a park residence and up to the El Dorado

Bridge to the Tower House Historic District

Mine. The wide, clear creek on your left is aptly named Clear Creek, and can run like a river in springtime.

El Dorado Mine, which was built around 1885 and operated until 1967, still has standing buildings filled with rusty mining machinery and a shaft that heads deep into the hillside. Rangers give tours of the mine on summer weekends. Even without a tour guide, you can peek into the assorted outbuildings and imagine what mining life might have been like.

After visiting the mine, you have two options: Ride the wide dirt road called the Camden Water Ditch Trail which loops around behind the mine, along Willow Creek and back to the Tower gravesite and the Camden House, or walk past the mine to the Mill Creek Trail, an incredible single-track trail that crosses and re-crosses Mill Creek 20 times in each direction. If you are going to explore Mill Creek, don't try to ride it, just lock up your bike and hike. It's a terrific little trail, up to 2.5 miles one-way through a mixed forest that is pretty in any season.

For a final side-trip, take a ride over to the Camden House and its outbuildings. Although the Tower House Hotel burned down in 1919, Camden's residence still stands. It has been beautifully restored.

In addition to the bike riding, hiking and historical tour, kids can try their luck at gold panning on Clear Creek, the same creek where the gold rush began at Whiskeytown when Pearson B. Reading discovered gold in 1848. It costs a buck to get a gold-panning permit from park headquarters, but the permit is good for one year, and when your six-year-old finds that really big nugget, maybe he'll pay you back.

Make it easier: Just cut your trip short, riding only the wide loop trail to the mine and back.

Trip notes: There is no fee. For more information and a free trail map, contact Whiskeytown National Recreation Area, P.O. Box 188, Whiskeytown, CA 96095-0188; (530) 241-6584 or (530) 246-1225.

Directions: From Interstate 5 at Redding, take Highway 299 west for 16.5 miles, passing Whiskeytown Lake and turning left at the sign for "Tower House Historic District." Park in the lot, walk your bike down the paved path and across the wooden bridge, then ride through the white picket gate and cross a second bridge. Take the wide dirt trail that leads south (straight), past a park residence and toward the El Dorado Mine.

---

13. WATER DITCH TRAIL
Whiskeytown National Recreation Area
Off Highway 299 west of Redding
4 miles/1.5 hours — dirt single-track/MB
steepness: ◉ ◉   skill level: ◉ ◉

If you like riding on single track and you like lakeside trails, the Water Ditch Trail is a perfect fit. Its rather unattractive name does it no justice, as the trail skirts the edge of Whiskeytown Lake, providing stunning lake views at almost every turn.

The water ditch itself was part of the original irrigation system— one of many ditches, flumes and pipes—that developer Levi Tower built to supply his hotel, farm and mining operations. The trail starts at the Oak Bottom campground and runs for two miles. It ends near the Carr Powerhouse, which is part of a huge water regulation system somewhat more complicated than Tower's was: It diverts water from the Trinity River, stores it in Trinity Lake, sends it by tunnel to Whiskeytown Lake, then sends it to Keswick Reservoir and into the Sacramento River, all in an effort to keep the Central Valley from looking like a desert.

The Water Ditch Trail does have some technically challenging parts. If you are riding with young children, a better option would be to ride the Tower House Historic District trails (see page 41). On this trail, be sure to keep your speed down and your bike in control.

Starting from the dirt pullout and trailhead along the Oak Bottom access road, you head downhill immediately for about 30 yards (it's a bit steep), to an intersection where bikers go to the right and hikers to the left. Follow the bikers' trail along the dirt single-track as it curves in and around the lakeshore. The entire length of trail runs between Whiskey-town Lake and Highway 299, so you are wowed by lake views the

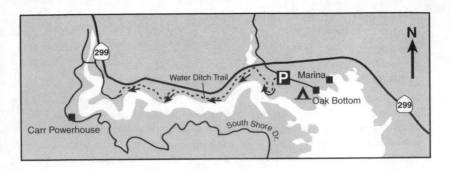

whole way. The only minus is road noise on roughly half the trip. One 300-yard section of the trail is actually right next to the road, but it's over with quickly and the rest of the time you're surrounded by oak trees and possibly the biggest manzanita bushes in all of Shasta-Trinity. Fall colors are good on this trail, and the lake is always populated with a variety of birds. We saw hundreds of duck pairs in October.

There is one major stream crossing, where, on our trip, the bridge had been washed out. It was replaced by a couple of planks, which we walked our bikes over. About 1.5 miles down the trail, there is a pumphouse with a locked gate which you have to carry your bike over, or you can walk your bike up the stairstepped trail off to the side. Shortly after the gate, you reach an intersection where a dirt road comes in from the right. Follow the road to the left for about 25 yards and then pick up the single-track again, next to the lake, continuing west to the trail's end at a paved road in one-half mile. Turn around here for a four-mile round-trip, or ride out-and-back on the pavement for one mile to the Carr Powerhouse. At the powerhouse, a few picnic tables are located right below the giant electric towers and power lines. Go figure.

Make it easier: Just cut your trip short, turning around sooner.

Trip notes: There is no fee. For more information and a free trail map, contact Whiskeytown National Recreation Area, P.O. Box 188, Whiskeytown, CA 96095-0188; (530) 241-6584 or (530) 246-1225.

Directions: From Interstate 5 at Redding, take Highway 299 west for 13.5 miles, passing Whiskeytown Lake Visitor Information Center and turning left at the sign for Oak Bottom campground and marina. (The Oak Bottom turnoff is five miles past the Visitor Information Center and 2.5 miles before the Tower House Historic District.) Drive two-tenths of a mile down the Oak Bottom access road, where there is a trailhead and dirt parking pullout for a few cars on the right side of the road. If this parking area is full, you can drive further down the access road and park near the campground. There is another trailhead across from the camp store.

14. SACRAMENTO RIVER TRAIL
City of Redding
Off Highway 299 in Redding
7 miles/1.25 hours — paved bike trail/RB or MB
steepness: ◉ ◉   skill level: ◉

If ever there were a perfect, easy trail for teaching someone how to ride a bike, or for going with a friend on a casual Sunday afternoon ride, the Sacramento River Trail is it. It's just the kind of trail you'd want in a riverside park: It's pretty all the way, it takes you away from the bustle of downtown, and it offers plenty of good places to sit on a bench and watch the water roll by. With a 10-mile-per-hour speed limit along the trail, you won't be going anywhere fast.

Not surprisingly, the multi-use trail is popular with Redding locals, and you'll see plenty of dog-walkers, anglers, baby strollers, and joggers in addition to dozens of squirrels and small flocks of quail, who don't seem to mind the humans in the least. If you visit in summer, you'll be able to pick a few handfuls of blackberries along the trail (careful, they stain your cycling gloves), and if you time your trip for fall, you'll get one of Redding's finest displays of autumn color. The trees with the compound, lance-shaped leaves are sumacs, which turn vibrant red in October, while the oaks prefer to wear gold.

The first mile of trail from Riverside Drive is so tame and suburban-feeling, you'll be a little surprised when you continue west along the river and find yourself in wide-open foothill country, where the paved trail seems out of place against the rugged landscape. At 2.5 miles, you reach the 418-foot-long, hiker and biker footbridge across the Sacramento River, just before Keswick Dam. The bridge is a technological wonder, considered an environmentally safe bridge because it is a "concrete stress-ribbon," supported by 200-plus steel cables in its concrete deck instead of concrete pilings or bridge piers dug into the riverbed. In addition to being constructed to avoid damage to the rock outcroppings along the river, it's really fun to ride on.

Cross the bridge and start looping back on the trail, now on the north side of the river. This side of the path is steeper and has more tight curves, making it more interesting for bike riders and less popular with walkers and joggers. After about 1.5 miles, the path is interrupted by a residential area where you ride down a neighborhood street for two-tenths of a mile. You pick up the trail again along the river, heading east to Benton Drive/Riverside Drive. At this intersection, turn right, cross the Diestleherst Bridge over the river and return to your

Hiker and biker footbridge across the Sacramento River

starting point on Riverside Drive.

You may want to bring your fishing rod along for this trip, as the Sacramento River has a good trout fishing section right along the bike path. However, be wary of neighboring cows who sometimes wade into the water to take a drink and cool off. They just ruin your chances of catching anything.

Make it more challenging: You can add three more miles to your trip by riding out-and-back on the trail extension from Diestleherst Bridge to Benton Ranch, heading towards downtown along the north side of the river, through Caldwell Park and under the Market Street bridge. Return to your starting point by crossing the Diestleherst Bridge back to Riverside Drive.

Trip notes: There is no fee. For more information and a free map, contact City of Redding Parks and Recreation, 760 Parkview Avenue, Redding, CA 96001-3396; (530) 225-4095.

Directions: From Interstate 5 at Redding, take Highway 299 west for two miles, until it connects with Highway 273 heading north (this is also North Market Street). Veer to the right on Highway 273, then turn left (west) on Riverside Drive. Don't cross over the river on Riverside, but instead continue straight into the parking area at Riverside Park. Start riding on the bike trail by heading west from the parking area.

Napa, Sonoma, & Mendocino

15—Old Haul Road, *MacKerricher State Park*...................................... 48

16   Fern Canyon & Falls Loop Trails, *Russian Gulch State Park* ...   50

17—Fern Canyon Trail, *Van Damme State Park* 52

18—Pygmy Forest Trail Loop, *Salt Point State Park* 53

19—Gerstle Cove to Stump Beach Cove Trail, *Salt Point State Park* ... 56

20—Sebastopol-Santa Rosa Multi-Use Trail,
   Sonoma County Regional Parks 58

21—Howarth Park & Spring Lake Park Trails,
   Sonoma County Regional Parks 59

22—Lake Ilsanjo Trail Loop, *Annadel State Park* 61

23—Meadow & Hillside Trail Loop, *Sugarloaf Ridge State Park* 63

24—Lake Trail, *Jack London State Historic Park*............................... 65

For locations of trails, see map on page 8.

15. OLD HAUL ROAD
MacKerricher State Park
Off Highway 1 near Fort Bragg
6 miles/1 hour — paved road/RB or MB
steepness: ⚙   skill level: ⚙

First, the good news: The beauty of MacKerricher is all the recreation options it provides—in one state park, and for free. Some visitors ride the bike trail with its exquisite ocean views while others fish in Lake Cleone. Some hike the lake's perimeter trail while others search the tidepools at Laguna Point. Some lie on the beach while others dive for abalone along the shoreline. All this, and no state park day-use fee. It's hard to believe.

Now for the bad news: The bike trail, called the Old Haul Road, has suffered some serious storm damage over the years, and parts of it are completely washed away, replaced by millions of grains of blowing sand. Sections of the trail are impossible to ride on. The state park people have been hoping for funding from Cal Trans so they can repair the trail, as well as fix an aged railroad trestle that connects the trail to Fort Bragg and beyond, but so far, they're still just hoping.

But that hasn't stopped the bikers on the Old Haul Road. They arrive in great numbers and ride the sections that can be ridden. They share the trail with hikers, baby strollers, dogs on leashes, even some

Old Haul Road, MacKerricher State Park

equestrians, and everybody has a good time. A three-mile oceanside section from Ward Avenue to the closed-off railroad trestle in Fort Bragg (over Pudding Creek) allows six miles round-trip of uninterrupted riding, and gets the most traffic. At the railroad trestle, mountain bikers have carved a trail down the embankment to an access road below, so those on fat tires can continue riding into town. Everyone else just turns around and gets to see the coastal vistas one more time.

The Old Haul Road was originally a railroad grade built in 1914 to haul logs and lumber. In 1945, the rails were removed and the trail became a paved road for logging trucks. Then as now, sand continually reclaimed the route, causing many people to scratch their hands and wonder why the road wasn't built somewhat farther inland.

As the Old Haul Road heads south from the park into town, it passes behind the backs of seaside motels and occasionally provides views of the Georgia-Pacific Lumber Company's rather unattractive smokestacks. But you're unlikely to mind, because the western, ocean side of the trail is still undeveloped—just grassy bluffs and rocky coastline. Ocean views are spectacular the whole way. Tempting spur trails veer off from the paved trail onto the bluffs, but stay off of them—they are used by the many equestrians who frequent this park.

If it's solitude you seek, the passable southern stretch of trail won't provide it. For peace and quiet, you must brave the more collapsed trail sections on the park's north side (only if you have a mountain bike and are prepared to do some walking). To access it, don't make the mistake of riding north from Ward Avenue. This section of trail is in bad repair. Instead, drive your car to the Ten Mile River parking area on Highway 1 (just south of the Ten Mile River bridge, on the west side of the road), where you'll find the trail's north terminus. If you start here and ride south, you can get in a couple miles of riding before having to walk through ankle-deep sand.

Make it more challenging: If you don't mind walking your bike in sand, you can attempt to ride/walk the entire trail, which is 10 miles one-way. Views are terrific along the entire route.

Trip notes: There is no fee. A free trail map/park brochure is available at the entrance station. For more information, contact MacKerricher State Park, P.O. Box 440, Mendocino, CA 95460; (707) 937-5804 or (707) 937-4296.

Directions: From Mendocino, drive 11.7 miles north on Highway 1 to the entrance to MacKerricher State Park on the left (three miles north of Fort Bragg). Turn left into the park, drive past the entrance station, and turn left again, heading toward the camping areas. In half a mile, you'll see Lake

Cleone on your left. Park in the lot by the lake or continue to the right, to the end of the road and the parking lot by the beach at Laguna Point. (You can also drive north of the park entrance and start riding at Ward Avenue.)

16. FERN CANYON & FALLS LOOP TRAILS
Russian Gulch State Park
Off Highway 1 near Mendocino
3.2 miles/1 hour — paved bike trail/RB or MB
steepness: ● skill level: ●

We arrived at the parking lot at Russian Gulch State Park just in time to hear a park ranger tell an inquiring visitor: "Generally speaking, mountain bikes are not welcome in the Mendocino state parks."

With that warm greeting, we pulled our bikes out of the car and began riding, feeling a little like pond scum.

Well, that ranger was overdoing the negative, because the truth is that there are terrific trails open to all kinds of bikes in Mendocino state parks, and the Fern Canyon Trail in Russian Gulch is one of the best. What he should have said is that mountain bikers have to stay on the designated paved bike trails, which is true at all the major Mendocino parks, including Russian Gulch, MacKerricher, and Van Damme. But these parks' trails are downright spectacular, and pavement doesn't diminish the experience in the slightest. Instead, it provides a quality experience for all kinds of bikers and their bikes: fat tires, skinny tires, tandems, wheelchairs, and even a few tricycles.

The Fern Canyon Trail at Russian Gulch is made even better because it combines an easy bike trip through a forested, streamside canyon with a short hike to Russian Gulch Falls, a gushing 36-foot waterfall that drops into a rocky fern grotto. The falls are framed by huge toppled tree trunks, some with hundreds of ferns growing right out of them. It's a terrific little waterfall in a lush, vibrant setting.

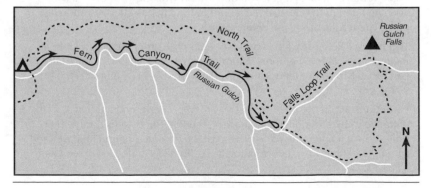

Some riders need a little assistance on the Fern Canyon Trail.

The trail directions are a breeze. Just get on your bike and ride from the trailhead at the edge of the campground, following the smooth paved trail for 1.6 miles to a trail junction, where there are a few picnic tables and a bike rack. Here you must lock up your bike and continue on foot to the waterfall. There are two options for getting there: You can take the short, seven-tenths of a mile route that reaches the falls from the north, or the longer, 2.3-mile route that reaches the falls from the south. After viewing the falls, you can either return the way you came or hike the other side of the loop back to the trail junction and your bike, then ride back to the campground. The three-mile round-trip bike ride will probably take you less than an hour, but figure on an hour extra to hike the short route to the waterfall, two hours extra to hike the long route.

Make it easier: You can skip the waterfall hike and just ride your bike through the canyon, which is pretty enough to be worth the trip by itself.

Trip notes: A $5 day-use fee is charged per vehicle. A free map is available at the entrance kiosk. For more information, contact Russian Gulch State Park, P.O. Box 440, Mendocino, CA 95460; (707) 937-5804 or (707) 937-4296.

Directions: From Mendocino, drive two miles north on Highway 1 to the entrance for Russian Gulch State Park on the left. Turn left and then left again immediately to reach the entrance kiosk. After paying, continue straight past the kiosk, crossing back under the highway to the eastern

side of the park. Drive past the recreation hall and through the campground to the parking area for the Fern Canyon Trail. Start hiking from the
trailhead on the east side of the parking area. (If the campground is closed
for the season, you must park near the recreation hall and walk through
the campground.)

---

17. FERN CANYON TRAIL
Van Damme State Park
Off Highway 1 near Mendocino
5 miles/2 hours — paved trail/RB or MB
steepness: ◉ ◉   skill level: ◉

This Fern Canyon business causes some confusion. Here we are in
the coastal resort town of Mendocino, eager to ride our bikes, and
everyone keeps telling us to ride the Fern Canyon Trail. The catch is
that there are two Fern Canyon Trails within five miles of Mendocino.
Both are paved bike trails, both are in state parks, and both carve their
way through flora-rich canyons, paralleling streams.

Here's the difference: The Fern Canyon Trail in Russian Gulch
State Park, just north of Mendocino, is the paved trail with an optional
add-on hike to a beautiful waterfall (see story on page 50). The Fern
Canyon Trail in Van Damme State Park, just south of Mendocino, is
the paved trail with many bridges that cross and re-cross Little River,
with an optional add-on hike (or mountain bike ride) to a pygmy
forest. Both Fern Canyon trails are excellent trips, well worth the long
drive to Mendocino for the chance to ride them.

The Fern Canyon Trail in Van Damme State Park has one big
catch, though—you have to ride it when the weather has been fair for a
while. The trail was closed for long periods off and on in the 1990s
because of wiped-out bridges and other storm damage from winter
rains. When it reopened late in the year, the rains came down again and
it was closed for two more weeks due to fallen trees. That's how it goes
during some winters here. The combination of the trail's several bridge
crossings over Little River and the thickness of the forest surrounding it
means that a period of hard rain can close the trail. Always call the park
before making a trip here, especially in winter.

When it's open, however, the Fern Canyon Trail offers plenty of
riding and hiking options. The first 2.5 miles are paved and nearly flat,
with only a gentle uphill grade, curving through Little River's lush
canyon lined with redwoods, firs, alders, and berry bushes, as well as
the inevitable ferns. Like its neighboring Fern Canyon Trail in Russian

Gulch State Park, this Fern Canyon Trail is covered with fir and pine needles, making you frequently forget you're riding on pavement. At 1./5 miles, you pass some hike-in campsites, and at 2.5 miles, the paved trail ends at a junction, where there are several choices. Mountain bikers can ride to the right on a dirt fire road for 1.2 miles to a pygmy forest, an interesting environment of sandy, highly acidic soil and miniature cypress and pine trees. Road bikers and those preferring to hike can lock up their bikes and hike on the trail to the left, which heads deeper into Fern Canyon, the trail getting narrower and the flora more dense with every step. One-and-a-half miles further, the trail begins to switchback out of the canyon and into a drier forest. Many people turn around at the switchbacks, preferring the cool green of the ferns, while others continue another mile to the pygmy forest. From there, you can return the way you came, or, for a shorter trip, walk back on the 1.2-mile mountain biker's route to the junction where you left your bike. (Mountain bikers can ride only the 1.2-mile route from Fern Canyon to the pygmy forest, not the longer hikers-only route.)

Make it easier: Skip the walk or ride to the pygmy forest. Instead, lock up your bike at the end of the paved trail and walk only a short way into the fern canyon, then turn around. If you want to see the pygmy forest, you can drive to it on Little River Airport Road, located half a mile south of the main park. The pygmy forest is 2.7 miles east on Little River Airport Road, on the left.

Trip notes: A $5 day-use fee is charged per vehicle. A free park map is available at the entrance kiosk. For more information, contact Van Damme State Park, P.O. Box 440, Mendocino, CA 95460; (707) 937-5804 or (707) 937-0851.

Directions: From Mendocino, drive three miles south on Highway 1 to the entrance for Van Damme State Park on the left. Turn left and stop at the entrance kiosk. After paying, continue straight past the kiosk to the parking area for the Fern Canyon Trail, located at the east end of the canyon campground. Start hiking from the signed trailhead.

18. PYGMY FOREST TRAIL LOOP
Salt Point State Park
Off Highway 1 near Jenner
4.5 miles/1.5 hours — dirt roads/MB
steepness: ● ● ●   skill level: ◐ ●

If you've been eating too much abalone with garlic and butter on your trip to Salt Point State Park, here's a ride where you'll work off some calories, guaranteed. The Pygmy Forest Trail's a workout, but it's

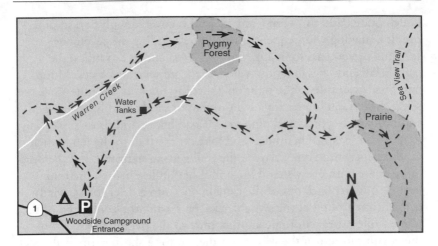

definitely worth the effort. When it's all over, you can have another serving of those tasty shellfish which this park—and this whole stretch of coast—is best known for.

Check your calendar before you go, however. The state park only opens its trails to mountain bikers from April to October in order to protect the trails in the wet and muddy months. (Abalone season runs from April to November, which coincides nicely, if you have friends who like to dive.)

Even if you're well-fed and raring to go, you may eye the uphill fire road leading from the parking lot with some suspicion, as I did. However, once you get through the first 200 yards of climbing, you can turn left onto a nice level stretch. (Ignore the trail sign that points straight uphill for the Pygmy Forest—you're taking a slightly easier route.) Enjoy the smooth ride through thick pine and fir trees, catch your breath, and at the next intersection, turn right. Climb. Climb some more. Walk your bike when you can't stand climbing any more. The trail is not terribly steep, but rather a slow, continual, relentless uphill, gaining about 500 feet in elevation.

As you climb, you may notice the forest around you changing. The soil starts to look different—drier and sandier—as you ascend the hillside. Rhododendrons begin to spring up among the trees, which appear less dense than they were earlier on the trail. You'll pass another junction on your right, where you can turn back if you feel completely pooped, but it's only one-half (grueling) mile more to the Pygmy Forest, so push on. Extensive grumbling is not allowed, since you can make the entire 1.5-mile climb in less than 30 minutes, even if you walk half of it (guess how I know).

Finally you reach the top of the ridge, at elevation 900 feet. The trail flattens out, and suddenly you're in the pygmy forest. Azaleas and rhododendrons flourish in the sandy, acidic soil, and cypress, pine, and redwood trees grow in dwarfed versions. It's a strange-looking place, a big contrast to the "normal" conifer and hardwood forest you've been riding in.

The trail narrows to single-track, with a few sandy and rocky spots to keep things interesting. Keep your speed down and watch out for other trail users who may be coming the opposite way through the dense pygmy forest. (I was listening to the wind in the tiny trees, marveling at nature's many oddities, when I was startled by a group of eight-year-olds singing "100 Bottles of Beer on the Wall." They were on 86 when they passed me.)

If you've made it this far, you might as well ride the rest of the loop instead of turning around, because the remainder is pure fun—all flat or downhill. The trail descends through the pygmy forest, then meets up with a fire road where you can turn left or right. Right goes straight home, but if you have any energy remaining, turn left instead for a flat half-mile. The trail leads to a wide and pretty meadow which is called a coastal prairie. (I call it a good picnic spot.) When you reach an intersection with Sea View Trail, you've gone far enough; turn your bike around and begin the descent back to the campground at Highway 1. When you reach two water tanks halfway down, stay to the left if you want to ride a slightly different route than the one you rode up.

Make it easier: The steepest part of the climb is the last half-mile to the pygmy forest, so if you have small kids who can't make the ascent, take the cutoff by the water tanks for a shorter loop ride. If they want to see pygmy trees, take them to Van Damme State Park (see "Make it easier" on page 53), where you can drive right to them.

Trip notes: A $5 day-use fee is charged per vehicle. A park map is available at the entrance station for 50 cents. For more information, contact Salt Point State Park, 25050 Coast Highway 1, Jenner, CA 95450; (707) 847-3221.

Directions: From U.S. 101 at Santa Rosa, drive west on Highway 116 for 33 miles, through Sebastopol and Guerneville, to Highway 116's intersection with Highway 1 near Jenner. Continue north on Highway 1 for 20 miles to Salt Point State Park. Look for the Woodside Campground entrance on your right (if you reach Gerstle Cove, you've gone too far) and enter there. Pay at the kiosk and then drive through, keeping to the left, heading toward the hike/bike camp. Park in the parking lot for the hike/bike camp and start riding on the dirt fire road that leads off from the far side of the lot. It is signed as "Pygmy Forest, 2 miles."

19. GERSTLE COVE to STUMP BEACH COVE TRAIL
Salt Point State Park
Off Highway 1 near Jenner
2.4 miles/45 minutes — dirt roads/MB
steepness: ⊛   skill level: ⊛

If you're prepared for some coastal wind, the Salt Point State Park trail from Gerstle Cove to Stump Beach Cove is a spectacular, flat bike trip across grassy bluffs, with classic ocean views every pedal-crank of the way. It's short enough and flat enough so that kids can enjoy the ride equally with adults, and with the Gerstle Cove Marine Reserve located just below the cliffs, the trail offers plenty of opportunities to get a look at some marine life.

While the coastal vistas here are unparalleled, you must time your trip right and dress properly to enjoy them. Otherwise, you can feel like you're riding in the middle of a hurricane. If 2.4 miles doesn't seem like much of a bike workout, try it when the wind is howling at 50 miles per hour, which it can do here.

For starters, make sure you arrive between April and October, the only months when the park's trails are open to bikes. Then, time your trip so that you are riding this trail as early in the morning as possible, before the wind picks up speed. If you arrive too late, you're better off riding the Pygmy Forest Trail (see the previous story), because it's protected by trees. On this trail, it's just you, the wind, the bluffs, and the wide, wide ocean. Bring a jacket with you, always.

Start riding from the parking area at Gerstle Cove. If the short paved path around the headlands (signed as the Salt Point Trail) is empty of people, you can ride it for 150 yards till it meets up with a dirt fire road, which you then follow. If there are lots of folks standing around on the paved path admiring the view, ride your bike from the parking lot back up the park road about 100 yards and pick up the dirt fire road there, which is signed as "Authorized Vehicles Only." That means you.

Now you're in business. Prepare to be awed by the rocky coastline, huge kelp beds washed up on shore, harbor seals swimming in the surf, and sea birds swooping and diving overhead. If you're very fortunate, you may even get to see a California gray whale passing by on its yearly migration. (Most sightings are between November and May.) Waves crash against the cliffs, sometimes causing a fine mist to dampen your face as you ride. The place is so beautiful, and so dramatic, chances are you won't even mind the wind.

Stump Beach Cove at Salt Point State Park

Ignore any trail spurs and stay on the main fire road, leaving the single-track for hikers. The surface is eroded in some places, but rock-hard from the constant, drying wind. Occasionally the route turns inland, moving away from the sea, which provides spectacular views of the forest backing Highway 1, and the grasslands between the forest and the sea. In springtime, these grasslands are profuse with blooms from lupine, poppies, and coastal paintbrush.

When you reach Stump Beach Cove, the trail loops around to the right, skirting the edge of the cove and coming to an end at Highway 1. You can ride all the way to the highway and then just turn around, enjoying all the views one more time on your return trip.

Make it more challenging: You can ride your bike from this parking area to the visitor center and Gerstle Cove picnic area, following the paved park road. Beware of park auto traffic, however.

Trip notes: A $5 day-use fee is charged per vehicle. A park map is available at the entrance station for 50 cents. For more information, contact Salt Point State Park, 25050 Coast Highway 1, Jenner, CA 95450; (707) 847-3221.

Directions: From U.S. 101 at Santa Rosa, drive west on Highway 116 for 33 miles, through Sebastopol and Guerneville, to Highway 116's intersection with Highway 1 near Jenner. Continue north on Highway 1 for 20 miles to Salt Point State Park. Look for the Gerstle Cove entrance on your left. Drive through the entrance kiosk, then head straight for seven-tenths of a mile to the day-use area.

20. SEBASTOPOL-SANTA ROSA MULTI-USE TRAIL
Sonoma County Regional Parks
Off Highway 116 between Sebastopol and Santa Rosa
6 miles/1 hour — paved bike trail/RB or MB
steepness: ◉   skill level: ◉

Sebastopol is the kind of unspoiled Sonoma town where you can still smell the apples in the fall. Sure, the city has grown up; sure, things aren't the way they used to be; but still, Sebastopol manages to retain its rural, small-town feel. The old rail trail that runs from Sebastopol to Santa Rosa is the perfect kind of bike trail for this town—a flat and easy route where you can ride through farmland and inhale the apple-scented air.

Pull that old beach cruiser out of your dusty garage—you know, the one that's so old, it only has three speeds—because on the Sebastopol-Santa Rosa Multi-Use Trail, you won't even have to shift. The trail's history is obvious (it's an old railroad line) because the route is completely straight and completely flat. It's exactly the kind of path that trains like.

Bikers like it, too, and so do rollerbladers, joggers, dog walkers, parents with baby strollers, and others of similar ilk. Luckily the trail starts near the Town Plaza in Sebastopol, which has both a bike store and an ice cream store, fulfilling all of a cyclist's basic needs.

The first part of the route is prettier than its latter miles, which enter less rural territory as you leave Sebastopol and near Santa Rosa. Although the entire trail parallels busy Highway 12, it is sheltered from the freeway by trees for the first mile and a half. Several benches are placed along the trail, nice spots to sit and look out to the south over farm country. There are no benches looking out to the north at the freeway, thank goodness.

The trail intersects with roads at a few points, but most are just ranch roads with little or no traffic. There is one major intersection about two miles in where you must stop and look carefully before crossing, but otherwise, you are mercifully separated from automobiles until the bike route comes to an abrupt end at Merced Avenue, one-half mile from the Santa Rosa city limit. The Sonoma County Regional Parks Department hopes to someday extend this trail into downtown Santa Rosa, but for now, everybody just rides to Merced Avenue and then turns around and rides back.

Make it easier: The trail gets much less attractive after the first major road crossing two miles in; you could turn around there if you wish.

Trip notes: There is no fee. For more information, contact Sonoma County Regional Parks Department, 2300 County Center, Suite 120A, Santa Rosa, CA 95403; (707) 527-2041.

Directions: From U.S. 101 at Santa Rosa, drive northwest on Highway 116 to downtown Sebastopol, just before Highway 116's junction with Highway 12. Turn left on Burnett Street in Sebastopol and park in the city lot, which allows three hours of free parking. Ride your bike out the east side of the parking lot and cross Petaluma Boulevard (the road you drove in on) to locate the start of the trail.

21. HOWARTH PARK & SPRING LAKE PARK TRAILS

Sonoma County Regional Parks

Off Highway 12 in Santa Rosa
5 miles/1 hour — paved bike trail/RB or MB
steepness. ⬤ ⬤   skill level: ⬤

Howarth Park and Spring Lake Parks are two adjacent parks, run by the city of Santa Rosa and county of Sonoma respectively, that are well-loved by locals but virtually unknown outside the Santa Rosa area. Thousands of people drive within five miles of them on their daily commute without knowing of their existence or their charms. In addition to a terrific paved bike trail, the parks have two lakes which are great for fishing, picnicking, and strolling around, as well as a campground, a boat ramp, hiking and horseback riding trails, and enough game courts and children's play sets to keep an entire family happy for a year.

The bike trail that runs through both parks

Lake Ralphine, Howarth Park

is perfect for a one-hour workout. It makes a nice loop that you can ride around once or twice, with a few small hills to get your leg muscles working. I know a family who comes here regularly on weekends; one parent plays with the kids while the other rides the bike trail, then they switch roles. There's even an amusement park called K Land at Howarth Park, with a carousel, a miniature train, an animal barn, and pony rides during summers and school vacations. With all this action, plus the possibility of rowboating or fishing on the lakes, everybody is guaranteed a good time.

If you start your ride at Howarth Park by Lake Ralphine, you can avoid paying the entrance fee at Spring Lake Park. Lake Ralphine is much smaller than Spring Lake, although still popular with anglers (especially young ones) who shorefish for bass, trout, and bluegill. The bike trail passes Lake Ralphine's southeast edge, heading through oak-studded hills to Spring Lake. The trail loops around Spring Lake; you can head either left or right to ride around it. I'd suggest riding to the left first, since the trail is routed up a hill and over the dam, offering great views of the 75-acre lake.

Constructed as a flood control reservoir in 1962, Spring Lake offers decent fishing prospects for trout and bass and plenty of picnic spots with views of ducks, reeds, and water. Although swimming is not allowed in the lake, there is a separate swimming lagoon on its east side. You ride past it on the bike trail on the way to the campground and boat ramp.

As you ride through the boat ramp parking area, the trail gets a little tricky to follow. You must go up a short hill, then turn right at the Jackrabbit Parcourse/Picnic Area and ride through it to pick up the bike path again (on your right). This is the only place where the trail is broken and you may have to contend with cars.

In less than a quarter of a mile you descend to the fork where you first entered the loop; turn right to ride the loop again or left to head back to Howarth Park, Lake Ralphine, and your car.

Make it more challenging: Many riders like to ride the loop around Spring Lake twice. Mountain bikers also have the option of heading off on various dirt trails which intersect with the paved trail. Be sure to get updated information on which dirt trails are open to bikes.

Trip notes: There is no fee. For more information, contact Sonoma County Regional Parks Department, 2300 County Center, Suite 120A, Santa Rosa, CA 95403; (707) 527-2041.

Directions: From U.S. 101 in Santa Rosa, take the Fairgrounds/Highway 12 exit. Highway 12 becomes Farmers Lane as it heads through downtown Santa Rosa. Turn right on Montgomery Drive and continue for one mile. Turn right on Summerfield Road and drive one-quarter mile, turning left into the entrance for Howarth Park. Drive straight up the hill to the upper parking lot, which is next to Lake Ralphine. The bike path begins on the right side of the lake.

22. LAKE ILSANJO TRAIL LOOP
Annadel State Park
Off Highway 12 in Santa Rosa
6.3 miles/1.5 hours — dirt roads/MB
steepness: ✹ ✹ ✹   skill level: ✹ ✹

Annadel State Park is a horsey kind of place. In fact, sometimes it seems there are more horses here than people, with numerous horse trailers in the parking lot, hoofprints all over the place, and horse "evidence" on the trail. Lucky thing is, those big hairy guys are generous, and they don't mind sharing the trail to Lake Ilsanjo with easy bikers, as long as we mind our trail manners.

So, when you see a horse and rider coming toward you on the trail, what do you do? Right—stop riding, pull over to the side, smile a lot, and let them pass. If you're heading in the same direction as they are and need to pass, call out gently and cheerfully, without shouting, and ask the rider's permission. Give the horse plenty of time to move off the trail. That way, you won't scare the daylights out of anyone.

Okay, now that we've brushed up on our horse etiquette, we can ride to Lake Ilsanjo, on one of the best mountain bike loops in Sonoma. The trip starts with a good climb over 1.5 miles on Warren P. Richardson Trail, with one tight hairpin turn and a couple of stretches where the route goes flat for a while so you can catch your breath. The wide, smooth trail is completely forested, thick with Douglas firs, bays, and ferns, a godsend in the warmer months. You know you're near the lake when you start to descend, heading into wide open canyonlands, with occasional oak trees dotting the meadows. The trail takes you to the east side of the lake, providing great views of blue water and plenty of waterfowl, and then circles around and over the dam. Expect lots of company, especially right by the lake and dam, because this route is popular with bikers, hikers, swimmers, and anglers. Fishing is fair in Lake Ilsanjo, with anglers lining up along the shore to cast for black bass and bluegill. More than a few people make this a combination biking/fishing trip, since the lake is a bit far for walking.

Bear right on Rough Go Trail and head away from the lake to Live Oak Trail. Turn right and ride for four-tenths of a mile to Burma Trail,

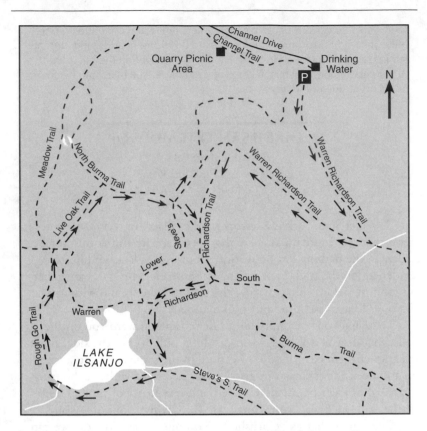

then bear right again, completing your loop. All of these trails are nearly flat, with wide open canyon views to the north and west, but Burma is extremely rocky, so much so that I had to stop and walk my bike for a short distance.

You can continue on Burma Trail straight back to Warren P. Richardson, or bear left on Steve's S Trail to get there as well. Either way, when you reach Richardson, it's an easy coast back down to the parking lot. Be sure to turn left at the hairpin turn that you rode through on the way up; when coasting downhill, it's easy to continue straight instead of making that turn, in which case you'll head off on Two Quarry Trail and probably won't be home in time for supper.

With all the possible bike routes in 5,000-acre Annadel State Park, a park map is essential for your trip; buy one at the self-registration station where you pay your park fee. And, if you see any horses on your ride, don't forget to mind your manners.

Make it easier: You can skip the loop and just ride up the hill to the lake's eastern edge and back, for a four-mile round-trip with no technical riding.

Trip notes: A $2 day-use fee is charged per vehicle. You must pay the fee at the self-registration station on Channel Drive. Park maps are available for 75 cents at the self-registration station. For more information, contact Annadel State Park, 6201 Channel Drive, Santa Rosa, CA 95409; (707) 539-3911 or (707) 938-1519.

Directions: From U.S. 101 in Santa Rosa, take the Fairgrounds/Highway 12 exit. Highway 12 becomes Farmers Lane as it heads through downtown Santa Rosa. Turn right on Montgomery Drive and follow it for 2.7 miles (veering to the right), then turn right on Channel Drive. Follow Channel Drive into the park, stop and pay the fee at the self-registration station halfway in, then drive to the end of the road and park in the lot. Look for the trail (a fire road) on the southwest side of the parking lot.

23. MEADOW & HILLSIDE TRAIL LOOP
Sugarloaf Ridge State Park
Off Highway 12 near Kenwood
2.5 miles/1 hour — dirt roads/MB
steepness: 🌑 🌑 🌑   skill level: 🌑 🌑

With its entrance set further off the main road, Sugarloaf Ridge is often overlooked in a cluster of close-together Sonoma state parks, including Annadel, Sugarloaf, and Jack London. Getting there requires a four-mile drive off Highway 12, leading to the park's entrance set 1,000 feet below the top of Sugarloaf Ridge, elevation 2,200 feet. If you make the trip, you'll find that much of the ascent is accomplished on the drive up, so you're rewarded with an easy ride in the park, along ridgeline meadows that offer spectacular views of the Sonoma Valley below.

There is still some climbing to be done, however. While the Meadow Trail is mostly flat, the Hillside Trail ascends about 350 feet in half a mile and then drops back down, reminding your heart and lungs of their respective functions.

From the day-use parking area, ride up the paved park road for one-quarter mile, toward the horse corral area, then ride through the horse camp gate. At the far end of the horse camp, the pavement ends, and on the right is a gate and gravel trail, signed as the Meadow Trail. Although it is marked as open to hikers and horses, bikers are welcome, too. Ride on it for eight-tenths of a mile, passing by the junctions with Gray Pine and Brushy Peaks trails on your left, and then loop to your right on Hillside Trail.

Hope you're warmed up, because now you're going to climb like a mountain goat. While the Meadow Trail was sunny and open, the

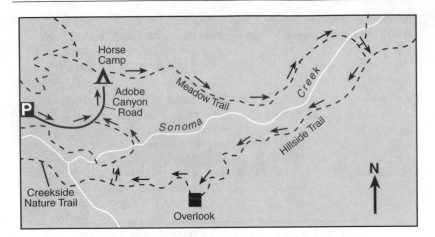

Hillside Trail is shaded by oaks, laurel, and madrone, and if it's at all warm outside, you'll be grateful for the canopy. Deer, like bike riders, favor the combination of meadows and forest here, and more than once I've startled a group of them while riding this part of the loop.

After climbing for six-tenths of a mile (pant, pant), you'll start to descend and pass a water storage tank. Don't rush downhill or you'll miss the best part of this ride, which is an overlook with a picnic table located about 100 yards after the tank. A little cutoff trail leads to the lookout (ride too fast and you'll miss it), where, lo and behold, there's a spring and a water spigot. Drink up and fill your bottle. Hopefully your biking partner remembered to pack along some good food, since you're here at this fine picnic table with a terrific view of the valley. Have lunch and celebrate making the climb to such a great spot.

On the downhill, the gravel service road turns to dirt, and eventually to single-track, so try to keep your eyes on the trail as you descend, even though you will be continually distracted by the views. When you reach an intersection where Hillside Trail heads to the right and a nature trail leads straight ahead, stay on Hillside. Pass another hiking trail, then cross Sonoma Creek and take a short jaunt through a meadow. The trail will lead you back to a gate at the horse corral area, just a few dozen yards from where you started. Ride back on the pavement to your left to the parking area and your car.

As with all the parks in Sonoma, it's not advisable to ride here in summer unless you get an early morning start. For the best all-day trip, arrive in late winter or spring and ride this loop, then lock up your bike and hike the short Canyon Trail from west of the entrance kiosk to the small waterfall on Sonoma Creek (see a park map for details).

Make it easier: To avoid any serious climbing, just ride out and back on the Meadow Trail.

Trip notes: A $5 day-use fee is charged per vehicle. A trail map is available from the entrance kiosk for 75 cents. For more information, contact Sugarloaf Ridge State Park, 2605 Adobe Canyon Road, Kenwood, CA 95452-9004; (707) 833-5712 or (707) 938-1519.

Directions: From U.S. 101 in Santa Rosa, take the Fairgrounds/Highway 12 exit. Highway 12 becomes Farmers Lane as it heads through downtown Santa Rosa. Continue on Highway 12 for 11 miles to Adobe Canyon Road. Turn left and drive 3.5 miles to the park entrance kiosk. Pay the entrance fee, then continue straight and park in the day-use parking area on the left. Ride your bike further up the park road, following the pavement to the far end of the horse camp. Where the pavement ends, take the gravel trail on the right, which is signed as the Meadow Trail.

24. LAKE TRAIL
Jack London State Historic Park
Off Highway 12 in Glen Ellen
2.7 miles/1 hour – dirt roads/MB
steepness: ⊛ ⊛ ⊛   skill level: ⊛ ⊛

Jack London wanted beauty, and so he "bought beauty, and was content with beauty for awhile." That's how he spoke of his ranch, and the hills surrounding it, which are now a part of Jack London State Historic Park. London's vision of beauty is the basis for a great bike trip from the ranch's vineyards to its lake, and then further beyond to a hillside clearing and vista point.

London, the most popular and highest paid fiction writer of the early 1900s, wanted to build his home in Glen Ellen to escape from city life. After two years of construction on his ranch dream house, it mysteriously caught fire and burned to the ground just days before he and his wife were to move in. London continued to live on the ranch property, in a small wood-frame house, until his death in 1916.

In the 1950s, several parcels of this land became state park property, and today, the park has grown to 800 acres with several miles of fire roads that are open to bikes. Many of the trails are quite steep as they rise toward the summit of Sonoma Mountain. For easy bikers, the best ride is the 2.7-mile round-trip to London's ranch lake and an overlook beyond. You can begin or end your trip with a visit to the Jack London Museum at the park's visitor center, which has interesting exhibits and photographs from the life of the author.

Even without the historical slant, this ride is a winner. Take the paved trail from the parking lot to the picnic area (walk your bike on this 100-yard section, since it can be crowded), then pick up the dirt fire road signed as the Lake Trail. Follow it to the right, past the winery ruins on your left and the trail to London's pig pens on your right, riding along acres of carefully tended grapevines. Shortly you'll begin to climb, and continue to climb for half a mile through mixed hardwoods and Douglas firs all the way to the lake. (You must stay to the left and pass through a gate at the edge of the vineyard; hikers can split off from bikers here and walk to the lake on single-track.)

Although London's lake is more of a pond nowadays—with sediment continually encroaching, it has shrunk to half its original size—the redwood log cabin he used as a bathhouse still stands. London and his wife would entertain guests at the lake; swimming and fishing were preferred activities. Ride around the lake's left side, following the trail that is signed "Mountain Trail to Mountain Summit." It's a hard, switchbacked climb over a third of a mile but worth the effort. When you reach an intersection with Fallen Bridge Trail, you're at the vista point in May's Clearing, and the view of the valley to the south is breathtaking.

Retrace your route when you're ready, but control your speed on the way downhill. The park has a strict 15-mile-per-hour speed limit, and with the number of horses and hikers on the trail and around the ranch grounds, it makes sense to obey it.

Make it more challenging: From the vista point at May's Clearing, you can continue to climb uphill on the Mountain Trail for another 1.5 miles to the next vista point.

Trip notes: A $6 day-use fee is charged per vehicle. A park map is available at the entrance station for $1. For more information, contact Jack London State Historic Park, 2400 London Ranch Road, Glen Ellen, CA 95442; (707) 938-5216 or (707) 938-1519.

Directions: From Sonoma, travel north on Highway 12 for 4.5 miles to Madrone Road and turn left. At the end of Madrone Road, turn right on Arnold Drive and follow it for three miles into Glen Ellen, then turn left on London Ranch Road. Follow London Ranch Road for one mile to the park entrance kiosk. Park in the day-use area on the right (not in the visitor center lot on the left). The trail leads from the parking area.

Sierra Foothills
& Central Valley

25—Bidwell Park Ride, *City of Chico* 68
26—Chico to Durham Bike Path, *Butte County* 70
27—Hardrock Trail, *Empire Mine State Historic Park* 71
28—Quarry Road Trail, *Auburn State Recreation Area* 73
29—American River Parkway: Beal's Point to Negro Bar,
    Folsom Lake State Recreation Area 75

🕸 For locations of trails, see map on page 8. 🕸

25. BIDWELL PARK RIDE
City of Chico
Off Highway 32 in Chico
6 miles/1 hour — paved bike trail/RB or MB
steepness: ⊛   skill level: ⊛

Chico is a bike riding kind of town. Take its downtown stretch on
Main Street, for example: bike racks on almost every corner, three bike
stores in the space of two blocks, and municipal buses rolling by with
bike carriers mounted on their backs. Like many other college cities,
Chico has made way for its bike-riding students at Cal State by adding
bike lanes to major streets and even printing up a local map with sug-
gested routes for bicyclists. But the town has gone beyond mere bike
accommodation with its conversion of rail trails to bicycle trails (see
story on page 70) and with its city park—Bidwell Park—which is
largely closed to vehicle traffic, so bicyclists can have a field day.

Visitors and locals alike enjoy Bidwell. Access is easy: Starting
from 4th and Main streets in downtown Chico, ride down 4th Street
straight into the park. (You can also drive into the park from 4th Street
and park in one of several small lots, but parking is limited.) In half a
mile, the park road is blocked off to cars and the route becomes blissfully free of auto traffic. Since this is a two-lane road (called South Park
Drive) and not a bike trail, there is plenty of room for bikers traveling
in both directions, as well as for the multitudes of walkers, joggers,
baby-stroller-pushers, and the like. Since this is a city park, there are
plenty of water fountains, picnic tables, benches, and children's play
areas along the route. The first main grouping of facilities is at the One
Mile Recreation Area, on your right, one mile in.

Although Bidwell Park can get quite hot in summer, it is well-
protected by shade trees, which make a great display of color in the fall.
Oaks, maples, sumacs, and other deciduous trees line the route, enough
of them to make you sometimes forget you are in the middle of a big
town. Because of the density of the trees, it's surprising when the route
suddenly intersects with a well-traveled city street, Manzanita Avenue.
With that dose of reality, you must make a decision: Cross the road and
continue onward into Upper Bidwell Park, or turn around and ride the
north side of the loop back to your starting place. Road bikers can ride
only one-half mile further into Upper Bidwell; the pavement ends at
Five Mile Recreation Area and numerous mountain bike trails continue
up into the hills (see "Make it more challenging").

To turn around at Manzanita Avenue and complete a six-mile loop ride on pavement, walk your bike to the left across the Manzanita bridge over Chico Creek (watch out for cars). Pick up the bike trail again on your left; it turns into a park road called Peterson Memorial Way. Now you're on the north side of the creek, heading west. The second leg of the loop is more of the same. To complete the trip, look for Mangrove Avenue near the park's west end; turn left and ride two blocks to be deposited back on 4th Street, near the park entrance.

Riding through Bidwell Park

Make it more challenging: Mountain bikers can use the paved loop as a warmup for the trails in Upper Bidwell Park, which are more wilderness-like than those of the lower park, and fairly steep. North Rim Trail offers the best views, and it begins on Wildwood Avenue. From the east end of the paved trail in the lower park, turn left on Manzanita Avenue, then right on Wildwood for one mile to the trailhead.

Trip notes: There is no fee. For more information, contact the City of Chico, 901 Fir Street, P.O. Box 3420, Chico, CA 95927; (530) 895-4972.

Directions: From the Sacramento area, drive north on Interstate 5 to Highway 32, 18 miles north of Willows. Turn east on Highway 32 for about 25 miles to Chico. Continue on Highway 32 as it becomes Nord Avenue, Walnut Street, and finally West 9th Street and turns left. Drive about 10 blocks on West 9th Street until you reach Main Street, then turn left. Turn right on East 4th Street and park your car along East 4th Street. Ride your bike along East 4th Street, continuing east for a few blocks into Bidwell Park. (You can also drive your car along 4th Street and into the park, but parking is limited.)

26. CHICO to DURHAM BIKE PATH
Butte County
Off Highway 32 near Chico
5 miles/1 hour — paved bike trail/RB or MB
steepness: ◉   skill level: ◉

I'd heard from a Chico native about the fabulous converted rail
trail that led out of town, through ranch lands rich with fragrant
almond groves. On my first day in Chico, by pure chance I thought I
spied the trail running parallel to the main street. I parked my car
immediately, unloaded my bike, jumped on and started pedaling—for
two tiresome miles through hundreds of back yards and then alongside
the highway to the Chico Municipal Airport. Hmm...perhaps this was
not the trail she'd intended.

Well, with a little asking around, I found a rail trail leading the
other way out of town, and this trail, from Chico south to the small
town of Durham, was reputed to be lined with almond trees, and to
have a great French bakery at its end. When easy biking involves croissants of any kind, you can be sure I'll be the first to saddle up, and you
should, too, because it turns out the ride is as good as the reward.

The trail's beginning does not look promising, as it starts in an
ugly industrial area, but things keep getting better as you ride. The
bikeway parallels Midway Road for its whole length (you can't have
everything), leaving urban Chico behind. As promised, it enters an
expanse of farmland and orchards.

An abandoned Sacramento Railroad line, the bikeway is flat and
straight—a typical converted rail trail. But unlike other rail trails, this
one sees little traffic except from bicyclists, since it isn't located in the
center of town with easy pedestrian access. That means you don't have
to dodge many novice rollerbladers, wayward dogs on long leashes, or
walkers strolling three- and four-abreast. Instead, you can relax and
enjoy the pastoral views of rural farms, and if you are lucky enough to
ride here in February or March, inhale the intoxicating fragrance of
almond trees in bloom. Some farmers plant their trees in alternating
rows of male and female trees, which makes for alternating rows of
pink and white flowers. It's quite a show in early spring.

The bike path ends at Jones Avenue, just shy of Durham. If you
don't mind riding on a quiet road with occasional car traffic, continue
south on Jones Avenue (don't ride on busy Midway Road) for two more
miles until you reach Durham-Dayton Highway. Turn right, cross the
railroad tracks, and ride about 300 yards into Durham. Turn right on

Midway and ride less than 50 yards to the aforementioned French bakery/cafe, on the right side of the road.

If you add on the two-mile road ride to the Durham bakery, your round-trip mileage will increase from five miles to nine. But there's gourmet coffee, incredible cinnamon pastries, and chocolate croissants awaiting you for the extra effort. For many, the payoff is adequate.

Make it easier: Just shorten your trip. You can start riding on the rail trail further south on Midway Road, and skip the road ride to Durham.

Trip notes: There is no fee. For more information, contact Butte County Department of Public Works, Oroville, CA 95965; (530) 538-7681.

Directions: From the Sacramento area, drive north on Interstate 5 to Highway 32, 18 miles north of Willows. Turn east on Highway 32 for about 25 miles to Chico. Continue on Highway 32 as it becomes Nord Avenue and Walnut Street. Turn left on West 2nd Street, drive about 10 blocks, then turn right on Broadway. In about one-half mile, Broadway will become Park Avenue (Highway 99), and in exactly one mile, Park Avenue veers left and Midway Road continues straight. Stay on Midway Road and park along the road. You will see the bike trail on the left. (It begins at the intersection of Midway and Hegan Lane.)

---

27. HARDROCK TRAIL
Empire Mine State Historic Park
Off Highway 20 in Grass Valley
3 miles/1 hour — dirt double-track/MB
steepness: ◉ ◉   skill level: ◉

Don't tell the park rangers, but the best reason to come to Empire Mine State Park has nothing to do with its mining history. Sure, when you come here you can visit the museum, pay two dollars, take the mine tour and learn all about the history of this gold-rich land. But when you hop on your bike and start riding on the park trails, you'll probably forget everything. In fact, as you cruise around on smooth dirt paths, oohing and aahing at the pretty Sierra foothills forest, you're likely to wonder why the mine owners didn't give up hardrock mining and invent mountain biking instead.

Well, they didn't, but luckily somebody else did, and now you can ride on land that made up one of the biggest and richest hardrock gold mines in the state from 1850 to 1957, with more than 300 miles of underground tunnels and shafts. Of course, the mine owners completely destroyed the land—environmentalism had not been invented yet, either—but Mother Nature has been healing herself, and what

Hardrock Trail, Empire Mine State Historic Park

stands today is a profusion of pines, white and black oak trees, big manzanita bushes, and the scattered remains of mine structures.

The Hardrock Trail, which begins three-quarters of a mile down the road from the park visitor center, is the best trail to start exploring on, and gives you the option of adding on a challenging one-mile loop trip to Osborn Hill. The route is well-signed and passes by several mines, the first of which is the W.Y.O.D. mine, which stood for "Work Your Own Diggins." This was the place where the wealthy mine owner allowed peon miners to lease sections of the mine, then work their own diggings. Not surprisingly, no one got rich in this fashion except the mine owner.

Past the W.Y.O.D. mine, turn left at the fork (one-half mile in), which is often unmarked but is the Short Loop Trail on the park map. After a brief climb, this trail brings you to an overlook where you can see the mine yard buildings. Head to the right, past the Orleans mine and stamp mill, and cross Little Wolf Creek on a wooden bridge. Here you have the option of continuing uphill to the Osborn Loop Trail (look for the turnoff on the left after the creek crossing), or turning right and heading back along the ridge on the Long Loop Trail. The Long Loop Trail cuts through a very flat and pretty section of forest; it's particularly spectacular in fall when all the oaks turn yellow.

If you decide to ride the Osborn Loop, take the left turnoff after the creek and head uphill, passing by several abandoned mine sites, on your way to a great lookout over the entire 700-acre park and the Sacramento Valley. Osborn Loop reconnects with the Long Loop Trail. Ride west on Long Loop Trail across the ridge and then downhill, past the cutoff for the Short Loop and the W.Y.O.D. mine, back to your starting point.

Make it easier: Skip the Osborn Loop, the only part of the trail that climbs substantially.

Trip notes: There is no fee for bike riding in Empire Mine State Historic Park, but if you want to take the mine tour, there is a $2 fee per person. Trail maps are available at the visitor center for 50 cents. For more information, contact Empire Mine State Historic Park, 10791 East Empire Street, Grass Valley, CA 95945; (530) 273-8522.

Directions: From the Sacramento area, drive east on Interstate 80 to Highway 49 near Auburn, then take Highway 49 north to Grass Valley and Highway 20. Exit on Highway 20 east (toward Grass Valley), which becomes Empire Street, and follow it for three miles to the Empire Mine State Historic Park visitor center. Buy a park map at the visitor center, then drive back down the road for three-quarters of a mile (the way you came in) and park in the dirt lot on the left (south) side of the road. The trailhead for the Hardrock Trail is clearly marked.

---

28. QUARRY ROAD TRAIL
Auburn State Recreation Area
Off Highway 49 near Auburn
10 miles/2.5 hours — dirt double-track and single-track/MB
steepness: ⊛ ⊛   skill level: ⊛ ⊛

The Quarry Road Trail is the trail to ride in Auburn State Recreation Area. If you attempt any of the several other trails in the park, you'll wish you hadn't, because they're hard—real hard. They climb with the average grade of a skyscraper. Their trail surfaces are little more than rock piles. The sun beats down upon them year-round. They offer no shade or relief anywhere. Of course, this makes them wildly popular with many mountain bikers, but not with easy bikers—we haven't lost our minds to the sport (yet).

Start your ride from the dirt parking lot on the south side of the Middle Fork of the American River, sandwiched in between the river and Highway 49. The lot may be filled with other cars, but chances are good that the occupants will be clustered on the first half-mile of trail and river, most of them looking for a good swimming hole, many carrying inner tubes and other floatation devices. You can ride further, deep into the river canyon, and your chances of company will decrease as you progress. Bring water and a snack with you, because this is dry country. Prepare to be awed by the stunning American River canyon, which you'll ride alongside for five miles each way (more or less as you desire).

The Quarry Road is a breeze to follow—wide and smooth and frequently marked with small posts that say "WST," which stands for Western States Trail. (The Quarry Road is one section of this longer trail.) A few spur trails lead off to the right, but all are clearly marked "No Bikes."

The American River from the Quarry Road Trail

The first notable landmark you pass is an old quarry, the trail's namesake, which has a trail fork with both options leading back to the main trail in less than 100 yards. The path gets a little more technical after the quarry, including one fairly rocky stretch before it smooths out again. Soon you pass an off-highway-vehicle area on the opposite side of the river, and if you're lucky, none of them will be around.

Quarry Road continues, rolling up and down tiny hills, for several miles of uninterrupted riding and great vistas of the often-steep river canyon. Hawks and turkey vultures fly over the blue-green water; diving mergansers sometimes make an appearance. The scenery is gorgeous the whole way, especially in spring when the wildflowers bloom. You'll see a few digger pines—kind of scraggly-looking conifers with gray-green needles—and some interesting rock outcrops, exhibiting the defined layers of sedimentary rocks. A few offshoot trails lead down to the river; take any of them if you want to cool off.

After several miles you'll leave the sunshine and the river views and head into thick oak and pine forest, where the trail narrows. Pick your own turnaround point—the trail eventually leads to a primitive camp called Cherokee Bar in about eight miles, with another dirt-and-gravel road (Sliger Mine Road) coming in to access it. We turned around long before the camp, at about five miles, where the trail crosses a big culvert and we had to dismount our bikes to get across. You can decide you've seen enough at any point, then head back the way you came.

Make it easier: A good turnaround point for families with young children is at the quarry. After this point, the trail gets a little more rough.

Trip notes: There is no fee. For more information and a free park map/brochure, contact Auburn State Recreation Area, P.O. Box 3266, Auburn, CA 95604; (530) 885-4527.

Directions: From the Sacramento area, drive east on Interstate 80 to Highway 49 near Auburn, then take Highway 49 southeast. In three miles, Highway 49 makes a hard right turn towards Cool and crosses a bridge over the American River. Set your odometer at the turn, and in four-tenths of a mile, you will see an unmarked dirt cutoff road on your left. (It's easy to miss, so go slow.) Turn left and park in the dirt parking area. The Quarry Road Trail is the gated dirt road by the parking area

29. AMERICAN RIVER PARKWAY: BEAL'S POINT to NEGRO BAR
Folsom Lake State Recreation Area
Off Interstate 80 at Folsom Lake
7 miles/1 hour — paved bike trail/RB or MB
steepness: ◉ ◉   skill level: ◉

I had been hearing about the American River Parkway for years, described as some sort of bicycling achievement, a 32.8-mile trail leading all the way from Discovery Park in Sacramento to Folsom Lake. Like a film you hear so much about that you never bother to see, I never rode my bike on the American River Parkway. I figured it had to be overrated.

But in researching this book, I made the trip all the way to the trail's east end at Beal's Point at Folsom Lake and started riding. And you know what? I felt the same way I felt when I saw *Titanic* two years after it came out: Hey, no wonder everybody likes this. The American River Parkway really *is* good.

You don't have to ride the whole thing, though. Some sections are far better than others, and conveniently, the first section is the best part of all. After leaving the Beal's Point parking area (which can be an absolute zoo on summer weekends because of the sandy beach and swimming areas), you ride to the left on the bike trail. The numbers painted on the trail's surface mark your mileage. Because you started at 32.8, the numbers will drop as you ride west—31, 30, 29, etc.

Your first vistas are of Folsom Lake, as you ride around its northwest edge on a wing dam of the huge, 340-foot Folsom Dam, to your left. If you've never seen it before, the immensity of Folsom Lake can come as quite a surprise. The 18,000-acre reservoir was created in 1955 by building a main concrete dam on the American River, as well as several wing dams and dikes. Here's a fact you can't live without knowing: The Folsom Dam contains enough concrete to build a sidewalk three feet wide from San Francisco to New York City.

Boating is the big draw at Folsom Lake, especially speedboating and waterskiing. But if you visit here in fall, the lake's water level is likely to be down so low, it will drive away almost everybody but those in rubber rafts. Fishing is also good for trout, bass, perch, and catfish.

What comes into view next is a place you've probably heard about but never thought you'd visit—Folsom State prison. It's kind of eerie to ride by on your bike, free as a bird, while all those inmates are locked behind bars, but as you continue onward, your surroundings quickly become less foreboding.

Hey, why is the American River suddenly so wide? Well, at three miles out on the bike trail, the river's been dammed again, this time by Nimbus Dam, and you're riding past Lake Natoma, smaller and quieter than Lake Folsom, and better for fishing. Just past the highway bridge before Negro Bar is one of the trail's prettiest overlooks, with little boats floating in the lake, people wading near the shore, and even a little bit of wilderness amid encroaching urbanization. A turnaround here, near mileage marker 29, will give you a seven-mile round-trip.

Make it more challenging: Just keep on riding, all the way to Sacramento in 32.8 miles, if you like.

Trip notes: A $6 day-use fee is charged per vehicle at Beal's Point. For more information and a free park map/brochure, contact Folsom Lake State Recreation Area, 7806 Folsom-Auburn Road, Folsom, CA 95630; (916) 988-0205.

Directions: From the Sacramento area, drive east on Interstate 80 to the Douglas Road exit near Loomis. Drive east on Douglas Road for 5.3 miles, then turn right on Auburn-Folsom Road and drive 1.7 miles to the left turnoff for Beal's Point. Turn left and drive down the park access road to the large parking lot. You will cross the beginning of the bike trail as you drive in to the lot.

Tahoe

30—Carr, Feely, & Island Lakes Trails, *Tahoe National Forest* 78
31—Watson Lake & Fibreboard Freeway Loop, *Northstar at Tahoe* 80
32—Burton Creek State Park Trails, *Burton Creek State Park* 83
33—Truckee River Recreation Trail, *Tahoe City Parks and Recreation* 85
34—Ward Creek Trail, *Tahoe National Forest* 87
35—Blackwood Canyon, *Tahoe National Forest* 88
36—General Creek Loop, *Sugar Pine Point State Park* 90
37—Pope-Baldwin Bike Path, *Lake Tahoe Basin Management Unit* 92
38—Fallen Leaf Lake Trails, *Tahoe National Forest* 94
39—Angora Lakes Trail, *Tahoe National Forest* 96

✺ For locations of trails, see map on page 8. ✺

30. CARR, FEELY, & ISLAND LAKES TRAIL
Tahoe National Forest
Off Highway 20 near Interstate 80
2 miles/1.5 hours — dirt single-track/MB
steepness: ⊛ ⊛ ⊛   skill level: ⊛ ⊛ ⊛

You may wonder why a trail that is only two miles long would be rated a three-wheeler for steepness and skill level. Two miles on a bike? Heck, anybody could ride that far. Maybe, but add in a heart-thumping hill and some very interesting technical sections, and I guarantee this short trail will give you a workout you'll remember.

Of course, that's nothing compared to the view you'll remember. This trail leads past three stunning alpine lakes and under huge moss-covered conifers to a rocky vista where you can look out over mountains, forest and a deep blue body of quiet water.

The ride is doable, even for beginners, as long as you're willing to walk a few sections where tree roots and rocks have overrun the trail. Even if you end up walking half the route, you'll still make it to beautiful Island Lake, a destination worth seeing under any conditions.

The thing is, the riding isn't the only part of the trip that's a little tricky. The drive to the trailhead is no cake walk—three miles in on a bumpy dirt road, with four-wheel-drive being more than just a good suggestion. Every time I visit here, there are a couple of ordinary passenger cars at the trailhead that somehow made it up the road, but I wouldn't try it unless you go *very* slowly and carry a spare tire.

The first time I came to Carr and Feely lakes was in late June after a heavy snow year. The road was snow-free for the first two miles, but the surrounding forest had heavy white patches everywhere. We rounded a corner and faced a wide snow field instead of the road, so we parked our car and hiked through the snow. At the trailhead, Carr Lake was ice-free, but Feely Lake was almost completely frozen, and the trail was impassable. At 6,600 feet in elevation, the season is short here, and you should time your trip carefully to avoid the snow. Visiting in late summer insures the best possible trail conditions—dry and hard.

After parking your car near Carr Lake, the most difficult part of your entire ride may be negotiating the one-tenth of a mile up to the dam and trailhead at Feely Lake. The Forest Service road from the parking lot to the dam is very rocky and steep and requires a stream crossing most of the year. Walk your bike if necessary, but get to the right side of Feely Lake Dam, where you'll see the trailhead for this trail. While Island Lake is only one mile away, the trail also leads to

Looking out over Island Lake, Tahoe National Forest

Round Lake (1.5 miles), Milk Lake (2 miles), and Grouse Ridge Campground (3 miles), which gives you some options if you want to extend your trip, either biking or hiking.

You ride through a forest of firs, with thick coats of staghorn moss growing up their trunks. The first flat section lulls you into a false sense of security before you start your healthy climb to the ridge. The trail is riddled with obstacles—mostly trees and rocks—but a few switchbacks make the ascent a little easier. After panting to the top, you reach a tiny pond, which the trail skirts around. Next is a trail junction at a small lake with an island, which surprisingly is not Island Lake. It is quite pretty, though, and surrounded by rocks and conifers. At the junction, the left fork heads to Penner Lake in two miles, and the straight path continues to Round and Milk lakes and Grouse Ridge Camp. If your ride has already worn you out, as mine did, head to the left, either riding or walking your bike on the Crooked Lakes Trail (Forest Service Trail 12E11) toward Penner Lake, with the false Island Lake on your left. In about 200 yards, which you can shortcut by climbing up a little granite hill on your right, you come to one of the most gorgeous lake vistas I have ever seen, up on a granite slab overlooking the real Island Lake. I took one look at the lake and its smooth rocky overlook and declared it to be one of the top 10 picnic spots in the universe. Spread out your tablecloth here, have lunch, enjoy the view, then take a vote to either venture onward or turn around and head back.

Make it more challenging: What, you're a glutton for punishment? Okay, ride straight at the junction, rather than turning left to the Island Lake overlook, and see if you can make it another half-mile to Round Lake or one mile to Milk Lake.

Trip notes: There is no fee. For more information, contact Tahoe National Forest, Nevada City Ranger District, P.O. Box 6003, Nevada City, CA 95959; (530) 265-4531.

Directions: From Auburn, drive east on Interstate 80 for four miles, past Emigrant Gap. Take the Highway 20 exit and head west for four miles to Bowman Lake Road (Forest Service Road 18). Turn right and drive 8.5 miles until you see the sign for "Lindsey Lake, Feely Lake, Carr Lake" and Forest Service Road 17. Turn right on Road 17 and follow the signs to the Carr Lake parking area (it's just under three miles), then walk your bike up to the dam and trailhead at Feely Lake. Road 17 can be very rough; four-wheel-drive is recommended.

---

31. WATSON LAKE & FIBREBOARD FREEWAY LOOP
Northstar at Tahoe
Off Highway 267 near Truckee
9.2 miles/2.5 hours — dirt roads/MB
steepness: ⊛ ⊛ ⊛   skill level: ⊛ ⊛

Several ski resorts around Lake Tahoe have jumped on the mountain biking bandwagon, opening up their ski hills to bike riders in the off-season in order to provide summer recreation options and produce year-round income. Northstar at Tahoe was the first and it is still the best of the lot, offering more than 100 miles of biking trails, plus chair lifts to carry bikers and their bikes high up the mountainside.

If you want simple, though, the key is not to throw away big bucks on the multi-ride ticket. Many of the park's trails are far from easy, with bumpy Tahoe-style rocks everywhere to jar your brains, and sandy patches that make your wheels grind to a halt. You probably won't want to ride a whole bunch of different trails here, especially in one day. But there's one excellent, easier loop trip to a mountain lake that covers 9.2 miles and will take you about 2.5 hours, plus some time on the chair lift. To ride it you need only buy the cheaper single-lift ticket. Besides saving money and having a nice bike ride, you can have a picnic lunch at the lake, hike around a little, and if you've brought your fishing rod, make a few casts for trout.

Exactly what route you'll take depends on which chairlifts are running when you go, but usually the trip requires a lift up the Echo chair from the village to mid-mountain, followed by a short, quarter-mile bike ride over to either Vista Express lift or Lookout lift where you'll be carried higher up the mountain. (Your bike usually rides on the chair immediately behind you or in front of you—the chairs have bike racks on the backs of them.) After your second chairlift, make your way over to a trail called Try-umph (their spelling), also called Road 500. Try-umph runs across the backside of Mount Pluto and has many nice open views to your right. It climbs almost imperceptibly for 1.6 miles till you reach a gate, which you pass through and head downhill until the trail dead-ends at Fibreboard Freeway (Road 100).

Just off your loop and less than a mile to the right is Watson Lake, probably the most popular destination at the bike park, even though it is technically outside the park in Tahoe National Forest. Keep an eye on your trail map if you decide to make the trip; there are actually two turns to get there and on my trip, the first was signed and the second was not. After the first right turn, turn left at the next intersection (a quarter-mile further), rather than continuing straight on Fibreboard, and ride downhill to the lake's border in seven-tenths of a mile.

You'll see plenty of other cyclists at the lake, as well as possibly a few cars that have driven in on Forest Service roads from the other side of the mountain. The lake is wide, pretty and shallow, the kind of place where kids like to look for frogs and usually find them. Some folks fish here, with mixed success, but most just have lunch and walk along the shore.

Riding to Watson Lake from Northstar at Tahoe

After your lake visit, backtrack up the trail and pick up the Fibreboard Freeway, turning right on it to complete your loop. This road is less rocky than other park trails, with smoother gravel and less big rocks, meaning you can just cruise along without having your eyes continually glued to the ground ahead of your front tire. Don't stop paying attention on this route, though. My biking partner, who is a much stronger rider than I am, zoned out for a while on the downhill and fell off his bike, even though the trail was flat and smooth, with no obstacles. (More evidence for the theory that if you snooze, you lose.) Even though his fall was minor and he suffered only a scrape on his forearm, he was well-attended to by a great first-aid woman who rode up to us on an all-terrain-vehicle. First-aid folks are out patrolling these trails all the time, and they can be radio-summoned by chairlift operators, so help is never far away—a comforting thought.

A three-mile stint on the Fibreboard Freeway brings you to Road 300 where you must turn left and ride past Northstar Reservoir, continuing until you intersect with roads 500 and 501, which bring you back to the top of the Echo lift. There you pick up Village Run to cruise back downhill to the village.

Note that a bike park map is essential for your trip, since there are so many trails and possible routes in the park. They're available for free when you buy your ticket, and a staff member can outline the Watson Lake loop for you.

Make it easier: An easier route is to ride to the picnic area at the caboose at Sawmill Flat, which has a view of Northstar Reservoir and surrounding mountains. The caboose is used as a warming hut during ski season, but is closed in summer. It's a three-mile round-trip.

Trip notes: The bike park is open daily from mid-June to Labor Day and weekends only in September and early October, weather permitting. Call to confirm exact opening and closing dates. Helmets are required for all riders. The fee is $14 for an adult single-ride ticket, $21 for an adult multi-ride ticket, $10 for a child-under-12 single-ride ticket, $15 for a child-under-12 multi-ride ticket. Bike rentals are available. Bike park maps are free. For more information, contact Northstar at Tahoe Mountain Adventure Shop, (530) 562-2248, or Northstar General Information, (530) 562-1010.

Directions: From Tahoe City, drive northeast on Highway 28 for seven miles to Highway 267 and turn left. Drive six miles to the turnoff for Northstar at Tahoe and turn left. Drive up the hill to Northstar Village and park in the lot. Walk your bike to the bike shop in the village, buy your lift ticket and get a trail map, then carry your bike up the stairs and around the back of the village to get on the chairlift.

32. BURTON CREEK STATE PARK TRAILS
Burton Creek State Park
Off Highway 28 near Tahoe City
7 miles/2 hours — dirt roads/MB
steepness: ⊛ ⊛   skill level: ⊛

Burton Creek State Park is a park-in-process, a marvelous strip of rare public land in North Tahoe which has not yet been fully developed by the state park system. That means there are no trail signs, no rest rooms, and no water. But it also means there are no day-use fees and no crowds, just a pristine pine and fir forest with miles of trails that are open to bikes. That, my friends, is a fair trade.

The tricky part is that it's hard to tell which way to go once you get to the park's main trailhead, because many dirt roads crisscross the area and currently, none are signed. To keep things simple, we made as few turns as possible. We rode straight past the state park sign, then turned left at the first junction (one-quarter mile in) and right at the next (one-tenth of a mile further). From there, we just rode straight for a few miles until we'd had enough, then turned around and rode back. The possibilities are endless, of course, but unless the park has posted trail signs or a trail map available by the time you visit, it's best to limit your turns so you don't get lost. (Rangers at nearby Tahoe State Recreation Area on Highway 89 can usually help you with updated Burton Creek trail information. Call them or stop in to see them before your bike ride.)

If you don't have to worry about directions, you can just focus on your surroundings, made up of a gorgeous forest of white fir, lodgepole and Jeffrey pines, with many singing birds. The forest here is more mixed than in other areas of Tahoe, and you will see plenty of wildflowers in summer—mostly big yellow mule's ears. Unlike many Tahoe dirt trails, this one is bordered closely by the trees, making it seem more like an intimate forest path than an old logging road.

It comes as no surprise that Burton Creek State Park land is adjacent to Burton Creek and Antone Meadows nature preserves, since flora and wildlife clearly flourish here. You aren't likely to have much human company, though, since the place is virtually unknown except to a few locals. The park is so new that even the Tahoe bed-and-breakfast owners who lodged us (and who live only a few miles from Burton Creek) didn't know where it was. We did see a couple of mountain bikers, including one woman riding with two happy dogs bounding along beside her, but that was all, even on a warm and perfect October

Sunday afternoon. In a place as popular as Lake Tahoe, a park with that kind of anonymity is a rare find.

Burton Creek State Park

Tahoe

Make it more challenging: You can ride much further in Burton Creek State Park, even making a loop out of your trip, but be sure to get updated trail information from Tahoe State Recreation Area before you go.

Trip notes: There is no fee. For more information, contact rangers at Tahoe State Recreation Area, (530) 525-7232. Currently, there is no Burton Creek State Park map available.

Directions: From Tahoe City, drive northeast on Highway 28 for 2.25 miles to Old Mill Road. Turn left and drive four-tenths of a mile on Old Mill Road, then turn left on Polaris and drive one-half mile to North Tahoe High School and the unmarked dirt road which begins by the school's parking lot. Park alongside the dirt road, but pull off the road and don't block the gate.

33. TRUCKEE RIVER RECREATION TRAIL
Tahoe City Parks and Recreation
Off Highway 89 near Tahoe City
9 miles/1.5 hours — paved bike trail/RB or MB
steepness: ●   skill level: ●

Of the three paved bike trails located in northwest Lake Tahoe, the Truckee River Recreation Trail is far and away the best. Here's what it does: It parallels the Truckee River for four miles, keeping the water in sight and only a few feet away. It affords you the opportunity to see wildlife—ducks and geese galore—even though you're on a paved trail. It provides a fun and easy ride that any level of rider, on any type of bike, can accomplish.

Now here's what it doesn't do: It doesn't require you to make a death-defying dash across busy Highway 89 in order to ride it. That is where other North Tahoe bike trails fail—even the famed West Shore trail. The whole point of being on a bike path is that you don't have to deal with cars, right? A bike path that crosses a major highway several times misses the point. The Truckee River Trail gets the point.

That doesn't mean you won't see the highway or hear its noise, because you will, since the bike trail runs parallel to it for its entire length. But with the pretty Truckee River running on the other side of the trail, you soon get skilled at looking only to the south and ignoring the north. Luckily, the highway is often 15 or 20 feet above you, as the trail is built lower than it in places, making the road seem to disappear. Sugar pines and Jeffreys, mixed with quaking aspen that turn yellow in September and October, also help to shield the route.

In the spring, the Truckee River can be a raging torrent of snow-melt, while in the fall, it's more of a lazy stream, often lined with big

Truckee River Trail

Canada geese flipping their tailfeathers in the air as they dunk their heads in the water, and fishermen making short casts into the stream. The river is tamest right by Tahoe City, and gets wider and stronger as you ride toward Squaw Valley ski resort. There are plenty of little cut-offs from the trail where you can walk your bike down to the river, and the last section of trail has a nice picnic area by the water.

You'll see everyone from little tykes on tricycles to gearheads on thousand-dollar bikes on this path, all of them getting the same good experience. With more than 150,000 people using the trail in the summer months, you get plenty of opportunity to practice saying, "Hello, on your left, thank you," as you ride. Watch out for roller-bladers and baby carriages in particular.

At the trail's end, you go under a bridge and end up on the opposite side of the river from Highway 89. The trail continues along the highway (but not separate from it) for a short distance to a trail parking area. Your best bet is to skip this section and instead turn around at the bridge, riding back to Tahoe City for a nine-mile round-trip.

Make it more challenging: At the end of the paved trail by the bridge, you can connect with the Western States Trail, a mountain-bikers-only dirt trail that switchbacks up a ridge and heads for miles to the west. Get a Forest Service map for details, or plan on riding only out-and-back for a short distance.

Trip notes: There is no fee. For more information and a free map of Tahoe City area bike paths, contact Tahoe City Department of Parks and Recreation, Tahoe City Public Utility District, P.O. Box 33, Tahoe City, CA 95730; (530) 583-5544.

Directions: From Tahoe City at the Highway 89/Highway 28 intersection, drive one-quarter mile south on Highway 89 to the bike trail parking area on the right. Ride your bike out of the parking area, back toward the intersection in Tahoe City, and pick up the paved bike trail that heads to your left (west) alongside the highway.

---

34. WARD CREEK TRAIL
Tahoe National Forest
Off Highway 89 near Tahoe City
6 miles/2 hours — dirt roads and single-track/MB
steepness: 🌑 🌑   skill level: 🌑 🌑

The Ward Creek Trail is part of a series of epic mountain biking loops, most of them more than 10 miles in length with gut-thumping climbs and treacherous stretches of rocky, narrow, single-track, which are greatly bragged about by Tahoe bikers. Now that you know, you can forget it, because our ride is simply out-and-back along the first stretch of Ward Creek. It's a spectacular streamside bike ride on a smooth dirt road, with an optional single-track continuation that will give you sweet mountain biking dreams for a long, long time.

Pack up your knapsack with a picnic and get ready. The first portion of the trail is easy enough for even young children to complete, provided you don't try to ride the route while snow is still on the ground. The second part is smooth single-track suitable for most beginners, and since this is an out-and-back venture, you can ride until you've had enough and then just turn around.

Cruise down the old logging road which parallels Ward Creek, passing by a fenced-off meadow with terrific open views of western mountains, often crested with snow into late summer. Ignore all cutoffs, staying on the main road. After about two miles, you'll reach a sign that says "Road Closed." Beyond the sign a bridge is out, but you can cross the stream by carrying your bike and walking on logs that have been placed across the gully. Ride to the left on the single-track, which is actually smoother than the logging road you were riding on. The route leads through streamside meadows, with some rocky, dry creek crossings that you may have to walk your bike across. (If you try to ride this trail before late summer or fall, the creeks may still be running, so take precautions.)

As the trail veers off to the left, you cross over to the south side of Ward Creek, and the trail climbs about 20 feet above the creek's canyon. Picnic spots are quite good along here, with nice views of the water running by, in case anyone is getting hungry. The trail finally heads into a thick pine forest, and for a six-mile round-trip, just ride into the trees for half a mile or so (the forest is very peaceful and beautiful—don't miss it), then turn around.

There are few forks in the single track, and no trail junctions. The easiest route is just to stay to your left at all forks (which is really just staying on the main trail), ride as far as you like, then retrace your tire treads when you are ready. The trail ascends slightly on the way out, so your return is almost all downhill, never too steep, just a perfect easy grade for gliding back.

Then the next time you're in a Tahoe bike shop and you overhear two gearheads bragging about conquering one of the epic Ward Creek loops, you too can casually say, "Yeah, Ward Creek, I've ridden there."

Make it easier: Turn around at the "Road Closed" sign, before the trail turns to single-track, and have your picnic near one of the fenced-in meadows.

Trip notes: There is no fee. For more information, contact Lake Tahoe Basin Management Unit, 870 Emerald Bay Road, South Lake Tahoe, CA 96150; (530) 573-2600.

Directions: From Tahoe City, drive approximately two miles south on Highway 89 to Pineland Drive, just north of Kilner Park. Turn right on Pineland Drive and continue for one-half mile to Twin Peaks Drive, where you turn left and travel for 1.7 miles. (Twin Peaks Drive becomes Ward Creek Boulevard). At 1.7 miles, there is a gravel pullout on the left at a gated dirt road, which is Forest Service Road 15N62 and the trailhead. Park and begin riding on the dirt road.

35. BLACKWOOD CANYON
Tahoe National Forest
Off Highway 89 near Tahoe City
4 miles/1 hour — dirt roads/MB
steepness: ◉ ◉   skill level: ◉ ◉

Bikers tend to be a little cynical about off-highway-vehicle riders, since the noise of screaming gas engines isn't exactly appealing to those who ride under their own power, looking for a peaceful outdoor experience. But at Blackwood Canyon, bikers have the North Tahoe Trail Dusters, an OHV club, to thank for the Blackwood Middle Fork Trail. When the Forest Service wanted to close down the trail, members of the club volunteered to maintain it and keep it open. So when you ride at Blackwood Canyon, you'll have to be a little tolerant if you hear the wail of an engine somewhere off in the distance.

Of course, you can always show up after Labor Day, in which case you'll probably have the whole place to yourself. On a warm September day, we parked at the off-highway-vehicle camping area and rode the Blackwood Middle Fork Trail for more than an hour, without seeing or hearing anyone.

A watershed restoration project is in process along Blackwood Creek. The canyon has had a long and unhappy history of flooding, grazing, logging and gravel mining, all of which took their toll on the stream and surrounding lands. In the 1960s, this beautiful canyon was nothing more than a quarry pit, as miners pulled out gravel for Tahoe-area roads and driveways. The Forest Service is in the process of reclaiming the land, and as usual, the prescribed course of action has been to protect the creek banks and do some revegetation work, but mostly to stay out of the way and let Mother Nature do her thing. The flow of Blackwood Creek has been returned to its original channel, and it's a strong running, pretty stream.

Starting at the off-highway-vehicle camping area, the trail runs flat for two miles through a thick mixed forest, with spectacular displays of wildflowers in the late spring and early summer. Then it begins to climb toward Barker Peak, elevation 8,166 feet, and I do

Blackwood Canyon near Barker Peak

mean climb, as in millions of switchbacks and a heady grade. Don't let it happen to you—be sure to turn around before the switchbacks. You'll pass another logging road off to your right (15N41, the North Fork Trail), but ignore it and stay to the left on the Middle Fork Trail (15N38). The trail surface is a little rocky, typical for North Tahoe, and you may have to walk across some of the creek crossings, whether they're wet or dry. We turned around at a wooden bridge that crosses the Middle Fork one mile after the North Fork Trail junction. From there, the trail climbs considerably.

After riding the canyon's dirt trail, you can go back and ride around on the flat part of paved Barker Pass Road (the road you drove in on). Although Barker Pass Road also climbs to Barker Peak, paralleling the Middle Fork Trail, the 2.2 miles from the off-highway-vehicle camp to Highway 89 is almost completely flat. There is some minimal car traffic, but the greatest hazard is from the number of rollerbladers who have made this road their home.

Make it easier: An option is to ride on the paved Blackwood Canyon Road only, which is smoother and easier to ride, although it has some car traffic. Ride the section from the off-highway-vehicle camp back to Highway 89.

Trip notes: There is no fee. For more information, contact Lake Tahoe Basin Management Unit, 870 Emerald Bay Road, South Lake Tahoe, CA 96150; (530) 573-2600.

Directions: From Tahoe City, drive approximately four miles south on Highway 89 to Forest Service Road 03, Barker Pass Road. It is also signed for Caspian Bicycle Camp/Blackwood Canyon. Turn right and drive 2.2 miles to the turnoff for the off-highway-vehicle camp on the right.

36. GENERAL CREEK LOOP
Sugar Pine Point State Park
Off Highway 89 on Lake Tahoe's west shore
6.5 miles/2 hours — dirt double-track/MB
steepness: ⊛ ⊛   skill level: ⊛

Cross-country skiers and easy mountain bike riders share a common affinity for smooth dirt trails that roll for miles and miles, with no steep grades and no disagreeable obstacles to interrupt their momentum. At Sugar Pine Point State Park, both groups find what they desire, skiers in the winter and bikers in the summer.

The General Creek Loop is a great trip, easy enough for families to ride together, with an optional lock-up-your-bike-and-hike trip to a tiny, marshy lake. It makes for a great morning or afternoon outing, just long enough to satisfy your urge for fresh air and exercise without completely exhausting you. The trip is pretty from snowmelt until snowfall, too, and is one of the first easy rides in the Tahoe area that opens up in late spring, since it doesn't have a lot of creek crossings.

You begin from campsite 149 in the General Creek Campground, and if you head straight, you will ride the loop counterclockwise. The trail is very smooth dirt and sand, with plenty of room for both hikers and bikers and only one hill, right at the beginning. It runs through a thick forest of the park's namesake sugar pines (as well as Jeffrey pines, lodgepoles and firs) on the first side of the loop; open meadows on the other. Cross-country skiing markers placed periodically along the trail assure that you're on the right track.

Head straight down the north side of General Creek (ignoring the left turnoff that goes over a bridge, which will be your return route) and simply cruise along through the sugar pines, with no turnoffs to distract you for a couple of miles until you reach the junction with the single-track option to Lily Lake. From here you can hike to the shallow lake, really more of a pond, but I recommend it because the surrounding forest is so gorgeous. You can lock your bike to the trail marker, or to a pine tree if necessary—there are plenty of them around. (Technically, you are allowed to ride your bike on the first half-mile of the one-

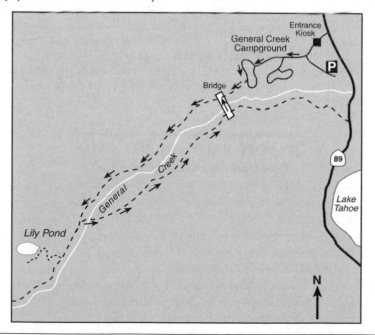

mile single-track to Lily Lake, but the trail quickly becomes impossible to negotiate because of rocks, tree roots and the like, so save yourself the frustration and ditch your bike here.)

True to its name, Lily Lake is completely covered with lilies. It covers a few acres but is very shallow, especially by late summer and fall, and is ringed by cottonwoods and aspen. In spring, wildflowers, corn lilies, and ferns in the meadow and surrounding forest can be quite lush. It's a peaceful spot, in any season.

After your lake visit, return on the same single-track, then connect back with your loop, heading to the right and crossing a couple of bridges and a neat 100-yard wooden walkway that is raised over a springtime marsh. The wooden planks are fun to ride on, and they soon deposit you on a wide dirt trail that brings you back along the south side of General Creek. When you come to a trail junction with a bridge to your left and the dirt road continuing straight, go left to complete your loop, then head right, back to the campground.

Make it easier: You may want to skip the hike to Lily Lake, as it adds almost an hour to your trip.

Trip notes: A $5 day-use fee is charged per vehicle. A map is available for $1 at the ranger kiosk. For more information, contact Sugar Pine Point State Park, P.O. Box 266, Tahoma, CA 96142; (530) 525-7982 or (530) 525-7232.

Directions: From Tahoe City, drive nine miles south on Highway 89 to the General Creek Campground entrance on the right. Park in one of the day-use parking areas near the kiosk, then ride your bike further down the park road to the campgrounds, staying to the right until you reach campsite 149 and the trail. (Don't be tempted to ride the single-track that leads from the day-use parking area to the General Creek Loop—it's for hikers only.)

37. POPE-BALDWIN BIKE PATH
Lake Tahoe Basin Management Unit
Off Highway 89 on Lake Tahoe's south shore
6.8 miles/1.5 hours — paved bike trail/RB or MB
steepness: ◉   skill level: ◉

If the Truckee River Recreation Trail is the best paved bike path in North Tahoe (see story on page 85), then the Pope-Baldwin Bike Path holds that honor in South Tahoe, outdistancing the competition by a long shot with some of the most stellar Lake Tahoe views imaginable. That, and it actually keeps you away from the road—really away, as in sometimes you can't even see it or hear it. Hallelujah.

The trail's west end is near Baldwin Beach, which can be your first stop if you are riding from the trail's west terminus at Spring Creek Road. A half-mile cutoff from the bike path on Forest Service Road 13N05 brings you to the picnic area at Baldwin Beach, and a short walk takes you to spectacular white sand beaches and lake views. Depending on how crowded it is, you may or may not want to hang around for long, so when you're ready, ride back to the bike trail and continue east.

Next stop is the bridge at Taylor Creek. If it's autumn, there's likely to be a crowd at the bridge, because this is where rainbow trout, brown trout, and kokanee salmon come to spawn each fall. On our trip, we saw hundreds of kokanees, colored bright red with green heads, laying their eggs and then slowly dying in the stream. The Forest Service has added more gravel to the streambed to make the spawning beds better for the eggs, which in a few short weeks will hatch small fry that make their way down Taylor Creek to Lake Tahoe.

It's a little sobering to watch fish meet their end, even as they are producing thousands of baby fish, so continue onward and turn left at the access road for the Tallac Historic Site, where there are several historic mansions. You can tour the houses and admire their opulence, if you're into that sort of thing. I walked out to the small pier instead, where I set my bike down and listened to Tahoe's water lapping on the shore. From the pier and its adjacent beach, you can see Richardson's Resort next door, a great place that has cabins for rent and a lakeside restaurant. You can also gaze at miles and miles of Lake Tahoe and its dramatic mountain backdrops to the south and north.

When you're ready, continue on the bike path, taking Forest Service Road 12N09 one-half mile to Pope Beach if you desire. Pope Beach has all the same amenities as Baldwin Beach: picnic area, swimming area, restrooms, and stellar lake views. The bike trail continues past the cutoff to Pope Beach for another half-mile, leading almost, but not quite, into the town of South Lake Tahoe. You can ride the bike lane into town, but it isn't separate from busy Highway 89, so I don't recommend it.

One tip to make your trip more enjoyable: If you ride this trail in October, you will find it largely deserted, and the Forest Service often closes the access roads to Pope and Baldwin beaches. Closes them to cars, that is—you can ride your bike right past the gates, down to the empty parking lots at the beaches, and see Lake Tahoe without the crowds.

Make it more challenging: Mountain bikers have the option of crossing the highway where the bike path ends near South Lake Tahoe and picking up any of the myriad trails that wind into Forest Service land. Get a Forest Service map before attempting the ride, as most trails are not marked.

Trip notes: There is no fee. For more information, contact Lake Tahoe Basin Management Unit, 870 Emerald Bay Road, South Lake Tahoe, CA 96150; (530) 573-2600.

Directions: From Tahoe City, drive south approximately 25 miles on Highway 89 to the southern end of the lake, past Eagle Falls and Emerald Bay. Turn right on Spring Creek Road, which is Forest Service Road 13N07, shortly before Baldwin Beach on the left. There are little sandy pullouts along the road where you can park. Walk your bike across Highway 89 to start on the bike route. (You can also park at Baldwin Beach or Tallac Historic Site and start riding from there.)

---

38. FALLEN LEAF LAKE TRAILS
Tahoe National Forest
Off Highway 89 near South Lake Tahoe
3 miles/1 hour — dirt roads/MB
steepness: ◉ ◉   skill level: ◉ ◉

People around the world rave about Lake Tahoe—sure, why not, it's North America's largest alpine lake and the 10th deepest lake on earth, as well as being clear blue and beautiful. But I like its smaller neighbor Fallen Leaf Lake at least as much and maybe more. It's a lake of manageable size, for one thing, at approximately three miles long. And since much of its shoreline is privately controlled, it's never over-crowded. It's as deep blue as Tahoe, and framed by groves of aspens that quake in the summer wind and turn golden in the fall chill. Combined with a backdrop of tall, craggy mountains, the scenery at Fallen Leaf Lake creates an impression that stays with you, and can keep you coming back season after season.

The Forest Service has built an assortment of short trails that run from Fallen Leaf Campground to the lake and partway around its northern border. Day-users can take the trail that begins on Fallen Leaf Lake Road, bypassing the campground and going straight to the lake. The route is single-track and sandy much of the way, but that's okay because it keeps your speed down, which is fortunate for the hikers who stroll around here. If you start from the day-use trailhead, you've got a decent hill to climb which brings you over a ridge to the lake. Even if you have to walk your bike on some of the rockier, hillier parts, you'll be at the lake in less than 15 minutes.

Once you reach the lake's edge, there are several riding options, as

Riding through the aspens near Fallen Leaf Lake

short trails shoot off to the left and right. We took the trail to the right around the lake, followed it to the dam over Taylor Creek, then walked our bikes across the dam. From there, we took the trail a little further to where it meets up with an old Forest Service road. We rode on that for a half-mile or so, then turned around and rode back in the other direction. Follow the trails as you like, but when faced with a choice at a junction, try to stay near the lake's edge, because the views are incredible. Fallen Leaf Lake's paths are some of the best in this book for simply looking out over gorgeous blue water.

If you visit here in summer, expect company from hikers and bikers staying at the campground. The lake can also get noisy with boaters, especially on summer weekends, which can put a crimp in your pastoral, non-motorized biking experience. If you arrive in late September or October, though, the lake is likely to be still and quiet, plus delicately framed by bright fall leaves on the cottonwoods and aspens.

Make it more challenging: You can combine this trip with a ride on the Pope-Baldwin bike path. After riding around Fallen Leaf Lake, ride your bike on Fallen Leaf Lake Road from the day-use parking area back to Highway 89, where you can pick up the bike path across the road.

Trip notes: There is no fee. For more information, contact Lake Tahoe Basin Management Unit, 870 Emerald Bay Road, South Lake Tahoe, CA 96150; (530) 573-2600.

Directions: From Tahoe City, drive south approximately 25 miles on Highway 89 to the southern end of the lake, past Eagle Falls, Emerald Bay and Baldwin Beach. Look for the turnoff on the right for Fallen Leaf Lake Road, located one mile past Camp Richardson. Turn right on Fallen Leaf Lake Road and drive eight-tenths of a mile to the trailhead for Fallen Leaf Lake Trail. The trail starts from the parking lot and is clearly marked.

39. ANGORA LAKES TRAIL
Tahoe National Forest
Off Highway 89 near Fallen Leaf Lake
2 miles/1 hour — dirt roads/MB
steepness: ⊛ ⊛   skill level: ⊛

The Angora Lakes are probably the most popular destination for families with small children in the entire Lake Tahoe region. This is so much the case, in fact, that when I walked the Angora Lakes Trail one summer weekday, I actually felt out of place without a four-year-old by my side. Kids are everywhere on this trail—on bikes, on their parents shoulders, on their own two feet, and on top of the many boulders surrounding the trail. When you get to the upper lake, kids are every-where there, too—on the beach, in the water, at the lemonade stand, and on the trail around the lake.

But show up after school starts in September and it's a different story. Things quiet down quite a bit here; in fact, there's hardly anyone around. That gives you some options: Take a family bike ride to Angora Lakes in the summer to give your kids instant companionship, or take a family bike ride to Angora Lakes in the fall to enjoy the scenery and the peace and quiet.

In any season, you get the same surroundings: Upper Angora Lake, set at 7,280 feet in elevation, is a perfectly bowl-shaped, glacial cirque lake, set in a pine forest with lots of rounded rock boulders sprinkled around. The granite wall on the lake's far side is snow-covered most of the year, and during much of late spring and summer, a water-fall of snowmelt flows down its face.

The trail to the lakes is simple to follow, with no turnoffs to con-fuse you—just follow the dirt road as it curves up the hill for one mile. Keep your speed down and watch out for hikers and other bikers, especially little ones, on the trail. Ride by the lower Angora Lake, which has a few private homes on its edge, and shortly you reach a log bike rack just before the upper lake and the Angora Lakes Resort. Lock up your bike (the resort management insists on this) and explore around. Built in 1917 on land leased from the Forest Service, Angora Lakes Resort has eight tiny cabins for rent right on the lakeshore, but they are so popular, it's almost impossible to get a reservation. No matter; the place is friendly toward day-users, too. They rent row-boats for $7 an hour and run a small refreshment stand, which pumps out lemonade by the gallon to thirsty hikers and bikers. A small sandy beach is popular for swimming and wading in summer, if you can stand the cold water. Some people try fishing for trout in Upper Angora Lake, with fair to medium success.

Trail alongside Lower Angora Lake

Make it more challenging: The dirt road that you drive in on is also suitable for riding, if you don't mind some car traffic. Many riders park their cars at the start of Road 12N14 and ride from there to Angora Lakes for a 6.6-mile round-trip.

Trip notes: There is no fee. For more information, contact Lake Tahoe Basin Management Unit, 870 Emerald Bay Road, South Lake Tahoe, CA 96150; (530) 573-2600.

Directions: From Tahoe City, drive south on Highway 89 approximately 25 miles to the southern end of the lake, past Eagle Falls, Emerald Bay and Baldwin Beach. Look for the turnoff on the right for Fallen Leaf Lake Road, located one mile past Camp Richardson. Turn right on Fallen Leaf Lake Road and drive eight-tenths of a mile to a fork in the road; stay to the left (do not head toward Fallen Leaf Lake) and continue for four-tenths of a mile. At the junction, turn right on to Forest Service Road 12N14, which alternates as paved and unpaved. Drive for 2.3 miles, past the Angora Fire Lookout, to the parking lot at road's end. The trailhead is on the left side of the farthest parking lot.

North San Francisco Bay Area

40—Marshall Beach Trail, *Point Reyes National Seashore* 100

41—Abbott's Lagoon Trail, *Point Reyes National Seashore* 101

42—Bull Point Trail, *Point Reyes National Seashore* 103

43—Estero Trail to Sunset Beach, *Point Reyes National Seashore* 105

44—Estero Trail to Drake's Head, *Point Reyes National Seashore* 108

45—Muddy Hollow Trail, *Point Reyes National Seashore* 110

46—Coast Trail, *Point Reyes National Seashore* 112

47—Bear Valley Trail to Arch Rock, *Point Reyes National Seashore* 114

48—Olema Valley Trail, *Golden Gate National Recreation Area* 116

49—Tomales Bay Trail, *Golden Gate National Recreation Area* 117

50—Bolinas Ridge Trail, *Golden Gate National Recreation Area* 119

51—Cross Marin Trail & Sir Francis Drake Bikeway, *Golden Gate
    National Recreation Area & Samuel P. Taylor State Park* 121

52—Devil's Gulch Trail, *Samuel P. Taylor State Park* 124

53—Kent Pump Road, *Marin Municipal Water District* 126

54—Lake Lagunitas Loop, *Marin Municipal Water District* 128

55—Phoenix Lake to Bolinas-Fairfax Road,
    Marin Municipal Water District 130

56—Las Gallinas Wildlife Ponds, *Las Gallinas Valley Sanitary District* .. 132

57—Shoreline Trail, *China Camp State Park* 134

58—Tiburon Bike Path, *City of Tiburon* 136

59—Perimeter Trail, *Angel Island State Park* 138

60—Laurel Dell Fire Road, *Marin Municipal Water District* 140

61—Old Stage Road: Pantoll to West Point Inn,
    Mount Tamalpais State Park 142

62—Old Railroad Grade: East Peak to West Point Inn,
    Mount Tamalpais State Park 144

63—Tennessee Valley Trail, *Golden Gate National Recreation Area* 146

64—Mill Valley & Sausalito Bike Path, *Marin County Parks* 148

🌐 For locations of trails, see map on page 9. 🌐

40. MARSHALL BEACH TRAIL

Point Reyes National Seashore

Off Highway 1 near Olema

2.4 miles/1 hour — dirt double-track/MB

steepness: ◉ ◉   skill level: ◉

The Marshall Beach Trail is one of the best kept secrets in Point
Reyes. Almost nobody comes out here, since the trailhead is situated on
a dirt road to nowhere at the northeastern tip of the Point Reyes Peninsula. While thousands of visitors pour into neighboring Tomales Bay
State Park for its protected bay waters and stunning white beaches, few
ever realize that right next door is Marshall Beach, with all the same
advantages but none of the crowds, and no day-use fee.

When you make the trip, you'll continually wonder if you are
following the right directions, because the road to the trailhead leads
through serious cattle country, with no beach or water in sight. The
paved road turns to dirt, and you continue driving along flat coastal
bluffs until you reach a nondescript trailhead in the middle of a cow
pasture. This is one trail where you have to keep a serious lookout for
meadow muffins, because the stuff can stay on your tires for days.

Cattle and dairy ranches have been operating in Point Reyes
since the 1850s. The 1962 law that authorized Point Reyes National
Seashore made allowances so that the original ranch owners could
continue operating within the seashore boundaries, as part of the
"cultural history" of the place. Currently, seven dairies operate within
Point Reyes, milking about 3,200 cows and producing over five million
gallons of milk each year. So wave and smile at Bessie as you ride to
the beach.

The ride is a simple out-and-back, with no trail junctions. Just
cruise down the wide ranch road, curving down the hillside and de-
scending to the water's edge. You can practically coast all the way down,
making for a good hill climb on the way back, ensuring you your
exercise for the day. Marshall Beach is a perfect beach, with coarse
white sand and azure blue Tomales Bay water, protected from the wind
by Inverness Ridge and framed by Bishop pine trees. Since you can't
drive here, there's rarely anybody around, except for occasional kayakers
making their way from the town of Marshall across the bay, or from
Tomales Bay State Park to the south. Bring a picnic, a bathing suit, a
good book, and some binoculars for birdwatching. Settle in for a perfect afternoon, then drag yourself away—and back up the hill—when
it's time to leave.

Make it more challenging: You can ride from the trailhead out-and-back on Marshall Beach Road, adding up to five miles on to your trip, but with the possibility of occasional car traffic.

Trip notes: There is no fee. A free map of Point Reyes National Seashore is available at the Bear Valley Visitor Center on Bear Valley Road. For more information, contact Point Reyes National Seashore, Point Reyes, CA 94956; (415) 663-1092.

Directions: From San Francisco, cross the Golden Gate Bridge on U.S. 101, then drive north for 7.5 miles. Take the Sir Francis Drake Boulevard exit west toward San Anselmo, and drive 20 miles to the town of Olema. At Olema, turn right (north) on Highway 1 for about 100 yards, then turn left on Bear Valley Road. Travel 2.2 miles on Bear Valley Road until it joins with Sir Francis Drake Highway. Continue northwest on Sir Francis Drake for 5.5 miles, then take the right cutoff for Pierce Point Road. In 1.2 miles, you come to the entrance road for Tomales Bay State Park. Immediately past it is Duck Cove/Marshall Beach Road, where you should turn right and travel for 2.6 miles. The road turns to gravel and dirt; stay to the left where it forks. Park in the gravel parking area, taking care not to block any of the dirt roads that connect here, and begin riding at the trailhead.

41. ABBOTT'S LAGOON TRAIL
Point Reyes National Seashore
Off Highway 1 near Olema
3 miles/1 hour — dirt single-track/MB
steepness: ⊛   skill level: ⊛

If the wind is howling and you've been nearly blown off your saddle on other rides at Point Reyes, drive over to the trailhead at Abbott's Lagoon for a trip through a sheltered watery paradise. The bike trail is not long, but it leads toward Point Reyes Beach, where you can lock up your wheels and continue walking along the sand in either direction for miles. The result is a spectacular two-part trip: First, a ride through protected lagoons teeming with bird life; then, a windswept walk along wide-open coastline.

Abbott's Lagoon is large—more than 200 acres—and joined by a spillway to two freshwater ponds. It is one of the many annexes of water that cradles the wide triangle of the Point Reyes Peninsula. The lagoon is only partially connected to the ocean, so it is rarely influenced by tides. This happens when harsh winter storms break through the western sand barrier of Abbott's Lagoon and open it to the ocean. Eventually sand accumulates and seals off the lagoon once again, but the result is that its water is continually brackish—a mix of saltwater

Abbott's Lagoon Trail, Point Reyes National Seashore

and freshwater. This type of mixed water environment is a haven for many species of birds, mammals, and plants.

You must ride slowly on this trail, so as not to scare the millions of birds or knock over any birdwatchers (who can be oblivious to everything except what they see in their binoculars). Many bird-fanciers and hikers use this trail, because it's level, gorgeous, and provides easy access to Point Reyes Beach. Stay alert and keep your speed down. If you want to try your hand at bird identification, look for these guys: western grebes (large gray and white diving birds with a long, swanlike neck and yellow bill), pie-billed grebes (similar to western grebes but with a short, rounded bill and no white patch), coots (dark grey/black hen-like birds that skitter across the water when they fly, dragging their feet), and caspian terns (like seagulls but more elegant and angular, with large red bills). You'll see notices warning you not to disturb the western snowy plover, a small sand-dweller that nests along the dunes of Point Reyes beach. Their population is in decline and their habitat is protected all along the Northern California coast.

The first 2,000 feet of trail is hard-packed for wheelchair use, and the rest of the route is wide, flat single-track—very easy to ride, although it can get a little sandy. The scenery is pretty right off, with a little bridge to cross and then a small pond on your left and the lagoon on your right. The sound of the ocean draws you straight ahead. A bucolic-looking white farmhouse, perched on a distant hillside over your right shoulder, watches over the whole scene.

Wildflower season from March through May brings spectacular shows of poppies and lupine, but perhaps the best time to visit is on a crystal-clear day in winter, when the fog has vanished and the rich, primary colors of water, sky, and grasslands are thoroughly saturated.

If you want to walk along Point Reyes Beach, look for the bike-lock post at the end of the trail, next to a wooden bridge, and secure your bike. A short foot trail leads away from the lagoon and to the ocean in less than a quarter of a mile. As you walk, watch for the seals and sea lions who sometimes haul out on the beach, and as always at Point Reyes, keep a lookout for passing gray whales.

Make it easier: Skip the walk along Point Reyes Beach and just take the ride back and forth along the lagoon.

Trip notes: There is no fee. A free map of Point Reyes National Seashore is available at the Bear Valley Visitor Center on Bear Valley Road. For more information, contact Point Reyes National Seashore, Point Reyes, CA 94956; (415) 663-1092.

Directions: Follow the directions on page 101 to the town of Olema in western Marin County. At Olema, turn right (north) on Highway 1 for about 100 yards, then turn left on Bear Valley Road. Travel 2.2 miles on Bear Valley Road until it joins with Sir Francis Drake Highway. Continue northwest on Sir Francis Drake for 5.5 miles, then take the right cutoff for Pierce Point Road. Drive 3.3 miles on Pierce Point Road to the Abbott's Lagoon Trailhead on the left.

42. BULL POINT TRAIL
Point Reyes National Seashore
Off Highway 1 near Olema
3.6 miles/1 hour — dirt double-track/MB
steepness: ⬤   skill level: ⬤

Bull Point is a mercurial trail—sometimes it shows up on Point Reyes park maps, sometimes it doesn't. Like the Marshall Beach Trail (see page 100), it's one of the forgotten Point Reyes trails, one that only the cows seem to know about. Even the Point Reyes cartographers occasionally forget it. It's just far enough out there so that not many people show up, and those who do usually pass it by on their way to more glamorous destinations like Drake's Beach or the Point Reyes Lighthouse.

But the trail is good—real good—and it's open to bikes, allowing you the opportunity to ride through a coastal prairie on your way to Drake's Estero. To get there, you ride on a wide strip of land between two arms of the estero: Creamery Bay and Schooner Bay, once the launching area for schooners carrying butter from Point Reyes dairies to dinner tables in San Francisco. Creamery and Schooner bays, as well as Barries and Home bays, are the four fingers of the hand that is Drake's Estero—the Spanish word for estuary, a place where saltwater and freshwater mix. Most scholars believe that Sir Francis Drake landed here in 1579, although there are still a few holdouts who insist he landed in San Francisco Bay, near Larkspur Landing, instead.

The trail begins on the left side of the parking lot, at a cattle gate which you must close behind you. You're likely to ride past some grazing moo-ers on the first section of the route. The trail is an old ranch road, which is rather indistinct at the trailhead but gets more distinct as you ride, becoming easier to follow as it leads toward the bay. Riding here makes you feel like you're in a Merchant-Ivory film; backdrops of green pastoral countryside are interwoven with vistas of wide, blue water. No, this is not 19th-century England, but rather late-20th-century Point Reyes, although it's easy to mistake the two.

There are no trail intersections to confuse you; it's just a straight shot to the waterway across grassy coastal bluffs. The last 20 feet of trail, right before you reach the cliff's edge over the bay, are caved in, so be ready to put the brakes on here, at the edge of the world. Looking toward the water, Creamery Bay is on your right and Schooner Bay is on your left. You can set your bike down on the grass and wander along

Bull Point Trail, Point Reyes National Seashore

North San Francisco Bay Area

the blufftops. When the tide is low, you can see poles sticking out of the waters of Schooner Bay, and grey mesh bags laying in the shallows and along the shoreline. Upon closer inspection, you'll find that the bags are filled with oysters—they're the property of Johnson's Oyster Farm, located across the bay. The farm is accessible by a side road off Sir Francis Drake Highway, and is worth a trip on your drive home.

As with all the bays, estuaries, lagoons and ponds at watery Point Reyes, the coves here are host to thousands of migratory birds. There are permanent residents as well; great egrets are among the most noticeable inhabitants. Their grand white plumage provides a stark, elegant contrast to the greens and blues of the landscape. Bring a pair of binoculars, a thermos of hot chocolate, and maybe a collection of Wordsworth with you. You can spend a pleasant morning or afternoon on the edge of the estero before hopping on your bike and riding home.

Make it more challenging: Since you've driven all the way out here on Sir Francis Drake Highway, you might want to combine this ride with one of the two Estero Trail rides that follow. The Estero Trailhead is three miles before the Bull Point Trailhead, on the south side of Sir Francis Drake.

Trip notes: There is no fee. A free map of Point Reyes National Seashore is available at the Bear Valley Visitor Center on Bear Valley Road. For more information, contact Point Reyes National Seashore, Point Reyes, CA 94956; (415) 663-1092.

Directions: Follow the directions on page 101 to the town of Olema in western Marin County. At Olema, turn right (north) on Highway 1 for about 100 yards, then turn left on Bear Valley Road. Travel 2.2 miles on Bear Valley Road until it joins with Sir Francis Drake Highway. Continue northwest on Sir Francis Drake and drive for 10.5 miles to the Bull Point parking area on the left side of the road. The trail leads from the left side of the parking area.

---

43. ESTERO TRAIL to SUNSET BEACH
Point Reyes National Seashore
Off Highway 1 near Olema
8 miles/2 hours — dirt single-track and double-track/MB
steepness: ◉ ◉   skill level: ◉ ◉ ◉

SPECIAL NOTE: A large section of the Estero Trail was badly damaged in the El Niño storms of early 1998. As of June 1999 (as this book goes to print) the Estero Trail is officially closed beyond the one-mile mark (the first causeway over Home Bay). The trail will require extensive repair and rerouting to steer clear of the eroded bluffs. I've included the following story on the Estero Trail because the park service has plans to repair the

---

Estero Trail to Sunset Beach, Point Reyes National Seashore

trail in the near future. Before planning a bike ride on the Estero Trail, please phone the park at 415/663-1092 for an update on trail conditions.

Of all the Point Reyes National Seashore bike trails in this book, the Estero Trail is the most challenging, with the toughest hills and the roughest trail surface. But if you're prepared for it, it's an absolute must-do bike ride. The Estero Trail leads you to trails that connect with either Sunset Beach or Drake's Head, both spectacular and distinct destinations. An out-and-back trip to Sunset Beach is slightly easier and shorter than the out-and-back to Drake's Head (detailed in the next story), so it's a better choice for novice riders. Riding either trail on an early morning, when the wildlife is abundant but people have not yet arrived, will produce a compelling desire to return again and again.

The Estero Trail is quintessential Point Reyes, which means that it's full of good surprises, so put your helmet on and get ready. The trail leads from the left side of the parking lot, lateraling a grassy hillside, with little or no indication of what lies ahead. As you coast down the hard-packed trail, take a look over your left shoulder at Inverness Ridge and central Point Reyes. In the process of regeneration after the terrible Mount Vision wildfire of October 1995, the hillsides have quickly turned from black to green again.

You'll round a corner and drop quickly into a stand of dense Monterey pines, with another one immediately following it. About this

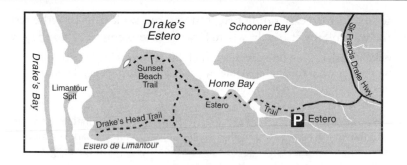

time, you may start wondering where the water is, this being the Estero Trail, after all. Another minute of riding and *wham*—the trail opens out to Home Bay, where you ride across a causeway on the edge of the bay, with water on either side of you. Stop for a moment along the causeway. This is a peaceful and protected spot, and you'll need to gather some energy for your first hill climb. It comes up next as you rise above Home Bay, on your way to a point overlooking the bay as it opens up to Drake's Estero. The incredible views will comfort you as you work your way up the short but steep hill, then descend rapidly down the other side and cross another levee, in another protected cove.

Keep riding along and above the waters of Drake's Estero, continuing straight until you come to the trail sign for Sunset Beach Trail at 2.4 miles. The route actually becomes easier to ride on Sunset Beach Trail, because it flattens out and is less vulnerable to erosion. (For the easiest riding on the hilly Estero Trail, visit in summer or after a dry spell in winter, when there is no mud on the trail and the dirt is hard-packed.)

Your chance of seeing wildlife along the route is excellent. In addition to the ever-present waterfowl and shorebirds, deer frequent this section of the park, including a small herd of white axis deer which were brought here by a rancher a generation ago. My riding partner and I spotted a pure white buck early one morning on the hillside above the Estero Trail. This was before we knew about the existence of white deer at Point Reyes, and we decided that either the animal was an apparition or we'd been blessed by a miraculous visitation. Nope, just a non-native white deer. More common black-tail deer are also abundant, with the males bearing impressive racks in the wintertime.

At 1.5 miles from the trail junction, you come within view of Sunset Beach. A large, quiet pond separates it from you. You can hear the ocean waves ahead, even though the pond water directly in front of you is completely calm and still. The trail becomes narrow and sometimes too wet for easy riding here, but you can walk your bike the rest of the way to Sunset Beach, where Drake's Estero empties into the sea.

Make it easier: Even riders with small children can tackle the first mile of the ride, down through the Monterey pines to the first levee. If you ride this far, then ride or walk up the trail above the levee for great views of Home Bay.

Trip notes: There is no fee. A free map of Point Reyes National Seashore is available at the Bear Valley Visitor Center on Bear Valley Road. For more information, contact Point Reyes National Seashore, Point Reyes, CA 94956; (415) 663-1092.

Directions: Follow the directions on page 101 to the town of Olema in western Marin County. At Olema, turn right (north) on Highway 1 for about 100 yards, then turn left on Bear Valley Road. Travel 2.2 miles on Bear Valley Road until it joins with Sir Francis Drake Highway. Continue northwest on Sir Francis Drake for 7.5 miles to the left turnoff for the Estero Trailhead. Turn left and drive one mile to the trailhead parking area.

44. ESTERO TRAIL to DRAKE'S HEAD
Point Reyes National Seashore
Off Highway 1 near Olema
9 miles/2.5 hours — dirt single-track and double-track/MB
steepness: ◉ ◉   skill level: ◉ ◉ ◉

SPECIAL NOTE: A large section of the Estero Trail was badly damaged in the El Niño storms of early 1998. As of June 1999 (as this book goes to print) the Estero Trail is officially closed beyond the one-mile mark (the first causeway over Home Bay). The trail will require extensive repair and rerouting to steer clear of the eroded bluffs. I've included the following story on the Estero Trail because the park service has plans to repair the trail in the near future. Before planning a bike ride on the Estero Trail, please phone the park at 415/663-1092 for an update on trail conditions.

The dictionary definition of an estero is a meeting of ocean salt-water and freshwater runoff, producing a rich habitat for waterfowl and shorebirds. Riding the Estero and Drake's Head trails gives you a double dose of these rich estuarine wetlands, as the Estero Trail parallels Home Bay and Drake's Estero, and the Drake's Head Trail delivers you to the edge of the Limantour Estero.

The nine-mile out-and-back trip is a challenge, though, and you must be prepared for it. The Estero Trail to Drake's Head Trail follows the same path as the previous ride for the first 2.4 miles, then at the junction with Sunset Beach Trail, it takes a left turn, leading away from Drake's Estero and over a small ridge. One-half mile later, you meet up with Drake's Head Trail at the intersection of a maze of cattle gates and fences, then take it southward (to the right), toward the ocean.

Rising above Home Bay on the Estero Trail

The end result is a trip that differs greatly from the ride on Estero Trail to Sunset Beach. This trail requires more climbing, which results in better views on your return trip downhill to the edge of Drake's Estero. Plus the riding is slightly more technical on the Drake's Head Trail. The narrow single-track path cuts right down the middle of a coastal prairie, with Limantour Estero on your left and Limantour spit—a long, narrow strip of sand separating the estero from the sea—straight ahead. The openness of the prairie can make the wind a challenge on many days.

Although the Estero Trail is popular with day-hikers, it is unlikely that you will have much company on the Drake's Head Trail. It is too far from any trailhead for most people to walk to, which makes it just about perfect for bikers and equestrians. Instead of other people, you're more likely to see wildlife. On one trip, I spotted the largest great blue heron of my whole birdwatching career. He slowly beat his wings, then took off from the ground like a huge mythical creature. I've also seen herds of 30-plus deer along the bluffs, and on one trip I was startled by a bobcat who was busily hunting mice or gophers in the grass.

The only tricky part of the trail comes after you climb the ridge on Estero Trail, heading away from Drake's Estero. At the top of the ridge you ride on a ranch road, then go through a cattle gate, then continue on the road to a fenced-in area. The ranch road parallels the fences, and it appears as though you should follow it, but watch for the posted blue and white trail arrows. They direct you to go through another cattle gate, into the fenced area, then ride on an indistinct trail inside the fence and along a cattle reservoir for about 150 yards. You exit out another cattle gate, where trail signs point you to the right along the bluffs for the Drake's Head Trail (signed as "not a through trail"). Just follow the blue and white arrows on the fences and you'll be fine.

Ride as far as you like along Drake's Head, taking the trail all or part of the way to its terminus at the edge of cliffs over Limantour Estero, but be sure to save some energy for the trip home. You may have to walk a couple of hills on the way back, depending on your energy level, but you won't mind because the views of the water are stunning all the way.

Make it easier: Ride only the Estero Trail portion of this ride. Turn around at the Sunset Beach Trail junction for a five-mile round-trip.

Trip notes: There is no fee. A free map of Point Reyes National Seashore is available at the Bear Valley Visitor Center on Bear Valley Road. For more information, contact Point Reyes National Seashore, Point Reyes, CA 94956; (415) 663-1092.

Directions: Follow the directions on page 101 to the town of Olema in western Marin County. At Olema, turn right (north) on Highway 1 for about 100 yards, then turn left on Bear Valley Road. Travel 2.2 miles on Bear Valley Road until it joins with Sir Francis Drake Highway. Continue northwest on Sir Francis Drake for 7.5 miles to the left turnoff for the Estero Trailhead. Turn left and drive one mile to the trailhead parking area.

45. MUDDY HOLLOW TRAIL
Point Reyes National Seashore
Off Highway 1 near Olema
4 miles/1 hour — dirt single-track/MB
steepness: ⊙   skill level: ⊙

"Traveling on the Muddy Hollow Trail is like visiting the thickest woods of Canada or the East Coast, where vines and trees grow so densely alongside moist ravines that if it weren't for the trail, you'd have to cut your way through the thicket with a machete."

This is what I wrote about the Muddy Hollow Trail in Point Reyes

National Seashore one month before the great Vision wildfire of October 1995. The fire burned for five days, destroying more than 12,000 acres, and Muddy Hollow was dead-center in the path of the blaze. Because this was one of my favorite trails in Point Reyes, I returned to ride it in the fire's aftermath with a large amount of trepidation.

But while the Muddy Hollow Trail is no longer a tunnel-like path through dense foliage, it is still an interesting route that leads to the edge of Limantour Estero and eventually to Limantour Beach, worth the trip for the nature lessons it provides. For those who knew the Muddy Hollow Trail in its previous incarnation, a ride here can offer a sense of hope, a tangible example of regeneration after devastation. New growth popped out of the blackened earth as soon as six weeks after the fire, and after only a few rains, the hills started to turn green.

Even for those who never visited Muddy Hollow before the fire, riding here is a fascinating education in the processes of a wildfire. Since the trail begins in what was once dense forest, then parallels a creek on its way to a small pond, the estero, and then the ocean, you can follow the course of the blaze all the way to the coast. When the fire reached the sparsely vegetated sand dunes at the sea, it had nothing left to burn, and depleted itself.

The fire cleared much of the brush from the pond's edge, making birdviewing from the trail easier. On my visit, the water was covered with hundreds of ducks. As you ride past the pond and estero, the trail veers to the left and meets the paved trail that leads from Limantour Beach parking lot to the sand. (It's paved to protect the nesting grounds of snowy plovers, so stay on the trail). You can lock up your bike and explore the beach or the estero.

Make it easier: Just ride out and back on the Muddy Hollow Trail, skipping the exploration of Limantour Beach.

Trip notes: There is no fee. A free map of Point Reyes National Seashore is available at the Bear Valley Visitor Center on Bear Valley Road. For more information, contact Point Reyes National Seashore, Point Reyes, CA 94956; (415) 663-1092.

Directions: Follow the directions on page 101 to the town of Olema in western Marin County. At Olema, turn right (north) on Highway 1 for about 100 yards, then turn left on Bear Valley Road. Travel 1.7 miles on Bear Valley Road, then turn left on Limantour Road. Drive 5.8 miles on Limantour Road to the right turnoff for the Muddy Hollow Trailhead. Turn right and drive one-quarter mile to the parking area. Start riding on the trail on the left that is signed "Muddy Hollow Trail," not the upper trail on the right that is signed "Muddy Hollow Road."

46. COAST TRAIL

Point Reyes National Seashore

Off Highway 1 near Olema
5.6 miles/2 hours — dirt double-track/MB
steepness: ● skill level: ●

If you've ever wanted to take someone on a mountain biking trip, then camp out overnight in a place that seems far removed from the hustle and bustle of the Bay Area, here's your chance. Then again, if you've ever wanted to ride your bike to a windswept beach, then find a private spot to sit on the sand and look out to sea for an hour before getting back to San Francisco in time for dinner, here's your chance, too. The Coast Trail, which runs roughly parallel to Muddy Hollow Trail in Point Reyes National Seashore (see the previous story), can provide either kind of trip. Bring a bike lock and the choice is yours.

Like Muddy Hollow, Coast Trail was badly burned in the Point Reyes fire of October 1995. But unlike Muddy Hollow, Coast Trail was never heavily forested to begin with, so the contrast of pre- and post-fire foliage is not as great. Within months, the grasslands and hillsides surrounding the Coast Trail turned green again, with millions of ferns, berry bushes, and vines poking out of the ground. Grasses quickly covered much of the blackened earth.

The Coast Trail is L-shaped, beginning at the Point Reyes Youth Hostel and making a beeline for the coast, then turning left (south) and running parallel to the beach for another mile to Coast Camp. It is wide open most of the way, except for a short section where you ride alongside a stream and its surrounding thicket of alders. In winter, the stream creates a few marshy areas, which are thick with cattails.

The riding is easy on the wide, dirt fire road, slightly downhill on the way to the beach and slightly uphill on the way back, but with no real climbs to slow you down. It's the perfect trail for riding side by side and conversing with a friend, since there are no blind corners or narrow turns. After 1.8 miles you reach the coast, and a trail marker notes that you can walk to your right along the beach to get to the Limantour parking lot in less than a mile. You will ride to your left instead, continuing along Coast Trail for 1.1 mile further to Coast Camp. You can actually see your destination from this trail marker, as there is a large rock outcropping just above the camp that is visible from a distance.

The trail continues beyond Coast Camp but isn't open to bikes, so lock up yours at the metal bike post next to the horse hitching posts, and take the narrow foot trail by the camp restrooms that leads to the

Coast Trail, Point Reyes National Seashore

beach. From there, you can walk as far as you like in either direction, either right toward Limantour Beach or left toward Sculptured Beach, with miles of uninterrupted sand in between.

If you choose to camp, be sure to make reservations, especially on summer weekends. Although the camp is free, you must have a camping permit from Point Reyes headquarters. The campground has 14 sites, piped water, restrooms and a few picnic tables. It can suddenly become windy, cold and foggy here at any time, so come prepared for any kind of weather if you're planning to spend the night.

Make it easier: Ride the Coast Trail only the first 1.8 miles to where it turns left at the beach, enjoy the ocean view, then return.

Trip notes: There is no fee. A free map of Point Reyes National Seashore is available at the Bear Valley Visitor Center on Bear Valley Road. For more information, contact Point Reyes National Seashore, Point Reyes, CA 94956; (415) 663-1092.

Directions: Follow the directions on page 101 to the town of Olema in western Marin County. At Olema, turn right (north) on Highway 1 for about 100 yards, then turn left on Bear Valley Road. Travel 1.7 miles on Bear Valley Road, then turn left on Limantour Road. Drive 5.8 miles on Limantour Road to the left turnoff for the Point Reyes Youth Hostel. Turn left, drive past the hostel and park in the lot on the right. Then ride your bike back up the access road, passing the hostel again, and begin riding on the dirt fire road just before and across the road from the youth hostel. It is signed as the Coast Trail to Coast Camp.

47. BEAR VALLEY TRAIL to ARCH ROCK
Point Reyes National Seashore
Off Highway 1 near Olema
6.4 miles/2 hours — dirt road/MB
steepness: ◉ ◉   skill level: ◉

The Bear Valley Trail is hands-down the most famous trail in Point Reyes, and for that reason alone I never rode or walked it. I feared the crowds at the trailhead, the noise of other chattering trail users, and the probable lack of peace in a place as sacred as Point Reyes.

But bypassing this trail could be the biggest mistake you can make in the North San Francisco Bay outdoors. I found this out when I finally rode the trail on a winter Sunday morning, then parked my bike at the trail's bike rack and walked the rest of the route to Arch Rock. The Bear Valley Trail is incredibly beautiful, and easy enough to be a perfect family bike trip. Most surprising of all is that if you arrive before 9 A.M., you can even get some solitude on the route. Winter is the best season for low crowds, and the trail is prettiest then anyway, with the stream running full and the forest dense and green.

Final steps to Arch Rock

The route is simple to follow, beginning just past the Bear Valley Visitor Center and Morgan Horse Ranch. There are several offshoot trails, none of which are open to bikes, so just stay on the main path and cruise your way down the forested trail. You'll pass along the border of Divide

Meadow at the midway point, with the trail leading slightly uphill on the way to it and slightly downhill after it. The entire route never gains more than 200 feet in elevation, making the trip rideable by almost anybody on fat tires.

At 3.2 miles you come to a bike rack and several trail junctions. Glen Trail goes off to the left and Baldy Trail to the right, but you will lock up your bike and continue straight on the Bear Valley Trail to Arch Rock. The walk is just under a mile, and for the first half you're deep in the forest canopy, with the trail surrounded by alders, laurel, fir and bay trees. Then suddenly the trail opens out to coastal marshlands, and you can see the ocean straight ahead.

Near the cliff's edge the trail splits off, meeting up with Coast Trail. You can take either trail to Arch Rock—continue straight ahead or head to the right and then jog to the left a tenth of a mile later. The junction is not always well-signed, so keep in mind that you want to end up at the edge of the bluffs looking out over the ocean. (If you keep heading to the right on Coast Trail, you'll miss Arch Rock altogether and wind up at Kelham Beach in seven-tenths of a mile.)

The final steps of the hike are extremely dramatic as you walk along the top of Arch Rock's jagged, jade-green bluff that juts out over the sea. Coast Creek, the gentle stream that you followed on the biking and hiking path, now cuts a deep and narrow gorge on its way to the ocean. The wind often howls with tremendous fury out here, which can come as a surprise after the protected forest trail.

A spur trail leads down the cliffs to the beach, worth hiking only during low tides, when there is room to explore. Many hikers are content to stay on top of Arch Rock and enjoy the view, which includes numerous other rock outcrops, the shoreline below, and the perpetually rolling surf.

Make it easier: Even the youngest riders can make the trip as far as Divide Meadow, once the site of an old hunting lodge and now a grassy picnic area with tables and restrooms. This makes a three-mile round-trip.

Trip notes: There is no fee. A free map of Point Reyes National Seashore is available at the Bear Valley Visitor Center on Bear Valley Road. For more information, contact Point Reyes National Seashore, Point Reyes, CA 94956; (415) 663-1092.

Directions: Follow the directions on page 101 to the town of Olema in western Marin County. At Olema, turn right (north) on Highway 1 for about 100 yards, then turn left on Bear Valley Road. Travel one-half mile on Bear Valley Road, then turn left at the sign for the Bear Valley Visitor Center. Park in the large lot on the left, past the visitor center, and ride your bike south along the park road to the signed "Bear Valley Trail."

48. OLEMA VALLEY TRAIL
Golden Gate National Recreation Area
Off Highway 1 near Olema
5 miles/2 hours — dirt single-track/MB
steepness: 🌀 🌀   skill level: 🌀 🌀

There is only one important point to remember when riding the Olema Valley Trail: Do not start from the well-known Five Brooks Trailhead, because the trail climbs like crazy within a mile of the parking area. Instead, start at the signed Olema Valley Trailhead just two miles south of the Five Brooks Trailhead, parking at the small pullout along the road. That done, prepare to have a good time as you ride through a flat valley at the base of a forested ridge.

One of the great things about the Olema Valley Trail is that it looks so inconspicuous on the Point Reyes trail map that it gets overlooked by most people. It appears to parallel the highway, which scares off many hikers, and it doesn't really *go* anywhere, which scares off many more. But therein lies its charm. Although it doesn't appear that way on the map, it's far enough off the road so that you rarely see or hear cars. Its trailhead is five miles from the main Point Reyes visitation areas, so you won't have to worry about having too much company, or running over any hikers, either. The flat, somewhat bumpy single-track is great for biking, and your chances of seeing birds and deer, maybe even a bobcat or a fox if you're very fortunate, are excellent.

The trail signs are just a little confusing at the trailhead; although you will be riding on the Olema Valley Trail, you must take the Randall Spur Trail for one-half mile to meet up with it. Just be certain not to ride on the Randall Trail on the east side of Highway 1, which climbs up a steep ridge, but rather the flat Randall Spur Trail on the west side of the highway. That taken care of, head across the meadow till you meet up with Olema Valley Trail, where you can choose to go left or right. On our trip, we headed right first, riding for 1.2 miles till the dirt single-track reached some old, broken pavement on the trail. Traveling in this direction, you are in the forest quite a bit, riding between big Douglas fir, California laurel, and live oaks. The forest alternates with wide meadows, wet enough for wild berries, cow parsnip, bush lupine and Canada thistles. The trail can get rather narrow and eroded in places. Shortly after the broken pavement section, the route climbs steeply up to an intersection with Bolema Trail, then beyond to the Five Brooks Trailhead.

Not feeling in the mood for the climb to Five Brooks, we turned around at the pavement and rode back to where Olema Valley Trail meets the Randall Spur Trail, then rode Olema Valley in the opposite (southerly) direction. After an immediate short climb to the far side of the meadow, the trail leads along the meadow's border for 2.5 miles to its terminus at Highway 1 near Dogtown. The trail ends shortly past the junction with Teixeira Trail, a ridge-climbing park trail that is no longer maintained. Traveling in this direction, Olema Valley Trail is out in the open the whole time, and can be very wet in some of the lower regions of the meadow, especially where it nears the junction with Teixeira. I've never been able to ride the complete length of this trail in winter or spring, as the water always comes sloshing up to my ankles in the last mile or so, but in dry weather, it can be done.

Make it easier: Just cut your trip short. The best route is to ride only to the right on the Olema Valley Trail, for the most varied and interesting terrain.

Trip notes: There is no fee. A free map of Point Reyes National Seashore that includes this section of Golden Gate National Recreation Area is available at the Bear Valley Visitor Center on Bear Valley Road. For more information, contact Point Reyes National Seashore, Point Reyes, CA 94956; (415) 663-1092.

Directions: Follow the directions on page 101 to the town of Olema in western Marin County. At Olema, turn left (south) on Highway 1 and drive for 5.5 miles to the trailhead for the Randall Trail on the left side of the road and the Olema Valley Trail on the right side of the road. (This trailhead is two miles past the Five Brooks Trailhead.) Park in the pullout along the road, then begin riding by the sign for the Olema Valley Trail.

49. TOMALES BAY TRAIL
Golden Gate National Recreation Area
Off Highway 1 near Point Reyes Station
2 miles/1 hour — dirt double-track/MB
steepness: ◉ ◉   skill level: ◉

Being an avid Point Reyes admirer and a mountain biker as well, over the years I've become fond of what I call "the lost trails of Point Reyes." Quite simply, these are low-profile, less-visited trails where you don't have to deal with a lot of other trail users. My way of avoiding the hiker versus mountain biker conflict is to stay off the most heavily hiked trails during the times they receive the most use. Not only does it prevent any possible discord with hikers, but I also cherish the solitude.

Although short in length, the Tomales Bay Trail is one of the best of the Point Reyes "lost trails." Part of it is an old rail trail that was

Tomales Bay Trail, Golden Gate National Recreation Area

built by the North Pacific Coast Railroad around the turn of the century and abandoned in the 1930s. Several levees and dikes are still in place from the railroad days.

The trail takes you from busy Highway 1 along rolling hills to a rich wetland area at the very south end of Tomales Bay, where the bay transitions into marshland. The trail is somewhat indistinct and has several minor offshoots, but stay on the main route and remember to keep heading for the water. You'll ride downhill first, then uphill again to the top of a ridge, with a wide view of Tomales Bay and the town of Inverness across the water. Just after topping the ridge, you'll curve downhill again and ride around a couple of pretty ponds surrounded by tall reeds and cattails. In the summer, red-winged blackbirds can be spotted here. Coots and mallards are present year-round.

At the bay's edge, you'll find an old trestle system and a bridge once used by the railroad. The levees, bridges and trestles were built to channel the flooded wetlands, allowing trains passage in high or low tides. Ride to the north along the water for a few hundred yards until you come to a fence across the trail. Here you can lock up your bike, then wander around the bay's edge, a great place for birdwatching. On one visit here, we were accompanied by four turkey vultures who sat sentry-like on fenceposts, silently observing our movements. They're very distinctive with their large dark bodies and red heads.

Try to time your trip for a low tide, when more land is available for walking and exploring, and be sure to bring binoculars to watch for birds. The view to the north up the length of Tomales Bay is always spectacular, whether it's a foggy and moody or crystal clear day.

Make it more challenging: If you drive north about one mile on Highway 1 to the Millerton Point parking area, you'll find another section of the old rail trail that can be explored on foot.

Trip notes: There is no fee. A free map of Point Reyes National Seashore that includes this section of Golden Gate National Recreation Area is available at the Bear Valley Visitor Center on Bear Valley Road. For more information, contact Point Reyes National Seashore, Point Reyes, CA 94956; (415) 663-1092.

Directions: Follow the directions on page 101 to the town of Olema in western Marin County. At Olema, turn right (north) on Highway 1 for two miles, passing through the town of Point Reyes Station. Continue on Highway 1 for 1.8 miles past Point Reyes Station to the Tomales Bay Trail parking area on your left.

---

50. BOLINAS RIDGE TRAIL
Golden Gate National Recreation Area
Off Sir Francis Drake Boulevard near Olema
7 miles/2 hours — dirt road/MB
steepness: ◉ ◉   skill level: ◉ ◉

Okay, everybody get in line and buy your "E" tickets, the roller-coaster ride at Bolinas Ridge is open for business.

The first time you ride it, you wonder how a trail could go up and down so much without ever going level. There are no pedal-and-cruise sections; you are either climbing up or coasting down the whole way. That's what makes Bolinas Ridge just plain fun, and also well-suited for all levels of riders because you can go as fast or as slow as you like. None of the hills in the first few miles are killers—they're all short and sweet—but they are just steep enough to give you some fast downhills.

The key is to start on the Olema side, at the Sir Francis Drake Boulevard trailhead, rather than starting on the Mount Tamalpais side at the Bolinas-Fairfax Road trailhead. If you start from Sir Francis Drake near Olema, you can ride southward for three to four miles with the trail climbing moderately as you go. Then when you are ready to turn around and head home, there is a fun descent ahead of you. Start at the Bolinas-Fairfax trailhead (11 miles south of here) and you descend right off, meaning you have to climb to get home, in which case you need more than an "E" ticket to ride.

There are two factors you should be prepared for: Number one, this is cow country, as in bovines everywhere you look, a regular cow-o-rama. They go their way; you go yours. Number two, because this is cow country, you've got to contend with a lot of cattle gates, which you must close behind you if you open them to ride through. The exact number of gates you must negotiate depends on whether the farmers are letting the cows roam or not; I've ridden here when there are only a few gates closed and I've ridden here when there are more than a dozen. Here's a little secret: The best way to get through the gates is not to open and close them, nor is it to lift your bike over the gate, set it down on the other side, then walk through the hikers' turnstile. The most efficient method is to lift your bike over your head (grab it firmly with both hands on the frame) and then walk through the turnstile with it. You and the bike arrive at the other side of the gate at the same time, and you get a five-second upper-body workout in the process, without straining your back.

You heard it here first, the patented Ann Marie Brown upper-body mountain-bike workout. Move over, Arnold Schwarzenegger.

You start your ride with a climb up to the ridge, and in about one mile pass the left turnoff for Jewell Trail, which connects Bolinas Ridge to the Cross Marin Trail/Sir Francis Drake Bikeway (see the following story). Continue straight on Bolinas Ridge Trail, gliding up and down one hill after another. The trail surface varies greatly; although it is always double-wide dirt, it is sometimes smooth and sometimes quite

Bolinas Ridge Trail, Golden Gate National Recreation Area

eroded and rocky. Stick to the worn tire tracks in the roughest parts of trail, and keep in mind that the first half-mile of trail is the rockiest—it gets better after that. Be prepared to give room to other trail users: equestrians, hikers, and mostly cows, who wander where they please along the trail. You'll want to keep your speed down, as the steepness of the downgrades can surprise you.

The furthest I've ever ridden from the Olema trailhead is to the Shafter Trail junction, five miles from the trailhead, with a total 1,000-foot elevation gain. Most often I've been content to turn around long before that, after an hour (or about 3.5 miles) of riding, near a tule-lined pond (for a total 800-foot elevation gain and seven-mile round-trip). The return trip offers a good amount of downhill, and views are terrific all the way home. From the top of the hills, you can see for miles in all directions, including all the way out to Tomales Bay.

Make it easier: Just cut your trip shorter, as the elevation keeps gradually increasing the farther you go. For less climbing, ride a shorter distance.

Trip notes: There is no fee. A free map of Point Reyes National Seashore that includes this section of Golden Gate National Recreation Area is available at the Bear Valley Visitor Center on Bear Valley Road. For more information, contact Point Reyes National Seashore, Point Reyes, CA 94956; (415) 663-1092.

Directions: From San Francisco, cross the Golden Gate Bridge on U.S. 101 and travel north toward San Rafael. Take the Sir Francis Drake Boulevard exit west toward San Anselmo, and drive 19.5 miles to the trailhead for the Bolinas Ridge Trail on the left side of the road. If you reach the town of Olema and Highway 1, you have gone one mile too far. (The trailhead is located exactly three-quarters of a mile past the right turnoff for Platform Bridge Road, and one mile before Olema.) Park in the pullout alongside the road and lift your bike over the cattle gate.

---

51. CROSS MARIN TRAIL & SIR FRANCIS DRAKE BIKEWAY

Golden Gate National Recreation Area & Samuel P. Taylor State Park

Off Sir Francis Drake Boulevard near Lagunitas

11 miles/2 hours — paved bike trail & gravel double-track/RB or MB

steepness: ◉ ◉   skill level: ◉ ◉

If you're yearning for a taste of big redwoods but don't have time to make the trip to the national and state redwood parks in the northwest corner of Northern California, the Cross Marin Trail/Sir Francis Drake Bikeway can fulfill your desires, just 30 miles from San Francisco and 20 miles from San Rafael. The trail is well-loved and well-used by

Cross Marin Trail/Sir Francis Drake Bikeway

both Marin County locals and vacationers staying at Samuel P. Taylor State Park and Point Reyes, but it's never so crowded that the experience is marred. In addition, it provides a gateway to several other hiking and biking trails, giving you plenty of options for extending your trip.

The Cross Marin Trail/Sir Francis Drake Bikeway is one trail with two names, under two different park jurisdictions. It's called the Cross Marin Trail when it's on Golden Gate National Recreation Area land, the Sir Francis Drake Bikeway when it's on Samuel P. Taylor State Park land. To further confuse things, some people call it the Samuel P. Taylor Bike Path. While many people start riding on it from within the state park, one of the best access points is at Platform Bridge Road, where you can park for free in roadside pullouts and start riding at the trail's western terminus.

The ride has offerings for skinny tires and fat tires alike, with 3.5 miles of smooth pavement and another two miles of rough pavement and dirt suitable for mountain bikes. Like many paved bike trails, the route is an old rail trail, built in 1874 by the North Pacific Coast Railroad, and abandoned in 1933. Samuel Taylor, the park's namesake, owned and operated a paper mill near the current park headquarters, and as he watched the narrow-gauge train with all its passengers chug by his mill, he got the bright idea to start an outdoor camping area right here along Lagunitas Creek (also called Papermill Creek).

The first section of trail is heavily wooded as it travels parallel to Lagunitas/Papermill Creek, then opens out into a broad meadow as Jewell Trail leads off on the right, one mile in. Stay on the paved path as it heads back into the trees, this time into *bigger* trees, as you enter the redwood stands near Samuel P. Taylor State Park. Quickly you are in a green redwood world, with only tall trees and low-growing sorrel and ferns. Right before you enter the main part of the park, you pass a large Sequoia on your left, an anomaly among all the coastal redwoods. I always wonder, is it lonely? Does it long for the Sierra, and the company of its own species?

Once you are in the park, your primeval redwood fantasy gets somewhat interrupted by campgrounds, signposts, and other indicators of civilization. You ride on park access roads for a short distance till you pass the camp restrooms, then the park road swings off to the left and you can continue straight, through a gate, on the bike path. The bike trail changes from smooth pavement to broken pavement and gravel, and most skinny-tire riders will have to turn around, making for a seven-mile round-trip. Mountain bikers can continue riding along the creek, crossing a footbridge over Sir Francis Drake Highway, till the trail ends two miles later at the fenced park boundary near Shafter Bridge. In summer, some hard-core bikers walk their bikes across the creek and continue riding across Sir Francis Drake on fire roads that lead to Kent Lake, but in winter, the stream is often too high to ford.

By far the best time of year to ride this trail is in winter after a good rain, when the campgrounds are empty, the creek is running full, and the trees and ferns are dripping with moisture. Your solitude will be interrupted only by the occasional sight and sound of cars on Sir Francis Drake, rather than crowds of people at the campgrounds and picnic areas of Samuel P. Taylor. For much of the route, you ride along with a feeling of wonderment, amazed that these beautiful redwoods are accessible on a paved bike trail, so close to an urban area.

Make it easier: Ride the paved section of trail only, for a seven-mile round-trip.

Trip notes: There is no fee if you park at Platform Bridge Road. A $5 per vehicle day-use fee is charged if you park in the main paved parking areas at Samuel P. Taylor State Park. A trail map/brochure is available at the ranger kiosk (at the main park entrance) for 75 cents. For more information, contact Samuel P. Taylor State Park, P.O. Box 251, Lagunitas, CA 94938; (415) 488-9897 or (415) 893-1580, or GGNRA/Point Reyes National Seashore, Point Reyes, CA 94956; (415) 663-1092.

Directions: From San Francisco, cross the Golden Gate Bridge on U.S. 101, then drive north for 7.5 miles. Take the Sir Francis Drake Boulevard exit west toward San Anselmo, and drive 18.7 miles to the right turnoff for Platform Bridge Road, located 3.4 miles past the main entrance to Samuel P. Taylor State Park. (If you reach the town of Olema and Highway 1, you have gone two miles too far.) Turn right on Platform Bridge Road and park in the pullout on the left side of the road. Begin riding on the paved connector path that leads from the pullout, cross a concrete bridge, ride about 30 yards and then turn left immediately on the signed Cross Marin Trail.

52. DEVIL'S GULCH TRAIL
Samuel P. Taylor State Park
Off Sir Francis Drake Boulevard near Lagunitas
2.5 miles/1 hour — dirt road/MB
steepness: ◉ ◉   skill level: ◉ ◉

So you tried the Riding and Hiking Trail to Barnaby Peak at Samuel P. Taylor State Park and got your butt kicked as it climbed more than 1,000 feet in less than two miles? Join the club. I'm convinced that the "Riding" part of the trail name means only if you are on a horse, who is dutifully doing all the work for you. Ride that sucker? I don't think so.

Ah, but there is still plenty to explore at Samuel P. Taylor, and mountain bikers can enjoy a spectacular little ride from Devil's Gulch Horse Camp to the boundary of the park, paralleling Devil's Gulch Creek the whole way. If you want to see more, simply lock up your bike and take a short hike to Stairstep Falls, a small and secret waterfall tucked into the back of Devil's Gulch canyon.

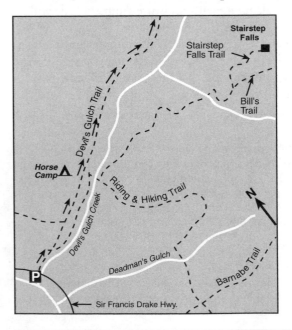

Begin your ride by carefully crossing Sir Francis Drake Highway from the dirt parking area across from Devil's Gulch Horse Camp. Ride up the paved access road to the camp, with Devil's Gulch Creek on your right. You'll see a hiking trail heading off from the paved road along the creek canyon, but stay where you are and ride straight ahead through the horse camp, being extra cautious if there are any horses around. (Never scare the big guys—they don't like it.) Ignore the Riding and Hiking Trail which begins on your right just before the picnic area, but shortly after it you can pick up a dirt road that continues straight into the canyon. Keep riding straight ahead with the grassy, bald hills of western Marin County on your left, and the lush, deep green stream canyon of Devil's Gulch on your right. You're right on the edge of two contrasting worlds, and the trail sometimes skirts into one and then back out into the other, alternating ferns and redwoods with grasslands and oaks. Both worlds offer spectacular views——one of lush riparian habitat, the other of miles of open hillside. The best time to visit is unquestionably in the spring, when the wildflowers put on their show and the meadows are green and beautiful.

The route is short and easy to follow as it contours Devil's Gulch canyon, and is smooth and flat enough for even the most novice riders. The only possible drawback is if horses have been using the trail after a period of rain; sometimes they can erode the trail with their deep hoof prints. If you ride after a dry spell, you'll have no problem.

The trail ends at a fence which marks the border of Samuel P. Taylor State Park, where you turn around and ride back. To extend your trip, you can lock up your bike at the horse camping area, then walk across the bridge over Devil's Gulch, turn left and hike to Stairstep Falls, a 40-foot waterfall that drops in three cascades over a rocky "staircase." (Follow the hikers-only trail marked "Bill's Trail to Barnaby Peak" for a half mile, then take the spur trail on the left for a few hundred yards to the falls.)

Make it easier: Just ride out and back on the trail, skipping the hike to Stairstep Falls.

Trip notes: There is no fee if you park across the road from Devil's Gulch Horse Camp. A $5 per vehicle day-use fee is charged if you park in the main paved parking areas at Samuel P. Taylor State Park. A trail map/ brochure is available at the ranger kiosk (at the main park entrance) for 75 cents. For more information, contact Samuel P. Taylor State Park, P.O. Box 251, Lagunitas, CA 94938; (415) 488-9897 or (415) 893-1580.

Directions: From San Francisco, cross the Golden Gate Bridge on U.S. 101, then drive north for 7.5 miles. Take the Sir Francis Drake Boulevard exit west toward San Anselmo and drive 15 miles to Samuel P. Taylor State Park. Continue exactly one mile past the main park entrance to the Devil's Gulch Horse Camp on the right, but park your car in the dirt parking area on the left side of the road. Walk your bike across Sir Francis Drake and through the access gate for Devil's Gulch.

53. KENT PUMP ROAD
Marin Municipal Water District
Off Bolinas-Fairfax Road near Fairfax
9 miles/2 hours — dirt road/MB
steepness: ◉ ◉   skill level: ◉

The Marin Watershed lands offer several epic mountain bike rides—the kind of trails that mountain bikes were first invented for. The Pine Mountain Loop is probably the most famous, complete with a downhill stint on the Repack Trail, so named because after you ride it, you'll probably have to repack your bearings. It's that severe.

Well, if extensive bike repair does not interest you in the slightest, head out to the Marin Watershed and ride the Kent Pump Road, the trail *next* to Pine Mountain, which is ever so much gentler and more forgiving. In fact, once I rode Pine Mountain and Kent Pump Road both in the same weekend, and not only did I not get my butt kicked on the latter, I actually had more fun.

Again and again, people miss this trail. They drive right past it on their way across the dam at Alpine Lake, and they miss out. The ride is flat, smooth and easy, and best of all, it travels through a gorgeous watershed canyon all the way to 460-acre Kent Lake. The only way to reach Kent Lake is to hike or bike there, which greatly limits the amount of company you'll have.

A few notes for the start of this trail: 1—Be careful not to park in front of the gate at the trailhead, since this is a protection road. 2—You have to crawl under the gate with your bike since there is no turnstile, but it's easier than it sounds. 3—When you begin riding, ignore the trail that leads immediately to the left, as it just loops back to the bottom of the dam. Stay straight on the main trail.

Kent Pump Road is basically flat, with only two short hills, one at the very beginning (going down on the way out) and one at trail's end at the lake (also going down on the way out). They are both short, manageable "ups" on the way home. The riding is very smooth gravel, so smooth it might as well be pavement, as the water district keeps the road well-maintained. The ravine drops off steeply to the left, so it's best to stay far from the road's edge when you're riding, but stop, take a break, and look over the edge every now and then. The canyon is very pristine and beautiful, with big mossy boulders, a pretty stream, and thick groves of trees draped with moss and lichens. Don't just whizz by and miss it. Also, pay attention to the many fragrances on the trail— the mix of firs, pine, and sage can be intoxicating.

End of the Kent Pump Road at Kent Lake

The only major trail junction you'll pass is Old Vee Road on your right, at two miles in; keep heading straight, snaking your way deeper into the canyon. Kent Pump Road curves a lot; it isn't arrow-straight like many fire roads, and you may surprise deer at turns in the road. They go bounding off down into the canyon, unbothered by the near-vertical slope.

When you finally reach the southeast end of Kent Lake, continue straight past a sign that reads "No Through Road in 0.5 Mile," ignoring two short right cutoffs. The downhill route drops you at the lake's edge, where there is a small pumphouse building. No water contact is permitted at Kent Lake, so forget swimming, but have a seat by the water's edge for a while and listen to the birds calling and the woodpeckers pecking. Many dead trees are sticking out of the water, silent victims that were swallowed up when the lake was dammed. The woodpeckers adore them.

When you've seen and heard enough, head back up the road to the trailhead.

Make it easier: This is about as easy as mountain biking gets, but if you're tiring out, just cut your trip short. The canyon is worth seeing even if you never make it to the lake.

Trip notes: There is no fee. For more information and a $2 map, contact Marin Municipal Water District at 220 Nellen Avenue, Corte Madera, CA 94925; (415) 924-4600. Or phone Sky Oaks Ranger Station at (415) 945-1181.

Directions: From San Francisco, cross the Golden Gate Bridge on U.S.
101 and travel north toward San Rafael. Take the Sir Francis Drake
Boulevard exit west toward San Anselmo and drive six miles to the town
of Fairfax. Turn left at the first gas station in Fairfax (at the "Fairfax" sign)
and then right immediately on Broadway. In one block, turn left on
Bolinas Road. Drive 7.8 miles on Bolinas Road to the dam at Alpine Lake.
Park as close to the right (north) side of the dam as possible, at any of the
pullouts along the road. The trailhead is on the right side of the dam, at the
gated fire road.

54. LAKE LAGUNITAS LOOP
Marin Municipal Water District
Off Bolinas-Fairfax Road near Fairfax
2 miles/1 hour — dirt single-track & dirt road/MB
steepness: ◉   skill level: ◉

Probably the greatest compliment you can pay Lake Lagunitas is
that it's a reservoir that somehow manages not to look like a reservoir.
Surrounded by oaks, madrones, pines and firs, it looks like a real lake, a
place that the earliest Marin inhabitants would have fished and used as
a water supply. It looks, well, natural.

It isn't, of course. This is Marin County, an area that is basically
semi-arid desert, so modern inhabitants have had to get smart about
storing water. Lagunitas is a small, 22-acre reservoir, part of the Mount
Tamalpais Watershed, managed by the Marin Municipal Water District.
It's the oldest of the Marin lakes and its dam was built in 1873. Luckily
the Water District people don't just horde water; they also open up their
land for outdoor recreation, and the lakes offer excellent fishing, hiking,
birdwatching, and bicycling.

The picnic area by the parking lot is often crowded, especially on
weekends, since it has fire grills, water, restrooms—the whole nine
yards. Ignore the throngs and start riding on the fire road to the left
of the picnic area (starting near the restrooms), heading past a small
abandoned house. I like to ride clockwise around the lake, which means
heading to the left of the dam. Your ride gets interrupted almost immediately when signs tell you to walk your bike for the first 300 feet
around the lake, including carrying it up a few stairsteps. There are a
couple more houses off to your left, which are clearly occupied, with tall
fences around them.

When the single-track widens to a one-lane dirt road, the signs
announce that you are allowed to ride again. Pedal through the oak
trees along the lake's edge, which is crowded with reeds, tules and cat-

tails. Since you are riding clockwise, facing east on this section, you get great views of the unmistakable profile of Mount Tamalpais. Various dirt roads come in from the left, but continue heading to the right to make a loop around the lake's edge. Cross the East Fork of Lagunitas Creek, either by riding through the dry creekbed in summer or taking the just-wide-enough-for-handlebars bridge in the wet season. This puts you on a wide single-track, continuing along the south side of the lake. Since it's shadier and cooler on this side, the oaks are covered with moss all winter and mixed in with more conifers. You can look between them to see little duck families floating on the surface of the lake.

Cross two more forks of Lagunitas Creek, then reach the pump-house for the lake by Rock Springs/Lagunitas Road. On the west side of the lake, you rise about 30 feet above the lakeshore, changing your view of the water. The trail never gains more than 70 feet in elevation, so it's an easy cruise, even for young riders. Watch out for hikers, though, who also enjoy this trail.

To complete your circle, ride past the dam. If you want to travel over it, you must walk your bike on the gravel walkway. (There's a wooden deck on the dam's left side, a great place to stop and look out over the lake.) Then you can return to the parking area the same way you came in, or take the fire road on the left side of the dam.

If you can visit Lake Lagunitas on a weekday, you'll have the best experience and the least crowds. On a midweek afternoon, it's so quiet here that you can ride the trail and hear ducks splashing in the water 100 yards away. Your only company may be a few anglers, fishing from shore. The lake is a testing ground for a wild trout fishery, so you'll meet only the most civilized breed of fisherperson. The rules are artificial lures only and single barbless hooks, with a two-fish limit. All trout over 14 inches must be returned to the lake, so they can keep spawning and naturally replenishing the fish population.

Make it more challenging: Rock Springs/Lagunitas Road leads off near the pumphouse, and climbs more than 1,000 feet in 2.5 miles to reach Potrero Meadows. You can ride that trail as far as you like. (The Bay Tree Junction is reachable in one mile, with a 600-foot elevation gain.) You can also just circle the lake's perimeter twice, for a few more flat miles.

Trip notes: The entrance fee (per vehicle) is $3 on weekdays, $4 on weekends from April to October, and $3 on weekends from November to March. For more information and a $2 map, contact Marin Municipal Water District at 220 Nellen Avenue, Corte Madera, CA 94925; (415) 924-4600. Or phone Sky Oaks Ranger Station at (415) 945-1181.

Directions: From San Francisco, cross the Golden Gate Bridge on U.S. 101 and travel north toward San Rafael. Take the Sir Francis Drake

Boulevard exit west toward San Anselmo and drive six miles to the town of Fairfax. Turn left at the first gas station in Fairfax (at the "Fairfax" sign) and then right immediately on Broadway. In one block, turn left on Bolinas Road. Drive 1.5 miles on Bolinas Road to Sky Oaks Road, where you bear left. Drive straight for one-half mile to the entrance kiosk, then continue and take the left fork that leads to Lake Lagunitas. Park at the far end of the parking lot, then begin riding on the unsigned fire road that begins near the restrooms and pay phone (to the left of the picnic area), which leads uphill to the lake.

55. PHOENIX LAKE to BOLINAS-FAIRFAX ROAD
Marin Municipal Water District
Off Sir Francis Drake Boulevard in Ross
7.5 miles/2 hours — dirt roads/MB
steepness: ◉ ◉   skill level: ◉ ◉

Why, why, why would the most popular lake in Marin County have the least amount of parking and poorest access? It's a question that mountain bikers ask themselves time and time again, as they search for a place to leave their cars and mount their bikes within a reasonable distance of Natalie Coffin Greene Park in Ross and the trailhead for Phoenix Lake. It's a tough call whether Phoenix Lake should even make it into this book, since getting to it on a Sunday afternoon can be darn near impossible. Still, the ride here is a perfect easy biking trip with plenty to offer everybody, and the trails provide a classic Marin outing, with a big lake, lush redwood forest, and oak-studded hills.

If you want easy, the best way to make this trip is to do it on a weekday, preferably in winter. On a Thursday morning in January, you can just drive right into the parking lot, no problem. If that doesn't fit your schedule, then arrive as early as possible on a Saturday or Sunday, and be prepared to park near the intersection of Sir Francis Drake Boulevard and Lagunitas Road, then ride your bike on city streets for a mile to the park entrance. It seems the town of Ross has gotten fed up with recreation enthusiasts parking along neighborhood streets every weekend, so they have signs up on roads all around the park that say "No Parking on Weekends and Holidays from 6 A.M. to 6 P.M."

Let's assume that you get to the trailhead, one way or another. The route leads uphill from the parking lot to Phoenix Lake in two-tenths of a mile, where you can ride to your left, around the east edge of Phoenix Lake, for one-half mile until the trail is closed to bikes. (This is a nice, quiet section of the lake, where you can often see a heron perched in a low tree, staring intently into the water, visualizing his

Phoenix Lake

lunch.) Turn around at the trail closure, then ride around the lake in the other direction, past the Phoenix Log Cabin, built in 1893 and currently not open to the public. Pick up Shaver Grade Trail just past the cabin, riding it to a multiple-trail junction called Five Corners. Be prepared to climb on the somewhat rocky trail, over one mile and a 300-foot elevation gain. It's a decent workout, but you won't mind because the trail takes you through a terrific redwood stand with the sound of busy woodpeckers echoing off the big trees.

When you reach Five Corners (puff, puff), continue slightly to the left on Concrete Pipe, a blessedly smooth and flat fire road. Riding on it feels like a reward after the work of climbing Shaver Grade. You are now in oak and grassland country, with highlights of bright red pyracantha berries in the wintertime. Ride to its completion at Bolinas-Fairfax Road, then turn around and ride back, for an easy downhill return to Phoenix Lake. When you reach the lake, you have the option of extending your trip by hiking on Yolanda Trail (my favorite) or on any of the many other trails that branch off from Phoenix Junction and the lake, or doing a little fishing from shore.

Make it easier: If you have small children who are not up to climbing, they can just ride around the north and east sides of the lake for a two-mile round-trip.

Trip notes: There is no fee. For more information and a $2 map, contact Marin Municipal Water District at 220 Nellen Avenue, Corte Madera, CA 94925; (415) 924-4600, or Sky Oaks Ranger Station at (415) 945-1181.

Directions: From San Francisco, cross the Golden Gate Bridge on U.S. 101 and travel north toward San Rafael. Take the Sir Francis Drake Boulevard exit west toward San Anselmo and drive 2.5 miles to Lagunitas Road on the left, across from the Marin Art and Garden Center. Turn left on Lagunitas Road and follow it for 1.1 miles to the parking area for Natalie Coffin Greene Park. (Drive through the intersection with Glenwood Avenue, where Lagunitas Road is signed "Not a Through Road," and past the Lagunitas Country Club.) There is parking for about 15 cars. A gated protection road leads to Phoenix Lake from the right side of the parking lot. (When the parking lot is full on weekends and holidays, you may have to park as far as a mile away on Lagunitas Road, as closer areas are signed "No Parking on Weekends and Holidays.")

56. LAS GALLINAS WILDLIFE PONDS
Las Gallinas Valley Sanitary District
Off U.S. 101 near San Rafael
6.5 miles/1.5 hours — dirt double-track/MB
steepness: ● skill level: ●

Sometimes unlikely places make good bike riding. So it is at the Las Gallinas Valley Sanitary District, where the important work of treating and disposing waste water gets done, as well as the equally important work of preserving wetlands. At this wastewater reclamation project you can find herons roosting in trees, a flock of white pelicans, and 3.5 miles of public access trails on the edge of San Pablo Bay.

The place may be alongside a sewage treatment plant, but it's wildlife heaven out here. In a two-hour trip, I saw several big jack rabbits, a flock of Canada geese, three hawks, numerous turkey vultures, a giant white egret, and a great blue heron. And this wasn't even autumn, which is the best season to see migrating birds.

The reclamation project in northeast San Rafael includes a freshwater marsh, an irrigated pasture, storage ponds, and a saltwater marsh. Yes, there are electrical towers. Yes, there is a barbed wire fence. But there's also uninterrupted San Pablo Bay shoreline with views of Mount Diablo to the east and Mount Tamalpais to the southwest. Plus there's a great trail surface for easy bike riding—wide, smooth, dirt and gravel— that makes the path accessible to anyone, even little kids.

You can begin riding by the playing fields at McInnis Park, if you wish, or you can park right by the sanitary district buildings and start from there. A large signboard by the bridge at the trail's start shows a map of the place and notes some of the wildlife you may see. Begin your ride, heading straight toward the bay. You cruise along on top of gravel levees that separate the sanitary district's storage ponds from the saltwater marshes along the bay. The presence of both of these natural and man-made habitats encourages wildlife. To make things more appealing for the birds, sanitary district personnel have planted willow and acacia trees to encourage nesting on the storage ponds' small islands. They also plant fish in the ponds to provide food for herons, cormorants, and egrets.

The result of all these good works is that the Marin Audubon Society has observed over 147 species of birds in the reclamation project area. Mallards, coots, and Canada geese nest and raise their young at the marshy pond. Cormorants, snowy and great egrets, night herons, great blue herons, long eared owls, and red-shouldered hawks show up to fish or hunt for small mammals. A flock of dozens of white pelicans frequent the marsh. (They're the favorites of regular visitors and birdwatchers.) Be sure to bring your binoculars, and stop your hike every now and then to listen to the variety of bird calls.

When you reach the edge of the bay, you can turn left and follow the Levee Trail for one mile to its end, then turn around and head back. At low tide, watch for shorebirds dipping their beaks in the mud at the edge of San Pablo Bay. On your return trip, be sure to circle around the freshwater ponds near the start of the trail and check out the resident population of ducks and coots.

Las Gallinas Wildlife Ponds

Make it easier: Skip the half-mile ride from the McInnis Park playing fields to the reclamation project lands. Instead, park in the lot right next to the sanitary district buildings and start riding from there.

Trip notes: There is no fee. For more information, contact Las Gallinas Valley Sanitary District, 300 Smith Ranch Road, San Rafael, CA 94901; (415) 472-1734.

Directions: From San Francisco, cross the Golden Gate Bridge on U.S. 101 and travel north to San Rafael. Take the Lucas Valley Road/Smith Ranch Road exit. At the stoplight, turn right on Smith Ranch Road and drive three-quarters of a mile to just before the entrance to John F. McInnis Park and Golf Course. Turn left and park in the pullout by the playing fields. Ride down the road for a half mile to the entrance to the wildlife pond trails, just to the left of the Las Gallinas Valley Sanitary District buildings. (There is a small parking lot for a few cars right by the entrance if you don't want to ride on the road.)

57. SHORELINE TRAIL
China Camp State Park
Off U.S. 101 near San Rafael
8 miles/2 hours — dirt single-track/MB
steepness: ◉   skill level: ◉ ◉

Most people think of China Camp State Park as being a historic preserve, showcasing the remains of a Chinese shrimp fishing village from the 19th century. It's the kind of place that is popular for school field trips. But don't forget about China Camp's scenic location on San Pablo Bay, which allows for blue-water vistas at every turn of the park's Shoreline Trail. Once you ride the trail and witness those views, you'll never think of China Camp State Park in quite the same way.

China Camp is also a rare animal in the California State Park system. It's one of the few state parks that keeps its single-track trails open to bikes. Partly that's because the park is rarely crowded, and bikers and hikers seem to mind their manners and get along just fine. Once when I hiked here, a woman rode by me on her mountain bike and called out merrily, "Oh, hello! I get to use my new toy!" as she dinged her handlebar bike bell. Even the testiest hiker (sometimes that's me) can't get annoyed with a biker using one of those cheery ringers.

So saddle up and begin riding from the campground parking area. You parallel San Pablo Bay as you ride to the east, heading for park headquarters in three miles or China Camp Village and the park's eastern boundary in just over four miles. As the trail leads from the parking area, you'll see Jake's Island and Turtle Back off to your left, on

San Pablo Bay and Rat Rock from China Camp State Park

the edge of the bay. These are shoreline hills that were once islands when bay waters were higher.

Stay on Shoreline Trail, roughly paralleling North San Pedro Road until the path heads inland through an oak and bay forest, then curves around into an open meadow and the park's group picnic area. As you ride through, your single-track trail will become a dirt road for a short distance, and you must make sure you head left, toward the bay, not back into the forest. (You actually end up on Miwok Fire Trail for about 100 feet.) Then you can pick up the single-track again, continuing eastward with more bay views all the way to the park ranger's headquarters, situated in a trailer along a service road.

From there, you can continue your trip on the Shoreline Trail to China Camp Village in seven-tenths of a mile, the trail crossing San Pedro Road to get there. The historic village is worth seeing, so lock up your bike and explore around the pier and four remaining buildings, filled with furniture and tools from the day-to-day life of the Chinese shrimp camp. A nice sandy beach to the west of China Camp Village is an excellent place for birdwatching, with great egrets fishing in the marshy edges of the bay. If you ride to the far eastern boundary of the park (two-tenths of a mile further, back on the south side of San Pedro Road), you rise up and above China Camp Village for a terrific view of Rat Rock (a tiny island), the pier at China Camp, and shrimp boats out in the bay. When you come to the park boundary sign, turn back.

By the way, don't be surprised if deer bound across the trail in front of you, or stare at you motionless from open fields. There are tons of them here, including new fawns every spring, and they've gotten used to bike riders and hikers. Often there is a family of deer right by the Back Ranch Meadows parking lot.

Make it easier: Just cut your trip short, riding only the group picnic area and back for a two-mile round-trip.

Trip notes: A $5 day-use fee is charged per vehicle. A free trail map is available at park headquarters (across from the Bullhead Flat parking area). For more information, contact China Camp State Park, 1455A East Francisco Boulevard, San Rafael, CA 94901; (415) 456-0766 or (415) 893-1580.

Directions: From San Francisco, cross the Golden Gate Bridge on U.S. 101 and travel north to San Rafael. Take the North San Pedro exit and go east for four miles on North San Pedro Road. Turn right at the sign for Back Ranch Meadows Campground and drive to the parking area. The trailhead for the Shoreline Trail is on the bay side of the parking lot.

58. TIBURON BIKE PATH
City of Tiburon
Off U.S. 101 in Tiburon
4.6 miles/1 hour — paved bike trail/RB or MB
steepness: ● skill level: ●

Okay, so it doesn't go very far and it sees a lot of use, but the Tiburon Bike Path provides the chance to ride around some prime real estate along scenic San Francisco Bay that 99 percent of us would never be able to afford in our wildest dreams. If you like stunning bay views, this ride is your ticket.

The path begins by the statue of Blackie the horse in Blackie's Pasture, just outside of the town of Tiburon, and ends where the paved, separate-from-traffic trail becomes a bike lane alongside busy Tiburon Boulevard, near the town center. The roadside bike lane is not recommended for families with small children, since the auto traffic can be quite hectic, but the 2.3-mile bike path is safe from cars and an enjoyable ride, making for a 4.6-mile round-trip.

For most riders, the trip begins with a two-part question: Who was Blackie the horse, and why is there a huge statue of him in the parking lot? Blackie was a fixture in Tiburon for decades, grazing in this pasture daily, long before it was a paved parking lot. He died at the ripe old age of 33 in 1966, and local admirers put up a gravestone in his memory. It has since been replaced by the handsome statue, and the entrance road and parking lot have been named after ol' Blackie.

The Northwestern Pacific Railroad used to travel the route of the Tiburon bike path, providing passenger and freight service from Corte Madera to Tiburon, and from there, transporting railroad cars across the bay to San Francisco. The abandoned rail right-of-way was converted to a paved multi-use trail, and is well-loved by bicyclists, rollerbladers, walkers, and baby-carriage-pushers. The entire route provides close-up bay views—the water laps within 20 feet of the trail at high tide—and glimpses of Sausalito, the Golden Gate Bridge, and Mount Tamalpais.

The trail leaves the parking lot and heads to the left, taking you past the Richardson Bay Wildlife Ponds. These small bird ponds, managed by the Richardson Bay Sanitary District, make good use of Tiburon's sewage. Huge cattails keep the ponds mostly hidden from view, but still you'll see many birds along the trail.

When you're not looking southward over the bay, your attention will often be captured by nearby human entertainment, which includes rowboaters and kayakers on the water, and people jogging by on the par course which borders part of this trail. You ride past some playing fields, scattered with soccer players on weekend afternoons, and next to them is the only trail fork. You must ride the lower route (closer to the water), as the upper route is closed to bikes.

Kids love getting off their bikes to explore around the coastal mudflats that edge the bay and the trail. There is plenty of opportunity for birdwatching, as long-legged types are perpetually digging in the mud for worms. Millions of migratory birds use the mudflats around San Francisco Bay as a safe haven and stopover on their long flights from cold climates to warm, and vice versa.

When you reach the bike trail's end near downtown Tiburon, you can lock up your bike and explore the downtown on foot—there are plenty of restaurants and shops to stop at—or just turn around and ride back to Blackie's Pasture.

Make it more challenging: You can combine this ride with a trip on the Tiburon ferry to Angel Island, then ride your bike on the Perimeter Trail there. (See the following story.) You will have to ride your bike on the roadside bike lane from the bike trail's terminus to downtown Tiburon, where the ferry leaves from 21 Main Street.

Trip notes: There is no fee. For more information, contact Department of Public Works, City of Tiburon, 1175 Tiburon Boulevard, Tiburon, CA 94920; (415) 435-7399.

Directions: From San Francisco, cross the Golden Gate Bridge on U.S. 101 and travel north toward San Rafael. Take the Highway 131/Belvedere/ Tiburon exit and travel east for 1.5 miles, then turn right at Blackie's Pasture Road and park in the large parking lot.

59. PERIMETER TRAIL
Angel Island State Park
In San Francisco Bay near Tiburon
5 miles/1.5 hours — gravel and paved road/RB or MB
steepness: ⊛ ⊛   skill level: ⊛ ⊛

The Perimeter Trail at Angel Island State Park is the most spectacular easy bike ride in the entire San Francisco Bay Area. This is high praise, because the Bay Area has plenty of first-rate rides, all perfect 10s in the scenery category. But what sets it apart is that Angel Island is an *island,* so going there adds an element of excitement to your trip that no mainland trail can provide. The 360-degree views alone are reason enough to make the journey.

What comes as a surprise to first-time visitors is how fun it is just getting to Angel Island—walking your bike up the ferry gangway, finding a spot on the ferry's top deck or inside the lower deck, smelling the salt air and watching as you depart the mainland. No matter how crowded the boat is, everybody is always smiling.

In about 25 minutes from Tiburon and 40 minutes from San Francisco, your ferry docks at Ayala Cove. Claim your bike from the holding area, buy a park map at the dock, then ride around to the right, past the island's cafe and a place where they rent mountain bikes. (If you don't feel like bringing your own, bike rentals start at $25 per day or $12 per hour. They also have bike trailers for rent, if your kids are too young to ride.) The picnic area ahead will be packed with people, but ride past them and take the gravel bike trail on the left, which switchbacks gently up a hill to join the main Perimeter Trail.

The Perimeter Trail is a paved road, with the pavement deteriorating to gravel and dirt in many places, but rideable on any kind of bike with any kind of tires. The trail sees so much use, it's been worn as smooth as a baby's behind. Since this is an island and the Perimeter Trail loops around it, you can head either right or left. I always ride to the left, heading clockwise around the island, working my way north to south. Heading this way, first you get views of Tiburon, then the Richmond Bridge and the top of the bay up towards Vallejo. You have to keep analyzing and re-analyzing what you are looking at, because your

Perimeter Trail, Angel Island State Park

perspective is so different from the middle of San Francisco Bay than it is from any of its edges. We landlubbers just aren't used to seeing the Bay Area this way.

Obviously, the views change as you move around the island. One of the best vistas is about two-thirds of the way around the loop, at an open stretch where you can see the Bay Bridge and the Golden Gate Bridge simultaneously, and everything in between and on either side, including Alcatraz, which is directly ahead. You're viewing the whole area from Berkeley to Sausalito, a 180-degree scene. On a clear day, it's beyond stunning.

The wind can blow at Angel Island, and the fog can come in on a moment's notice, so come prepared with an extra jacket, even on sunny days. Usually the trail is windiest on the west side of the island, where you are facing the Golden Gate. The trail also has its only major hill heading in this direction, but the Golden Gate views make the ascent worth the effort.

There are all kinds of historical side-trips possible on the Perimeter Trail, since Angel Island has a long and varied history as a military outpost, a Russian sea otter hunters' site, and an immigrant detention center. The visitors center near the picnic area at Ayala Cove has all the information you can ask for. For those who seek only pretty views and a nice bike ride, you can cap off your trip with lunch or a snack at the cafe near the ferry dock, which serves surprisingly good food and has an outside deck. Small rental lockers are also available at the ferry dock, in case you want to bring your own picnic but don't want to schlep it around, as well as restrooms and pay telephones.

Make it more challenging: A second loop trail is available at Angel Island, inside the Perimeter Trail. You can ride the double loop for a 10-mile round-trip by turning right on the Fire Road at the Angel Island Fire Station. Get a park map for details.

Trip notes: From Tiburon, the ferry costs $7 for adults. Your bike costs $1 extra. From San Francisco, the ferry costs $11 for adults. The ferry crossing fee includes day-use of Angel Island State Park. A park map/brochure is available for $2 at the ferry landing on the island. For more information, contact Angel Island State Park at (415) 435-1915 or (415) 893-1580.

Directions: Ferry service to Angel Island is available from Tiburon via the Tiburon Ferry; and from San Francisco, Oakland/Alameda, and Vallejo via the Blue & Gold Fleet. For departures from Tiburon, phone the Tiburon Ferry at (415) 435-2131. For the Blue & Gold Fleet, phone (415) 773-1188 for San Francisco departures, (510) 522-3300 for Oakland/Alameda departures, and (707) 64-FERRY for Vallejo departures.

---

60. LAUREL DELL FIRE ROAD
Marin Municipal Water District
On Mount Tamalpais near Mill Valley
6.5 miles/2 hours — dirt road/MB
steepness: ◉ ◉   skill level: ◉ ◉

Mount Tamalpais is known as the birthplace of mountain biking, and geologically speaking, it's perfectly shaped for it. Years ago, those first mountain bikers took their old beach cruisers out of their garages, had someone drive them to the top of Mount Tam, then let 'er rip, all the way down. It was only later that the idea came up to add gears to the bikes so they could climb back up the mountain.

Well, I'm grateful to those first daring and creative souls, but somehow, the whole climbing thing has never really caught on with me. Luckily, the Laurel Dell Fire Road can be the ticket for a Mount Tamalpais mountain biking experience that is *not* completely vertical in nature. Laurel Dell is a rolling, up-and-down track that laterals the mountain, never gaining more than 300 feet, giving you the chance to ride through a fir and redwood canyon, over a serpentine knoll, and into grassy hillsides just below the west peak of the mountain. Hey, if you like a ride that has a little bit of everything, this one's for you.

The first section of trail drops 300 feet immediately on its way to Laurel Dell, so right off you have a fun downhill through thick forest.

Laurel Dell is a meadow and picnic area on your left, and in winter, you'll probably have to cross a stream to reach it. In summer, the trail is dry. Next comes a series of short hills, one after another, providing a little interval training for your heart and lungs. Take a break from climbing any time you want and smell the Christmas-tree aroma of the dense fir trees.

Luckily all the hard work takes place in the shade, and when finally you come out into the open, you're on top of a rocky ridge. Notice the green serpentine (California's state rock) and dry, acidic soil, which supports only dwarf trees and scrub plants. Riding along the ridge, you get some great valley views down the north slopes of Mount Tam, especially after you pass the right turnoff for Barth's Retreat. You can barely make out the Fairfax golf course far below, and the blue water of Bon Tempe Lake. The large mountain that stands out in the distance on clear days is Mount Saint Helena in Napa, at just over 4,000 feet in elevation.

Keep riding straight, heading into open meadow country. Your first glimpse of Potrero Camp is an unmarked cutoff on the left that can take you there, if you like. I prefer to keep riding to the end of Laurel Dell Fire Road at Potrero Meadows, where it joins with Lagunitas/Rock Springs Fire Road. If you look up just before the junction of the two fire roads, you can see the radar station buildings on the top of the west peak of Mount Tam, at 2,560 feet in elevation. If neither Potrero Camp nor Potrero Meadows suits your rest-stopping fancy, ride to the left for one-quarter mile on Lagunitas/Rock Springs Fire Road, until you come to Rifle Camp, a great little forested picnic area with a restroom nearby. (Legend has it that the camp was named for an old rifle that was dug up there by a dog named Schneider, but don't quote me on this.)

Lagunitas/Rock Springs begins to descend here, leading all the way to the lakes of the Mount Tamalpais watershed, so turn around and ride back to Laurel Dell Fire Road, then turn right and ride back the way you came. Your return trip is mostly downhill through all the changes of scenery you passed on the way in, except for a final half-mile climb from Laurel Dell back to the parking area.

Make it more challenging: There are numerous great add-on hikes for this trip, including the Cataract Trail from Laurel Dell, leading northwest to a series of cascades. Bring a bike lock and explore.

Trip notes: There is no fee. For more information and a $2 map, contact Marin Municipal Water District at 220 Nellen Avenue, Corte Madera, CA 94925; (415) 924-4600. Or phone Sky Oaks Ranger Station at (415) 945-1181. Because this trip borders Mount Tamalpais State Park, rangers there can also help you. Contact Mount Tamalpais State Park, 801 Panoramic Highway, Mill Valley, CA 94941; (415) 388-2070.

Directions: From San Francisco, take U.S. 101 North over the Golden Gate Bridge to the Mill Valley/Stinson Beach/Highway 1 exit. Continue straight for about one mile until you reach a stoplight at Shoreline Highway. Turn left and drive uphill on Shoreline Highway for 2.5 miles, then turn right on Panoramic Highway. Drive for nine-tenths of a mile until you reach an intersection where you can go left, straight, or right. Take the middle road (straight), continuing on Panoramic Highway for 4.3 more miles to Pantoll Road. Turn right on Pantoll Road and drive 1.4 miles to its intersection with Ridgecrest Boulevard. Turn left on West Ridgecrest Boulevard and drive 1.6 miles to a small parking area on the right. Park there and take the trail downhill that is marked "Laurel Dell."

---

61. OLD STAGE ROAD: PANTOLL to WEST POINT INN
Mount Tamalpais State Park
Off Panoramic Highway near Mill Valley
4 miles/1 hour — paved and dirt road/MB
steepness: ◉ ◉   skill level: ◉ ◉

Pantoll has always been my favorite trailhead at Mount Tamalpais, providing a jumpoff point for outstanding hikes down fern-filled Steep Ravine and the view-lover's Coastal Trail, among other excellent trails. But somehow I never made a trip on Old Stage Road, which starts just across the road from the Pantoll Ranger Station. Since the trail is paved at its start, a lot of bikers and hikers pass it by, thinking it's just a park access road.

But the Old Stage Road is the easy biker's ally, a perfect route for an easy climb to West Point Inn, with the option of continuing up Old Railroad Grade to the East Peak of Mount Tamalpais. (See "Make it more challenging" below.) The trail is, literally, an old stage road, which passengers on the Mount Tamalpais Scenic Railway once used to go to Stinson Beach and Bolinas. In the early 1900s, they'd get off the train at West Point Inn, then make connections with the stage coach.

Today the Old Stage Road is a smooth, double-wide trail that makes for perfect family biking on Mount Tam. Start riding on the paved trail across from Pantoll that is signed "To East Peak." When the pavement meets a dirt road in less than half a mile, continue on the dirt. Views of San Francisco Bay and the Bay Bridge are incredible; look over your right shoulder as you make the slow but smooth climb. The grade is so gradual, and so full of interesting twists and turns, you often forget you are climbing.

In less than half an hour you will reach West Point Inn, previously owned by the railroad but now under Marin Water District jurisdiction, and leased and operated by a non-profit group. The inn has several bike racks and picnic tables, but the real draw is the great view from its deck, which takes in the Mountain Home Inn down below, a wide expanse of the bay, the Bay Bridge and Richmond Bridge, Larkspur

Old Stage Road, Mount Tamalpais State Park

Landing and San Francisco. The inn sells lemonade and granola bars, hot coffee and tea, and has an old stone water fountain out front where bikers stop to fill up their bottles. A great insider's tip is that West Point Inn has four cabins and seven rooms for rent, and although there is no electricity, there is propane for light, heat, and refrigeration.

If you want to add a hike to your trip, from West Point Inn you can pick up the Nora Trail to Matt Davis Trail, which has great views in either direction, or hike Old Railroad Grade to the east, heading toward Mountain Home Inn.

West Point Inn can get to be a zoo on summer weekends, especially in the afternoons. Also, it can be hard to park at Pantoll after 10 A.M. on many weekend days, so get an early start, or make your trip during the week.

Make it more challenging: To combine this ride with the following ride, take Old Railroad Grade from West Point Inn to East Peak. Make a hard left turn in front of the inn and continue uphill on Old Railroad Grade. Turn right on to the pavement when Old Railroad Grade ends near the East Peak loop. Note: This is a steeper, more technical grade than Old Stage Road.

Trip notes: A $5 day-use fee is charged per vehicle to park at Pantoll Ranger Station. A trail map/brochure is available for $1 at the ranger station. For more information, contact Mount Tamalpais State Park, 801 Panoramic Highway, Mill Valley, CA 94941; (415) 388-2070. For information about West Point Inn, phone (415) 388-9955.

Directions: From San Francisco, take U.S. 101 North over the Golden Gate Bridge to the Mill Valley/Stinson Beach/Highway 1 exit. Continue straight for about one mile until you reach a stoplight at Shoreline Highway. Turn left and drive uphill on Shoreline Highway for 2.5 miles, then turn right on Panoramic Highway. Drive for nine-tenths of a mile until you reach an intersection where you can go left, straight, or right. Take the middle road (straight), continuing on Panoramic Highway for 4.3 more miles to Pantoll Ranger Station and parking area. Turn left to park in the lot, then walk across Panoramic Highway to the start of Pantoll Road. On the right is a paved road that is signed "Old Stage Road to East Peak."

---

62. OLD RAILROAD GRADE: EAST PEAK to WEST POINT INN
Mount Tamalpais State Park
Off Panoramic Highway near Mill Valley
4 miles/1 hour — dirt road/MB
steepness: ◉ ◉ ◉   skill level: ◉ ◉

If you've heard the "war stories" about the Old Railroad Grade on Mount Tamalpais, you may approach the trail with some trepidation. If you've been told that Old Railroad Grade is long, rocky, and steep, you've been told truth. However, the key is to ride only a section of it, not the whole eight miles from the bottom of the mountain to the top. The best place to start is at the summit, the 2,571-foot East Peak of Mount Tam. If you're going to take a bike ride that's famous for its spectacular views, you might as well begin with a doozy.

At the parking area, take a look around before you mount your bike. From near the mountaintop visitor center, you can look east across the bay and south to San Francisco and its bridges. All of Marin County and San Francisco is spread out below you. If you want to go even higher and see even more, you can hike up the stairs to the lookout, perched above the visitor center, or walk the Verna Dunshee Trail that loops around the peak, an easy, one-mile hike. There are bike racks, picnic tables, and restrooms by the visitor center—all of a bicyclist's basic necessities.

When you've been adequately awed by the view, mount your bike and ride out of the parking lot, picking up Old Railroad Grade on the left side of East Ridgecrest Boulevard, just past the paved loop at the East Peak. (You passed the trail on your way in.) Keep in mind that Old Railroad Grade is not your average rail trail; in fact, it was part of what was known as the Crookedest Railroad in the World—the Mount Tamalpais Scenic Railway with 281 turns and curves. Even with all those switchbacks, the trail is still as steep as a ski slope in many spots. It's also somewhat rough and rocky, so prepare to brake a lot and keep your speed down, or risk losing your balance on the rocky surface. This trail is a great place to practice your downhill riding skills. Stay alert for people coming the other way around the curves, as the route is popular with bikers, and if you have kids with you, be sure they stay on the inside track, hugging the mountain. The outside track has some steep and dramatic dropoffs.

You won't pedal at all on the short, sweet trip down to West Point Inn, but that means the trip uphill will be a lot more time-consuming and energy-consuming, and gives your thighs a good workout. Enjoy the free ride while you've got it. West Point Inn was built by the railroad in 1914 as a restaurant and stopover for railway passengers who were getting off the train and picking up the stagecoach to ride down to Stinson Beach or Bolinas. After the rail days ended, the building

Rest stop at the picnic tables by West Point Inn

came under the jurisdiction of the Marin Water District, and is now leased and operated by a nonprofit group. You can purchase drinks and snacks at the inn, which is open all day on weekends, and afternoons only on weekdays (closed on Mondays). Restrooms and picnic areas are available all the time. A small sign on West Point Inn's front door conveys its philosophy: "You may use the parlor if you keep it tidy." Or just hang out on the inn's deck and enjoy the view, gathering energy for the climb back up to East Peak.

Make it more challenging: Combine this ride with the previous ride, continuing from West Point Inn to Pantoll Ranger Station.

Trip notes: A $5 day-use fee is charged per vehicle to park at East Peak. A trail map/brochure is available for $1 at the visitor center. For more information, contact Mount Tamalpais State Park, 801 Panoramic Highway, Mill Valley, CA 94941; (415) 388-2070.

Directions: From San Francisco, take U.S. 101 North over the Golden Gate Bridge to the Mill Valley/Stinson Beach/Highway 1 exit. Continue straight for about one mile until you reach a stoplight at Shoreline Highway. Turn left and drive uphill on Shoreline Highway for 2.5 miles, then turn right on Panoramic Highway. Drive for nine-tenths of a mile until you reach an intersection where you can go left, straight, or right. Take the middle road (straight), continuing on Panoramic Highway for 4.3 more miles to Pantoll Road. Turn right on Pantoll Road and drive 1.4 miles to its intersection with Ridgecrest Boulevard. Turn right on East Ridgecrest Boulevard and drive just over two miles to the parking area for East Peak. (Drive around the loop and park, then ride your bike out of the loop and pick up Old Railroad Grade on the left, just outside of the loop.)

63. TENNESSEE VALLEY TRAIL
Golden Gate National Recreation Area
Off U.S. 101 near Mill Valley
4 miles/1.5 hours — paved and dirt road/MB
steepness: ◉ ◉   skill level: ◉

After Angel Island's Perimeter Trail, the Tennessee Valley Trail is probably the most written about hiking/biking trail in all of the San Francisco Bay Area. But all that publicity is not without cause—the Tennessee Valley Trail is a stellar route, and easy enough even for small children. I suggest riding here only on weekdays, or early in the morning on weekends, to minimize your chance of facing crowds. But by all means, you should make the trip at one time or another, as the scenery is spectacular both along the route and at its destination, Tennessee Valley Beach.

Tennessee Valley Beach, Golden Gate National Recreation Area

Besides the views, the main reason for the crowds at Tennessee Valley is its proximity to the homes of thousands of San Francisco and Marin residents. Although Mount Tamalpais is just a few miles up the road from Tennessee Valley, it is a long, steep, winding drive to get there, while Tennessee Valley is in the flats, not far from town. This is the local outdoors spot, where everyone goes when they don't have all day to make a trip to Point Reyes, or they don't want to face the drive up Mount Tam. Tennessee Valley has trails for horseback riders, hikers, dog-walkers, and mountain bikers—a bit of everything for everybody.

Tennessee Valley Road begins as a paved route by Miwok Stables, where you can rent horses for a long or short trail ride. Then the pavement forks left and the trail turns to dirt, heading southwest to Tennessee Cove. That's where the 1853 steamship *Tennessee,* carrying cargo, mail, and 600 passengers, wrecked in dense fog on its way to San Francisco. Fortunately, all lives were saved.

The trail is a wide fire road that follows a creekbed between grassy ridges, leading for two miles to small, black sand Tennessee Beach, bracketed by high cliffs. While the beach is the prime attraction, a bird-filled lagoon along the route is a close runner-up in the scenery category. A fork in the trail shortly before the lagoon is designated so that bikers must go to the right, above the lagoon, while hikers are permitted to walk to the left, alongside it. The trail rejoins again a half-mile later as it nears the beach.

While Tennessee Beach is a great spot for surf-watching, don't think about swimming there, even on rare days when the air and sun are warm enough. The surf is extremely treacherous. There is a bike rack on the beach, though, so bring a lock with you and explore the area. A trail leads up the northwestern bluff to nearly 200 feet above the sea for an impressive overlook.

The ride back has a bit more climb to it, including one pretty good hill that comes as a surprise after all the flat riding you've been doing. Still, I've seen six-year-olds manage it, although the tricycle set tends to dismount and walk a lot on the way home.

Make it easier: You can just ride the trail to near the lagoon, then lock up your bike and walk around the marshy edges. There are plenty of great nature lessons to be had, and excellent birdwatching.

Trip notes: There is no fee. A free map/brochure is available by contacting Golden Gate National Recreation Area, Building 1056, Fort Cronkite, Sausalito, CA 94965; (415) 331-1540 or (415) 556-0560.

Directions: From San Francisco, take U.S. 101 North over the Golden Gate Bridge to the Mill Valley/Stinson Beach/Highway 1 exit. Continue straight for six-tenths of a mile to Tennessee Valley Road on the left. Turn left and drive two miles on Tennessee Valley Road to the trailhead.

64. MILL VALLEY & SAUSALITO BIKE PATH
Marin County Parks
Off U.S. 101 in Mill Valley and Sausalito
7 miles/1.5 hours — paved bike trail/RB or MB
steepness: ◉   skill level: ◉

People love paved bike paths, separated from car traffic. The better the trail's scenery, the more it is loved. That explains why the Mill Valley/Sausalito Bike Path, like the Tiburon Bike Path, gets packed with people on weekend afternoons, while the other Marin County bike paths like Corte Madera and Larkspur see comparatively little use. If you're choosing between riding along the bay's tidal waters or around a shopping center and freeway, it's not a difficult choice.

The Mill Valley/Sausalito Bike Path gives you a good tour of the area, starting from Sycamore Park near downtown Mill Valley and running all the way into central Sausalito. Sycamore Park is like a train depot for bikes, with trails running in three directions and bikers milling about. Although there are three trail options, for recreation purposes there is really only one way to go, which is south (to the right as you face the park), to Sausalito. The northern (left) bike path goes

All kinds of riders use the Mill Valley & Sausalito bike path

for only a mile to Lomita Drive, where it becomes a bike lane along the road. It's really just a connecting trail for bikers traveling north to Corte Madera, Larkspur, and beyond. The eastern (straight) bike path leads a very short distance to the other side of Sycamore Park and some housing developments and apartment complexes.

So southward we go, paralleling the edge of Bothin Marsh and Richardson Bay for three-plus miles to Harbor Drive in Sausalito. Unfortunately, the trail also parallels U.S. 101 for a mile of the route near Manzanita Junction in Marin City, but keep your eyes on the bay to your left and don't look at the freeway over your right shoulder. You will actually ride underneath the freeway by Manzanita Junction.

Despite how built up this urban corridor is, nature manages to thrive on the edges of the bay. If you ride during a low tide, you will see the mudflats, where birdviewing is excellent. Two wooden bridges allow the trail to cross over sections of the marsh, where you can see egrets, herons, and sandpipers by the hundreds. If you ride during a high tide, the bay water is pretty and blue, but there are fewer birds. Mount Tam is behind you; you get a fine view of its outline on your return trip.

There is one paved turnoff from the trail, just before Manzanita Junction, which leads to the right toward Tennessee Valley Road and Tamalpais Junction. Many local people use this route to ride their bikes to brunch or shopping in the Tam Junction area, or to continue biking on Tennessee Valley Road, connecting to dirt trails there.

If you continue straight instead of taking this turnoff, the main part of the bike path ends in 1.5 miles at Harbor Drive, near the bike store in Sausalito and Waldo Point Harbor, although you can keep riding into town along sidewalks and side roads through the boat yards.

Make it more challenging: Bikers who don't mind riding with auto traffic can combine this ride with a ride across the Golden Gate Bridge, by following Bridgeway through Sausalito and to the base of the bridge. The road turns into Second Street, then South Street, climbing uphill. At the top of the hill, the road turns right and becomes Alexander Drive, which leads to the bridge.

Trip notes: There is no fee. For more information, contact Marin County Department of Parks, Marin Civic Center, Room 417, 3501 Civic Center Drive, San Rafael, CA 94903; (415) 499-6387.

Directions: From San Francisco, take U.S. 101 North over the Golden Gate Bridge to the East Blithedale exit in Mill Valley. Exit and turn left on East Blithedale, then left on Camino Alto and left again on Sycamore Avenue. Follow Sycamore to its end at the park.

East San Francisco Bay Area

65—Point Pinole Road & Bay View Trail,
   Point Pinole Regional Shoreline 152
66—Wildcat Creek Trail, *Wildcat Canyon Regional Park* 154
67—Nimitz Way Bike Trail, *Tilden Regional Park* 156
68—Lafayette Reservoir Trail, *East Bay Municipal Utility District* 158
69—Lafayette-Moraga Regional Trail,
   East Bay Regional Park District 161
70—Iron Horse Regional Trail to Danville,
   East Bay Regional Park District 163
71—Eastern Contra Costa Regional Trails,
   East Bay Regional Park District 164
72—Round Valley Regional Preserve,
   East Bay Regional Park District 166
73—Morgan Territory Regional Preserve,
   East Bay Regional Park District 168
74—Lake Chabot West & East Shore Trails,
   Anthony Chabot Regional Park 171
75—Bay View Trail, *Coyote Hills Regional Park* 173
76—Tidelands Loop & Newark Slough Trail,
   San Francisco Bay National Wildlife Refuge 175

For locations of trails, see map on page 9.

65. POINT PINOLE ROAD & BAY VIEW TRAIL
Point Pinole Regional Shoreline
Off Interstate 80 near Richmond
6 miles/2 hours — dirt double-track and paved bike trail/RB or MB
steepness: ⊛ ⊛   skill level: ⊛

Point Pinole Regional Shoreline is a little park with a big heart, a place of tranquility not far from the urban bustle of the East Bay. Few people other than local anglers make the trip out here to the very edge of Point Pinole, but those who do are surprised at how much their three-fifty admission can buy. In addition to spectacular views to the north and west and good pier fishing for striped bass, sturgeon, and kingfish, the park offers volleyball courts, picnic areas, a three-mile round-trip paved bike path and more than 10 miles of winding dirt trails suitable for mountain bikers or hikers.

What that means is guaranteed fun for everybody. Skinny-tire types can ride up and back on the paved bike path, checking out the

Point Pinole Regional Shoreline

bay views first over their left shoulder and then over their right shoulder. The path makes a straight shot right up the narrow peninsula to a quarter-mile-long pier which juts out into the bay. You can ride your bike to the very end of the pier, then drop a line in the water or just sit and smell the salty air, admiring the views of Mount Diablo on your right and Mount Tamalpais on your left.

Fat-tire riders should start out on the paved path as well, then veer off on any of several double-track dirt trails. The Bay View Trail is the best of the lot, leading along the western edge of the peninsula with great views of Mount Tam, the Richmond Bridge, and the East and West Brothers Islands. The Marsh Trail is the other favorite, providing views to the north of Napa, San Pablo Bay, and the Carquinez Bridge.

The scenery at Point Pinole is an interesting mix. Far off in the distance, you can see plumes of smoke from factories and oil refineries. From the end of the pier looking back toward shore, you can see what looks like uninhabited coastal bluffs—rugged cliffs that rise 100 feet above the bay. Point Pinole is the only place on this side of the Bay that has shoreline cliffs; everywhere else the water's edge is surrounded

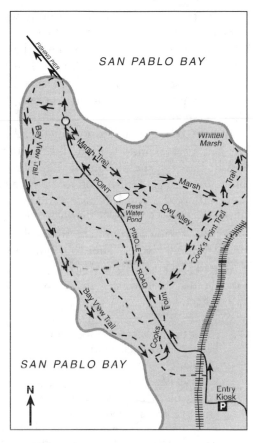

by flatlands. Most of the terrain is grasslands and eucalyptus, but there is also a large salt marsh which the Marsh Trail borders. But the main draw here are the wide-open bay views, which you get from just about everywhere in the park.

Start riding from the parking lot, picking up the paved bike trail near the ranger kiosk. You'll see a small mound planted with flowers, and a plaque marking the site of the Giant Powder Company from 1892 to 1960. When terrible explosions ruined its San Francisco and Berkeley factories, Giant moved to remote Point Pinole to manufacture dynamite, and built a thriving company town and railroad.

Ride to your left, over a railroad bridge, through a picnic area that is planted with both palm trees and eucalyptus (a funny looking combination) and some volleyball courts and playing fields. Now you're on your way to more remote land as you ride along the peninsula's length. Pass a paved loop with a bus shelter; shuttle buses ride this route every

30 minutes for those who don't want to walk all the way to the pier. Ride out to the pier's end where the views are terrific and there are plexiglas shelters for fishermen to hide behind when the wind howls. One great thing about pier fishing at Point Pinole is that you don't need a license, although all other Fish and Game regulations apply. The other great thing is that it's so pretty, you won't care much if you don't catch anything.

Road bikers should just turn around at the pier and ride back to the parking area, but mountain bikers can return to just north of the shuttle bus stop and pick up the Bay View Trail, leading west across the bluffs for a longer return loop to the paved trail. Or they can ride to just south of the shuttle bus stop and pick up the Marsh Trail, riding along the edge of Whittell Marsh and connecting to Cook's Point Trail to return. Taking both of these trails, plus riding the paved trail out-and-back, will give you about a six-mile round-trip.

Make it easier: Just ride the paved trail out to the pier for a three-mile round-trip. Be sure to go to the end of the pier for the great views in all directions.

Trip notes: A $3.50 entrance fee is charged per vehicle. A free map is available at the entrance kiosk. For more information, contact East Bay Regional Park District, 2950 Peralta Oaks Court, P.O. Box 5381, Oakland, CA 94605-0381; (510) 237-6896, (510) 562-PARK, or (510) 635-0135.

Directions: From Marin County, take the San Rafael-Richmond Bridge east (Interstate 580), then take the first exit east of the bridge, signed for Castro Street and Richmond Parkway. Drive five miles on Richmond Parkway to the Giant Highway exit. Take the exit and drive a half-mile, then turn right on Giant Highway. Drive three-quarters of a mile to the park entrance on the left.

Alternatively, from Interstate 80 in Richmond, take the Hilltop Drive exit west. Turn right on San Pablo Avenue, then left on Richmond Parkway. Follow Richmond Parkway to the Giant Highway exit. Turn right, drive a half mile and turn left onto the access road for Point Pinole.

---

66. WILDCAT CREEK TRAIL
Wildcat Canyon Regional Park
Off Interstate 80 near Richmond
8 miles/2 hours — dirt double-track/MB
steepness: ◉ ◉   skill level: ◉

Wildcat Canyon Regional Park is an oasis of wild land amid urban sprawl, a treasure of open space and a safe haven for wildlife and plant life. It is well-loved but not overused by its neighbors, and offers East

Wildcat Creek Trail, Wildcat Canyon Regional Park

Bay residents 10 miles of mostly dirt trails for mountain bike riding, horseback riding, dog walking and exploring. While hikers and hill-loving cyclists may take to the higher ridges of the park for stunning East Bay views, easy biking enthusiasts can have a great morning or afternoon riding the Wildcat Creek Trail along the park's canyon.

Bunny enthusiasts take note: You will see literally hundreds of furry hoppers on this trail, especially if you ride in the morning before the sun gets too hot. They scurry off the trail at almost every curve. Plenty of birds will accompany you, too, from large raptors to small songbirds.

But the thing you will notice the most, the one natural element that really stands out, is the biggest and oddest-looking collection of cardoon thistle plants this side of Pluto. They're everywhere, these huge thistles-on-steroids, entire armies of them standing in loose formations on the hillsides. On a foggy day they are quite an impressive sight, poking up through the grasses.

From the parking lot, the first mile of the Wildcat Creek Trail alternates as pavement and dirt, then it turns to dirt only. The trail is part of an old roadbed, abandoned because it lies along an earthquake fault and didn't hold up too well against the forces of entropy.

The ride is an easy rollercoaster, with only one big hill by the trail spur to Rifle Range Road. You come around the corner and you think, oh geez, I have to climb that (!?), but it's not as bad as it looks.

The creek canyon is quite pretty, forested on one side and with open hillsides on the other. Creekside trees include alders, willows, and California bays. The hillsides are a mix of native and nonnative grasses, studded with those ubiquitous thistles.

You will encounter other users on the trail, but with the nice wide double-track there is plenty of room for everybody. Just keep riding till you come to Tilden Nature Area, not to be confused with Tilden Park (see the following story). The trail becomes even smoother here, the dirt surface more hard-packed. A pretty little pond comes up on your right, as well as lots of trail spurs that are clearly marked "no bikes."

Ride all the way through the nature area to the parking lot just before the visitor center. If you like, you can lock up your bike there or walk it through the visitor center yard, where there is a miniature farm. If you ever wanted to pet a cow, here's your chance. They even have pony rides. When you are ready, turn around and ride back.

Make it more challenging: If you're up for some hill climbing, you can connect this trail to the paved Nimitz Way Bike Trail (see story that follows) by taking either the Havey Canyon Trail or Conlon Trail cutoffs. Both are opposite Rifle Range Road.

Trip notes: There is no fee. A free map is available at the trailhead. For more information, contact East Bay Regional Park District, 2950 Peralta Oaks Court, P.O. Box 5381, Oakland, CA 94605-0381; (510) 635-0135.

Directions: From Interstate 80 in Richmond, take the Amador/Solano exit and drive three blocks on Amador. Turn right on McBryde Avenue and head east. After passing Arlington Boulevard, continue straight (the road becomes Park Avenue) and bear left into the Wildcat Canyon parking area. The Wildcat Creek Trail begins on the far side of the parking lot.

---

67. NIMITZ WAY BIKE TRAIL
Tilden Regional Park
Off Highway 24 near Berkeley
7.5 miles/1.5 hours — paved bike trail/RB or MB
steepness: ✹ ✹   skill level: ✹

Here's a rare bike trail, one which bridges the philosophical gap between fat-tire bikers and skinny-tire bikers, a trail that all kinds of riders love equally. Nimitz Way is a paved bike route along the tip-top of San Pablo Ridge that gives skinny-tire riders the wildland scenery of mountain biking—far from the suburbs below—and fat-tire riders the cheap and easy thrill of gliding along on pavement while they cruise up and down the ridge.

I lived in the Bay Area for more than a decade before I finally rode Nimitz Way. I had heard plenty of good things about the trail—people from the East Bay always rave about it—but something always kept me away. Maybe it's because its name sounds more like a freeway than a bike path. Boy, was I missing out. It's free, it's easy, it has great views, and it's really fun.

You start at the well-marked gate by the Inspiration Point parking lot, which looks like Bike City on weekends. This entire area is well-loved for biking, with dozens of possible rides starting from one staging area. Its popularity is no surprise—if you think the view is good from Inspiration Point, wait till you head out on the trail. The vistas keep changing and getting more interesting: There's San Pablo Reservoir, and behind it is Briones Reservoir, plus looming Mount Diablo—all on your right. Then there's San Francisco Bay, the Golden Gate Bridge, and Angel Island on your left. At every turn in the trail, over every hill, you get a slightly different twist on the view: the Richmond Bridge drops into sight, the Gold Coast comes into frame up ahead, then San Francisco disappears and the Brothers Islands come into view. All of a sudden Napa and Carquinez show up to the north. And so it goes.

You just cruise along on pavement, stopping when you feel like it to enjoy the sights from your top-of-the-ridge perch. At strategic points along the trail there are benches dedicated to bygone Nimitz-lovers whose names are engraved on tiny plaques.

You'll confront only one steep hill, right before the pavement ends

View of San Pablo Reservoir from Nimitz Way Bike Trail

at 3.8 miles, which will make you say a hearty hello to your cardiovascular system. When the paved trail ends, skinny-tire riders turn around and head back, and mountain bikers can continue riding on the dirt trail that leads through a cattle gate and along San Pablo Ridge. If you continue on dirt, you can ride for 1.5 miles more to the end of the San Pablo Ridge Trail in Wildcat Canyon Regional Park, then ride back or connect to other trails there. It's gorgeous all the way.

Hey, you even get to see some wildlife on this trail. Last time I parked at Inspiration Point, I watched a bobcat slowly moving down a dirt path about 100 yards away. Then I set out on the trail and saw squirrels, bunnies, Cooper's hawks, and raptors galore. And of course the inevitable bovines made an appearance.

Don't forget to bring along a jacket, even on warm days, because it can get quite windy on top of the ridge. And as always, be prepared to share the trail with hikers and lots of other cyclists. Keep your speed down and call out when you need to pass.

Make it more challenging: If you have a mountain bike, continue on dirt on the San Pablo Ridge Trail. You can ride three miles out-and-back or make a five-mile loop back to the pavement by riding along San Pablo Ridge, turning left on Belgum, left again on Wildcat Creek Trail, then left on Conlon Trail back to Nimitz Way. This involves some decent climbs, so be prepared.

Trip notes: There is no fee. A free map is available at the trailhead. For more information, contact East Bay Regional Park District, 2950 Peralta Oaks Court, P.O. Box 5381, Oakland, CA 94605-0381; (510) 562-PARK or (510) 635-0135. Or phone Tilden Regional Park at (510) 544-2711.

Directions: From Interstate 580 in Oakland, take Highway 24 east. Go through the Caldecott Tunnel and exit at Orinda. Turn left on Camino Pablo. Drive north for about two miles, then turn left on Wildcat Canyon Road, following it for 2.5 miles to Inspiration Point's parking area on the right. The trail begins from the far edge of the parking lot.

68. LAFAYETTE RESERVOIR TRAIL
East Bay Municipal Utility District
Off Highway 24 near Lafayette
3 miles/1 hour — paved bike trail/RB or MB
steepness: ◉   skill level: ◉

Lafayette Reservoir is like San Pablo Reservoir's kid brother, and is often overshadowed by the larger, older reservoir's reputation for excellent boating and fishing and high catch rates. Both East Bay watershed lakes are open to many kinds of recreation, including allowing bikers to ride on paved trails along their edges. The foothill scenery at both lakes makes the riding pleasant and pastoral, with plenty of wildlife to watch and the option of bringing along your spinning rod to fish from shore.

But a real downer at San Pablo is that every year from November to mid-February, the place is closed down. That's usually just about the time you want a paved trail to ride on, when all the dirt trails in the Bay Area have turned to mud. So that's also usually about the time that people get around to appreciating Lafayette Reservoir, which stays open all year-round, and unlike San Pablo, is rarely overcrowded.

The managers at Lafayette have done a few other things right, too. Since the paved bike trail around the lake is short, just a three-mile loop, they instituted a rule that makes it safe for bikers and all other kinds of users to share the trail. Biking is permitted only on Tuesday and Thursday afternoons, from noon until closing at dusk, and on Sunday mornings, from opening (about 7 A.M., but the time varies with the season) until 11 A.M. While that may sound restrictive, it actually works out pretty well for most people.

Visiting here on a Sunday morning is just about perfect. You can ride the loop one or more times, then take your family out on the lake in a rental boat (pedal boats and row boats go for eight to ten bucks an hour, which is about all you need on the 50-acre lake), and have a great outing before the afternoon crowds show up. In summer, the reservoir is open until 8:30 P.M., so you can come by for an after-work ride on Tuesdays and Thursdays.

The key is not to overpay for your admission. The $5 fee at the entrance kiosk is only worth it if you're going to spend the whole day at the lake. If you're just coming for a bike ride or a short visit, park in the metered spots by the dam and pay only $1 per hour. Just be sure to bring along plenty of quarters.

The bike trail begins right from the parking area over the dam, and you can ride in either direction. If you're a first-time visitor, it's a good idea to ride to the right first (as you face the lake), because that direction takes you past the visitor center and boat rental area almost immediately, in case you want to sample the park's other offerings. (You'll ride along a park access road till you get past the visitor center, then the trail becomes a regular paved bike route.) The south and east edges of the lake are the most undeveloped, with acres of grasslands and a mixed forest, plus pretty lake views interrupted only by the occasional picnic area or fishing dock. Several dirt hiking trails branch off from the paved trail, but these are closed to bikes, so don't get any ideas (unless you've brought your bike lock.)

Lafayette Reservoir

The best time to visit Lafayette Reservoir is unquestionably in winter and spring, when the air is cool, the hillsides are green, and wildflowers pop out among the grasses. The lake is almost always full and pretty, and there are many birds and deer who make their homes here, providing a chance to teach children about wildlife.

Make it more challenging: This is a fun loop to ride two or three times around, since it is smooth and flat.

Trip notes: A $5 fee is charged per vehicle for all-day entrance to the park, or you can park in metered parking spots for $1 per hour (quarters only, two-hour limit). A free map is available at the visitor center. For more information, contact Lafayette Reservoir at (925) 284-9669. Or contact the East Bay Municipal Utility District, P.O. Box 24055, Oakland, CA 94623; (510) 287-0407.

Directions: From Interstate 580 in Oakland, take Highway 24 east toward Walnut Creek. Go through the Caldecott Tunnel and exit at Acalanes Road/Mount Diablo Boulevard. Veer to the right, then continue straight on Mount Diablo Boulevard for one mile to the reservoir entrance on the right. (Don't turn right on Acalanes Road.) Drive up the hill and park on top of the dam. The bike trail runs across the dam, near the parking area. Start riding near the restrooms, to the right of the metered parking spots.

69. LAFAYETTE-MORAGA REGIONAL TRAIL

East Bay Regional Park District

Off Highway 24 near Lafayette/Moraga
15.5 miles/2.5 hours — paved bike trail/RB or MB
steepness: ⊛   skill level: ⊛

When a lot of people have to live together in a small space, when suburbs grow so large that they connect town to town without any buffer of open land in between, one of the smartest things that city planners can do is open up spaces where folks can get a little fresh air and sunshine, places that are protected from cars and traffic and urban noise. The Lafayette-Moraga Trail is a place just like this, an open corridor between two East Bay cities, where all users under their own power —whether it's a bicycle, rollerblades, hiking boots or a wheelchair—are welcome.

It's not exactly a trip to the wilderness, but you will see plenty of deciduous trees on the first half of the trip, and then plenty of foothills and grasslands on the second half. Squirrels are omnipresent along the trail—not plain old Bay Area gray squirrels, but cute and chubby red squirrels with shiny, rust-colored coats. We saw a few busily burying nuts in flower beds, their genetic instinct preparing them for the long, hard, snowbound winter that will never come to sunny Moraga.

Also in the cute category, an entire pack of cub scouts cycled by us, dressed in their smart navy blue uniforms and little bicycle helmets, riding the Lafayette-Moraga Trail to earn their physical fitness badges.

That's just the kind of trail this is. A paved-over portion of the old San Francisco-Sacramento Railroad, the Lafayette-Moraga Trail is bordered by suburban neighborhoods and open space lands, and is well-used and well-loved by East Bay residents. A neat feature of the Lafayette-Moraga Trail is that it retains some of its railroad history. Unlike many converted railroad trails, this one proudly displays signs of its railroad past, with white train crossing signs at every intersection in the first few miles out of Lafayette.

Unfortunately, the trail crosses many roads, but only one is likely to have any serious traffic. It's near the Lafayette Community Center, at the trail's midpoint, where a spur trail goes straight ahead to the center, but you want to continue to the right, crossing St. Mary's Road. Be very careful as you cross, because the cars come quickly around a curve.

After the Lafayette Community Center, your surroundings get more rural, you see less of parallel St. Mary's Road, and you leave most of the houses behind. The trail leads past St. Mary's College, which has

Lafayette-Moraga Regional Trail

a pretty white church tower set in the hillside, surrounded by green playing fields. Shortly thereafter you come to Moraga Commons, a town park with a play area, restrooms, par course, and the like. The park also has an interesting waterfall sculpture and a sign that notes that the Lafayette-Moraga Trail was opened in 1976 and dedicated in 1992 as one of America's first 500 rail trails.

The final section of trail leads out to the country, from Moraga Commons to the Valle Vista Staging Area on Canyon Road. At Valle Vista, several East Bay Municipal Utility District trails lead off in all directions, but bikes are not permitted on these routes, so turn your wheels around.

Make it easier: Just ride to Moraga Commons, where kids can take a break in the play area, then turn around. From Lafayette to Moraga Commons is a 12-mile round-trip, taking about two hours to ride.

Trip notes: There is no fee. A free map is available at Moraga Commons or Lafayette Community Center. For more information, contact East Bay Regional Park District, 2950 Peralta Oaks Court, P.O. Box 5381, Oakland, CA 94605-0381; (510) 562-PARK or (510) 635-0135.

Directions: From Interstate 580 in Oakland, take Highway 24 east toward Walnut Creek. Go through the Caldecott Tunnel and take the Pleasant Hill Road exit south. Drive seven-tenths of a mile to Olympic Boulevard. Turn right on Olympic and the parking lot is on your right in about 50 yards. If the first lot is full, there is another one shortly after it.

70. IRON HORSE REGIONAL TRAIL to DANVILLE
East Bay Regional Park District
Off Interstate 680 near Walnut Creek/Danville
10 miles/1.5 hours — paved bike trail/RB or MB
steepness: ⬤   skill level: ⬤

The East San Francisco Bay Area has scads of paved bike paths, but at the risk of sounding a bit disparaging, let's be honest: Most of them leave something to be desired in the aesthetics department. The Contra Costa Canal Trail, the Alameda Creek Trail, and the Iron Horse Regional Trail are all easily-accessible trails which extend at least 10 miles one-way. They are suburban trails, however, and the landscape that surrounds them is a long way from the "great outdoors." Ride them without doing your homework first and you might find yourself in the middle of a huge industrial complex, or underneath a freeway cloverleaf, or in a residential neighborhood where you have to cross streets every two minutes. Your trip can feel more like work than a weekend excursion.

So, before you ride, get informed. Here's the scoop on one of the most popular East Bay paved bike trails, the San Ramon Valley Iron Horse Trail: At present, it runs 12.5 miles between Walnut Creek and San Ramon, but someday it will run all the way from Pleasanton to Suisun Bay, a distance of 33 miles. The Iron Horse Trail is a trail-in-progress, following the route of the 1890 Southern Pacific Railroad. When the railroad was abandoned in 1977, various citizen and government groups worked together to preserve the right-of-way and develop a recreational trail. Now they continue working to extend it; the Iron Horse Trail should be rideable in its entirety by 2010.

But be aware of a few things: 1) The trail is 75 feet wide in places, and there are stretches without a single tree or bush in sight; 2) It can get as hot as Hades in Contra Costa County in the summer; 3) Unless you are a big fan of concrete and corporate business parks, the best riding is found in the five miles from Walnut Creek to Danville. In the remaining seven miles from Danville to San Ramon, the trail is best suited for those commuting to work at one of the many corporations located there. It's straight, flat, hot, and dull as dishwater.

But from Walnut Creek to Danville the ride is a perfect family bicycling jaunt. In fact, on a nice Sunday you'll see more bikes pulling baby trailers on this trail than probably anywhere in the Bay Area. Plus you'll find the usual collection of kids on tricycles, closely followed by parents on single or tandem bikes, and rollerbladers and dog-walkers.

The trail begins officially at Newell and Broadway avenues in Walnut Creek, although many people start a half-mile further at the Park and Ride at Rudgear Road and Interstate 680, or on any of the little side streets that cut off Danville Boulevard, which runs parallel to the trail. The first mile has far too many road intersections to cross, but at least they're quiet residential streets with little car traffic. After passing through the Alamo Square shopping area at 2.5 miles, the trail gets noticeably prettier, traversing greener, shadier areas and heading into the town of Danville. A city parking area at Prospect Avenue is your destination, where you can lock up your bike and explore the cute old railroad town. Just turn left on Prospect and walk around the neighborhood for a few blocks.

After Prospect Avenue, the Iron Horse Trail crosses Danville Boulevard (in a rather dangerous manner), passes under Interstate 680 (in a rather ugly manner), then continues south to Pine Valley Road in San Ramon, with endless vistas of concrete buildings. That's what makes Prospect Avenue in Danville a great turnaround point on the trail, with many shops in the town center open for brunch, coffee, or snacks.

Make it more challenging: You can ride a full 25 miles out-and-back on this trail, traveling all the way from Walnut Creek to San Ramon, but don't expect to be awed by the scenery.

Trip notes: There is no fee. A free map is available by contacting East Bay Regional Park District, 2950 Peralta Oaks Court, P.O. Box 5381, Oakland, CA 94605-0381; (510) 562-PARK or (510) 635-0135.

Directions: From Interstate 680 in Danville, take the Rudgear Road exit and park at either the Park and Ride lot (on the east side of the freeway) or the Staging Area (west side). Note that Danville Boulevard runs parallel to the bike path. At any of the streets that intersect Danville Boulevard between Rudgear Road and Danville, you can drive one block west and reach the bike path. Along most of these streets there is parking for a few cars right next to the bike trail.

71. EASTERN CONTRA COSTA REGIONAL TRAILS
East Bay Regional Park District
Off Highway 4 near Antioch
17 miles/2.5 hours — paved bike trail/RB or MB
steepness: (●)   skill level: (●)

The East Bay Regional Park District deserves high praise and loud applause for the number of paved multi-use trails it has made available for public use. Many of its trails serve as important corridors for commuters on bicycles or on foot. All of them are heavily used by

Marsh Creek Trail, Eastern Contra Costa Regional Trails

recreationists seeking a safe place to ride bikes, push baby strollers, jog, walk dogs, ride rollerblades, and so on.

The Marsh Creek Regional Trail, the newest addition to the East Bay Regional Park District multi-use trail system, is no exception. It's the hub of a system of trails in eastern Contra Costa County. Currently the Marsh Creek Trail runs six miles from Highway 4 in Oakley to Creekside Park in Brentwood. In Oakley, it connects with the Big Break Regional Trail, which runs 2.5 miles along the Big Break shoreline of the San Joaquin Delta. The Marsh Creek Trail also connects with a section of the partially constructed Delta De Anza Regional Trail. When completed, the latter path will make most of Contra Costa County accessible by paved multi-use trail.

But the thorough coverage and usefulness of the trails in eastern Contra Costa County are not their only selling points. If you stick to the Marsh Creek Trail and the Big Break Trail, the paved paths are also surprisingly scenic and interesting. You can bicycle both trails out and back for a total 17-mile round-trip that feels like a ride in the country.

You can start your trip any number of places. If you don't live in the area, you're most likely to begin near the junction of Highway 4 and Cypress Road in Oakley, where the Delta De Anza Regional Trail and the Marsh Creek Regional Trail intersect. My first choice would be to ride north along Marsh Creek, heading for the San Joaquin Delta and the Big Break Regional Trail. This trail section leads through farmlands, heading nearly to the water's edge. It is excellent for spotting birds and other wildlife; we saw hundreds of coots, a great blue heron, and numerous ground squirrels. Although the trail never quite reaches the delta's shoreline, you ride close enough to sense it and smell it. Where the Big Break Trail ends rather abruptly in a suburban neighborhood, simply turn around and ride back to join the Marsh Creek Trail.

To continue on your trek, you'll have to cross Cypress Road at the traffic light (near where you parked your car), then stay on Marsh Creek Trail all the way to Brentwood. Marsh Creek flows with a surprising amount of water, especially in winter and spring, and it attracts white egrets by the dozens. They take their fishing seriously.

South of Cypress Road the Marsh Creek Trail crosses only a few roads; the intersections are mostly in quiet neighborhoods. (Remember to look before you cross.) For the most part the trail leads through peaceful farmlands and suburbs. One of the trail's highlights is found near the Marsh Creek Staging Area in Brentwood, where the trail passes a private school. The school has a small petting zoo, including several goats, peacocks, and a pig. The animals' enclosures are lined up right along the bike trail, so you can say "hi" to Miss Piggy as you ride by.

Make it easier: Just ride the northern tip of the Marsh Creek Trail and the Big Break Trail, starting from Cypress Road in Oakley, for a five-mile round-trip.

Trip notes: There is no fee. Free trail maps are available at signposts along the trail. For more information, contact East Bay Regional Park District, 2950 Peralta Oaks Court, P.O. Box 5381, Oakland, CA 94605-0381; (510) 562-PARK or (510) 635-0135. Or phone the East Contra Costa County Regional Trails Office at (925) 625-5479.

Directions: From Antioch, take Highway 4 east for five miles toward Oakley. (Highway 4 becomes Main Street.) In Oakley, turn left on Cypress Road. There is a parking pullout on the left, next to the bike trail, just after turning on to Cypress Road.

72. ROUND VALLEY REGIONAL PRESERVE
East Bay Regional Park District
Off Interstate 580 near Livermore
10 miles/2 hours — dirt double-track/MB
steepness: ◉ ◉   skill level: ◉ ◉

If you ever start to feel like the East Bay is too crowded, too congested, and has too much concrete, take a trip a little further east to the back side of Mount Diablo. Here, on the far eastern edge of the San

Francisco Bay Area, just before the bay's geography converges with that of the San Joaquin Valley, are wide open spaces, spring wildflowers, and stately oaks.

Welcome to Round Valley Regional Preserve, one of the newest additions to the East Bay Regional Park system. It's the 2,000-acre home of nesting golden eagles, burrowing owls, chubby ground squirrels, and the endangered San Joaquin kit fox. In spring, the grassy hills of Round Valley turn a brilliant green and are sprinkled with grassland wildflowers. The small miracle of Round Valley Creek flows with unmodulated passion until late spring or early summer, when it drops to meager pools along the streambed. In midsummer, temperatures at Round Valley can soar to more than 100 degrees, so be sure to plan your bike ride for the cooler months.

From the preserve staging area, the trail starts out with a long bridge over Marsh Creek. At the far side of the bridge, a right turn puts you on Miwok Trail.

Round Valley Regional Preserve

Right away you face the only two serious ascents of the day. Get yourself up and over those two hills any way you can, but don't be daunted by them—the remaining miles of trails in the preserve are almost completely level.

Within a half-mile on Miwok Trail, the wide dirt road starts to parallel Round Valley Creek. If you've timed your trip for the right season, the stream will be running cool and clear alongside you for much of your ride. You'll notice the remains of old farming equipment along the dirt trail; this land was farmed by the Murphy family from 1873 until 1988 when it was donated to the East Bay Regional Park District. Prior to the Murphys' ownership, the Round Valley area was home to Native Americans, who probably used the land as a meeting and trading place between San Joaquin valley tribes and East Bay hill tribes.

Stay on Miwok Trail through the entire length of the preserve—almost three miles—then turn right on Murphy's Meadow Trail. In a mile, turn right again, staying on Murphy's Meadow Trail and starting to loop back on the far side of Round Valley Creek. When you reach a junction with Fox Trail, take it for a short out and back excursion of under a mile each way. (Fox Trail climbs a bit, so skip it if you're not in the mood.) You have now covered the entire preserve, so pick a good spot for a picnic lunch. All that's left to do is retrace your tire tracks back to the staging area, or follow the "Make it easier" directions below.

Make it easier: Near the junction with Fox Trail, look for a good place to cross Round Valley Creek (you'll have to carry your bike) and rejoin the Miwok Trail on the other side. Currently the park's trails do not make a loop, but the two main trails are only about 100 feet apart near the Fox Trail junction.

Trip notes: There is no fee. Free trail maps are available at the trailhead parking area. For more information, contact East Bay Regional Park District, 2950 Peralta Oaks Court, P.O. Box 5381, Oakland, CA 94605-0381; (510) 562-PARK or (510) 635-0135.

Directions: From Interstate 580 in Livermore, take the Vasco Road exit and drive north for 14 miles. Turn left (west) on Camino Diablo Road and drive 2.1 miles. Camino Diablo Road becomes Marsh Creek Road; continue 1.6 miles to the Round Valley parking area on the left.

Or, from Interstate 680 in Walnut Creek, take the Ygnacio Valley Road exit and drive east for about nine miles to Clayton Road. Turn right on Clayton Road. In the town of Clayton, Clayton Road becomes Marsh Creek Road; continue east past Morgan Territory Road and Deer Valley Road to the Round Valley parking area on the right. (It's about 12 miles from Clayton.)

---

73. MORGAN TERRITORY REGIONAL PRESERVE
East Bay Regional Park District
Off Interstate 580 near Livermore
7 miles/2 hours — dirt double-track/MB
steepness: ◉ ◉   skill level: ◉ ◉

Morgan Territory—just the name sounds wild, like some kind of holdover from the Old West. If you're wondering if anything wild could still exist in Contra Costa County, wonder no more. Come to

Morgan Territory Regional Preserve

Morgan Territory and rediscover the wild East Bay.

The drive to the trailhead is a trip in itself. First, make sure you're traveling in the cooler months of the year, because the hills around Livermore bake in the summer. (If you're visiting in the warm season, make sure it is *very* early in the morning.) Then, follow narrow, winding Morgan Territory Road north of Livermore to the preserve's main trailhead. Try not to get so wowed by the views that you drive right off the curvy road. Watch for cars coming in the opposite direction; the road is so narrow that somebody usually has to pull over to let the other guy pass.

At the trailhead parking lot, you've climbed to 1,900 feet in elevation. (Actually, your car has.) You're greeted by grassy hillsides and often a fair breeze. Pick up a free trail map and follow Volvon Trail uphill and through a cattle gate. This first climb allows for no warmup, but fear not, the trail gets mellower at the top. (If you want to skip this first hill, take the dirt road to the right of the parking lot; it has a mellower grade and soon meets up with Volvon Trail.)

After a half-mile on Volvon Trail, bear right on Blue Oak Trail, and prepare yourself for a few glimpses of the San Joaquin Valley far to the east. When you aren't facing east, you have great views of Mount Diablo to the west. The dirt road rolls gently up and down small hills; you just glide along. The only difficulty for mountain bikers is the ruts and holes caused by the trampling feet of cattle. The roads are the roughest in spring after they've been wet from winter rains. If ruts and rough surfaces bother you, wait to ride at Morgan Territory until fall, when the road has been smoothed out by dry air and frequent spring and summer use.

True to its name, Blue Oak Trail features some magnificent oak trees, interspersed with rocks covered with colorful lichens. Dozens of spots invite you to throw down your bike, wander among the trees, and spread out a picnic.

Stay on Blue Oak Trail for 1.3 miles until you reach a cattle gate and a porta-potty. This is the turnaround point for the "make it easier" option (see below). But if you're feeling fine, continue through the cattle gate and turn right on Valley View Trail. (The trail straight ahead of the gate will be the return of your loop.) A rather quick and steep descent on Valley View Trail leads you to remarkable views of the San Joaquin Valley. After relishing the vista, turn right on Volvon Loop Trail to start your return, climbing back up to the cattle gate and porta-potty. From here you have an easy ride on Volvon Trail all the way back to the trailhead parking lot.

There are only a couple of tips to make your biking trip to Morgan Territory ideal: One, pick a cool day. Two, make sure you carry one of the park's free maps, because there are numerous trail junctions. And three, carry plenty of water and a suitable picnic to spread out under the shade of the biggest oak you can find.

Make it easier: This trip is a figure-eight loop; to cut it short, just ride half of the figure-eight. Turn around when you reach the cattle gate and porta-potty at the junction of Blue Oak, Volvon, and Valley View trails. Ride back on Volvon Trail for a four-mile loop.

Trip notes: There is no fee. Free trail maps are available at the trailhead parking area. For more information, contact East Bay Regional Park District, 2950 Peralta Oaks Court, P.O. Box 5381, Oakland, CA 94605-0381; (510) 562-PARK or (510) 635-0135.

Directions: From Interstate 580 in Livermore, take the North Livermore Avenue exit and turn left (north). Drive north for four miles, then turn right on Morgan Territory Road. Drive 5.6 miles to the entrance to Morgan Territory Preserve on the right. (The road is narrow and steep.)

Or, from Interstate 680 in Walnut Creek, take the Ygnacio Valley Road exit and drive east for about nine miles to Clayton Road. Turn right on Clayton Road. In the town of Clayton, Clayton Road becomes Marsh Creek Road; continue east for about five miles and turn right (south) on Morgan Territory Road. Drive about 9.5 miles to the entrance to Morgan Territory Preserve on the left.

74. LAKE CHABOT WEST & EAST SHORE TRAILS
Anthony Chabot Regional Park

Off Interstate 580 near San Leandro
8.5 miles/1 hour — paved bike trail/RB or MB
steepness: ◉ ◉   skill level: ◉

The biggest surprise you get while cruising the Lake Chabot paved trail is how much of a roller coaster ride it is. Lakeside trails are usually level and somewhat predictable, but the West and East Shore trails around Lake Chabot never stop turning, twisting, climbing, and diving. You're either braking hard or pedaling hard the whole way; you're rarely just coasting. This is more of a workout than many paved trails, yet at the same time it's not too hard for families or the not-so-fit.

There are many ways to customize the Lake Chabot trails according to your desires and abilities. Mountain bikers in decent shape may want to ride the entire 14.5-mile Lake Chabot Loop, which combines the paved West and East Shore Trails with several dirt fire roads (see "Make it more challenging"). Easy bikers will get the most out of the trip by parking at San Leandro's Chabot Park, just outside the border of Anthony Chabot Regional Park, where the West Shore Trail begins. From there you can ride out-and-back for an 8.5-mile trip on the West and East Shore Trails. Those seeking an even easier, shorter ride may want to park at

Lake Chabot

the Lake Chabot Marina, the midway point on the paved trail, and ride only the East Shore Trail, which is less hilly than the West Shore Trail.

Both the West and East Shore trails skirt the lake's edge, sometimes rising up along its steep walls, sometimes tracing just a few feet from the water. After the initial steep hill climb from Chabot Park to Lake Chabot's dam, the lake is always within view. Many riders bring their fishing rods along on the trail; the lake is frequently stocked and shorefishing prospects for trout, bass, and catfish are excellent. A $3 Chabot fishing permit, plus a state Fish and Game license, allow you to drop a line in anywhere you please.

A few forks branch off from the main trail, but if you stay along the water's edge, you'll do fine. One important junction is a half-mile in, at the top of the hill by the dam, where you must stay right on West Shore Trail. Otherwise, you can ride without concerns about junctions until the paved trail ends at a gate two miles beyond Lake Chabot Marina. Then just turn your bike around and ride back, or take a park map with you to continue riding the rest of the loop on dirt.

If you want to turn your bike ride into a day at the park, the marina has boats for rent, plus a small cafe that sells hot dogs and coffee along with the Power Bait. There is a large picnic area near the marina, and several hiking trails branch off from the paved bike trails.

Make it more challenging: The paved East Shore Trail ends at the dirt Cameron Loop, and mountain bikers can continue to the left on Cameron to connect with Live Oak, Towhee and Brandon Trails, then loop back to Chabot Park and the West Shore Trail on Goldenrod and Bass Cove Trails. The 14.5-mile route is well-signed along the way as the "Lake Chabot Loop."

Trip notes: There is no fee for parking at San Leandro's Chabot Park on Estudillo Avenue (see directions below). If you park at Lake Chabot Marina, a $3.50 fee is charged per vehicle. A free park map is available at Lake Chabot Marina. For more information, contact East Bay Regional Park District, 2950 Peralta Oaks Court, P.O. Box 5381, Oakland, CA 94605-0381; (510) 562-PARK or (510) 635-0135. Or phone Lake Chabot Marina at (510) 582-2198.

Directions: From Oakland, drive east on Interstate 580 to the Dutton/ Estudillo Avenue exit in San Leandro. Take that exit and drive straight for one-half mile, then turn left on Estudillo Avenue. Follow Estudillo for just under one-half mile, bearing left when the road forms a "Y" with Lake Chabot Road, then bearing right at the next "Y" and turning right into Chabot Park. Park just inside the gates; the paved trail begins on your left. (To park at Lake Chabot Marina instead, bear right onto Lake Chabot Road from Estudillo Avenue, then drive for 2.5 miles to the marina on the left.)

75. BAY VIEW TRAIL
Coyote Hills Regional Park
Off Highway 84 near Newark
4.5 miles/1 hour — paved bike trail/RB or MB
steepness: ⚙ ⚙   skill level: ⚙

Driving across the Dumbarton Bridge from San Francisco's South Bay to the East Bay, you notice a few things. Huge electrical towers straddle the water. An old railroad bridge parallels Dumbarton, a dismantled reminder of an earlier era. The bay itself seems impossibly huge and blue, in contrast to the density of the cities and freeways that surround it. But urban-weary eyes come to rest on the soft green knolls of Coyote Hills Regional Park, just ahead and to your left as you cross the bay. Its tule marshes, creeks, and acres of grasslands look fresh and inviting, beckoning you to pull off the freeway and explore.

A 1,000-acre patch of open space along the edge of the bay, Coyote Hills was the homeland of Ohlone Indians for more than 2,000 years. They fished bay waters for food and cut willow branches along the creeks to build their homes. Today the park is a wildlife sanctuary, both a permanent home and a temporary rest stop for thousands of resident and migratory birds. As a bonus, the park has a paved bike trail lateraling its hillsides, providing a great 3.5-mile loop trip with marsh and bay views. There is also a half-mile extension up a long hill (still

Bay View Trail, Coyote Hills Regional Park

more views) and a connection to the Alameda Creek Trail, where there are many more miles of riding possibilities.

To ride the trail, park in the Quarry/Dairy Glen Trail parking lot and pick up the paved Bay View Trail across the road. (It actually begins by the entrance kiosk, but there is no parking there.) Riding to your left, you immediately pass the Alameda Creek Ponding Area, with its many water birds, and a wooden hiker's boardwalk over the marsh. Watch for car traffic as you pass the visitor center, because for a few hundred yards the trail follows directly alongside the park road. Then continue past a connecting route to the Alameda Creek Trail (see "Make it more challenging").

The Bay View Trail contours around the park's hillsides, with plenty of curves but little climbing. At a sharp left curve, you pass a wooden outlook over the bay, with stairs that lead down to a hiking trail along a levee. Here your bay views begin to open up, and they stay open as you ride southward along the water. On a clear day, the sparkle of sunshine on the bay can be glorious.

Making a long loop around the bay's edge, you'll come around to an intersection with Meadowlark Trail, a paved trail which goes up a steep hill to some water district buildings and TV towers. If you want a quick but tough workout, ride up Meadowlark for great views of the bay and flatlands below. (I can almost guarantee you'll need at least one rest stop along the way—although it's short, it's *that* steep.) Then have fun cruising back down to rejoin the Bay View Trail loop.

You'll pass plenty of dirt trail intersections, all of which are signed and many of which are open to bikes, if you have your fat tires on. The Apay Way Trail leads to the San Francisco Bay National Wildlife Refuge visitor center (see the following story). The Nike Trail and Red Hill Trail climb to the higher areas of the park for panoramic views and a close-up look at some odd rock formations—outcrops of reddish-gold chert that were once part of the ocean floor. Binoculars are an excellent accessory for this trail, and if you have children with you, ask them how many white egrets they can count. Two of the largest egret nesting colonies in Northern California are located in neighboring San Francisco Bay National Wildlife Refuge. Their numbers are plentiful at Coyote Hills.

Make it more challenging: Bay View Trail connects with the 12-mile-long Alameda Creek Trail via a short dirt trail. Ride the loop as described above, then look for the signed Alameda Creek Trail turnoff on your right, less than one mile from the start of the loop. This is the north end of the paved trail, so you can ride southward on pavement, or ride to the north along a gravel levee into the San Francisco Bay National Wildlife Refuge.

Trip notes: A $3.50 entrance fee is charged per vehicle. A free map is available at the entrance kiosk and parking areas. For more information, contact East Bay Regional Park District, 2950 Peralta Oaks Court, P.O. Box 5381, Oakland, CA 94605-0381; (510) 562-PARK or (510) 635-0135.

Directions: From Highway 84 westbound in Fremont, take the Paseo Padre Parkway exit, turn right (north) and drive one mile to Patterson Ranch Road. Turn left and continue to the first parking lot on the left (before the visitor center), which is signed for Quarry/Dairy Glen Trails.

---

76. TIDELANDS LOOP & NEWARK SLOUGH TRAIL
San Francisco Bay National Wildlife Refuge
Off Highway 84 near Newark
7 miles/2 hours — dirt double-track/MB
steepness: 🌑 🌑   skill level: 🌑

If you want to combine a perfectly easy mountain bike ride with some bayside nature lessons, saddle up to ride at the San Francisco Bay National Wildlife Refuge. Riding a bike is the perfect way to see the place, because the refuge is big—over 20,000 acres of open space set aside to protect wildlife, the nation's largest urban wildlife refuge. If you walk, you can't get very far. If you ride, you can combine the Tidelands Trail with the Newark Slough Trail for a seven-mile round-trip loop along a slough, mudflats, wetlands, and levees, giving you a good schooling in what San Francisco Bay is all about.

Time your trip so you arrive any day except Monday, so you can drop in at the visitor center at the refuge. It's loaded with exhibits and information about bayside habitats and the plants and animals who live there. Your ride begins by the visitor center parking lot, and as you climb up the paved road, follow the signs for the Tidelands Trail. Don't worry too much about the short but steep hill you must ascend, because it's the only one you'll see all day.

The view from the top is worth the effort, anyway. From an overlook just above the visitor center, you can see across the expanse of the South Bay. The most noticeable landmark is the Dumbarton Bridge, with thousands of cars streaming across it. With all the freeways and industrial areas in this part of the bay, the wildlife refuge feels like an oasis for human beings as well as for animals.

Keep riding, using the 1.3-mile Tidelands Trail to get to the longer Newark Slough Trail. One loop connects to the other via a wooden bridge over the slough. While the Tidelands Trail is well-marked, the Newark Slough Trail has little to identify it except small brown hiker

---

signs with no trail names. Don't worry, all the trails at the refuge are open to bikes, so just ride as you please on the flat gravel double-track. You can never get lost, because the slough and surrounding marshlands are so wide open that the visitor center buildings can be seen from almost everywhere on the trail.

Newark Slough Trail makes a wide loop, just over five miles in length. After crossing the wooden slough bridge, ride clockwise (to your left), heading south toward Marshlands Road (the road you drove in on), then riding west along the slough and finally northward, looping back by the Dumbarton Bridge. Near Marshlands Road and Thornton Avenue you may see canoeists or kayakers putting in at a launch ramp on the slough, then paddling along the shallow waters.

The ride is a mix of smells, sounds, and sights. Close to the grassy hill near the visitor center, the scent of anise and sage prevails, while out along the tidelands, there are only the smells of the bay. On the northern part of the loop, your ears pick up the rush of cars on the highway, while a mile or so southward, there is only the sound of birds and lapping water. The further you travel on the loop, the greater variety of birds you will see, including willets, avocets, sandpipers, ducks, and snowy egrets. Winter is the best time for viewing large flocks, and for seeing occasional visitors, like Canada geese. Don't forget your binoculars on this trip, and also remember to keep your eyes open for small ground animals like rabbits and red foxes, who also inhabit the marshes.

Make it more challenging: You can also ride from the visitor center parking lot along the three-mile paved road that leads to the pier alongside Dumbarton Bridge. (Be forewarned: There can be cars along this route during some months of the year.) Ride out of the parking lot the way you drove in, then turn left at the sign for the pier, staying in the bike lane.

Trip notes: There is no fee. For more information, contact San Francisco Bay National Wildlife Refuge, P.O. Box 524, Newark, CA 94560; (510) 792-0222 or (510) 792-4275.

Directions: From U.S. 101 south, take the Highway 84 East exit. In just under one mile, turn right at the stoplight to continue on Highway 84 across the Dumbarton Bridge. Take the Thornton Avenue exit and turn right at the stop sign. Drive one-half mile and turn right at the San Francisco Bay National Wildlife Refuge sign (Marshlands Road), then follow the signs to the visitor center parking lot. Ride your bike on the gravel trail to the right of the wooden stairs, then turn left on the paved road that goes to the visitor center. You'll see signs for the Tidelands Trail along this road.

San Francisco
& South Bay Area

77—Coastal Trail & Great Highway Bike Path,
  Golden Gate National Recreation Area 178
78—Lake Merced Bike Path, *San Francisco Parks & Recreation* 180
79—Saddle & Old Guadalupe Trails,
  San Bruno Mountain State & County Park 182
80—Sweeney Ridge Paved Trail,
  Golden Gate National Recreation Area 184
81—Sawyer Camp Recreation Trail, *San Mateo County Parks* 186
82—Cañada Road Bicycle Sundays, *San Mateo County Parks* 188
83—Ranch Trail, *Burleigh Murray Ranch State Park* 190
84—Half Moon Bay Bike Path, *Half Moon Bay State Beach* 192
85—Corte Madera Trail, *Arastradero Preserve* 193
86—Dumbarton Bridge Ride,
  San Francisco Bay National Wildlife Refuge 195
87—Mountain View to Palo Alto Baylands,
  Mountain View Shoreline Park 196
88—Alviso Slough Trail, *San Francisco Bay National Wildlife Refuge* ... 199
89—Penitencia Creek Trail, *Alum Rock Park* 200
90—Los Gatos Creek Trail, *Vasona Lake County Park* 202
91—Coyote Creek Trail, *Coyote Hellyer County Park* 204
92—Russian Ridge Loop, *Russian Ridge Open Space Preserve* 206
93—Old Haul Road, *Pescadero Creek County Park* 208
94—Skyline-to-the-Sea Trail, *Big Basin Redwoods State Park* 209
95—Wilder Ridge & Zane Gray Loop, *Wilder Ranch State Park* 212
96—Old Landing Cove Trail, *Wilder Ranch State Park* 214
97—Pipeline Road, *Henry Cowell Redwoods State Park* 216
98—Aptos Creek Fire Road, *Forest of Nisene Marks State Park* 219
99—Monterey Peninsula Recreational Trail,
  Monterey & Pacific Grove 220

⚙ For locations of trails, see maps on pages 8 & 9. ⚙

77. COASTAL TRAIL & GREAT HIGHWAY BIKE PATH
Golden Gate National Recreation Area
Off Highway 1 on the San Francisco coast
8 miles/2 hours — dirt double-track and paved bike trail/RB or MB
steepness: ✹ ✹   skill level: ✹

The Coastal Trail in San Francisco is much like the city itself—a mixture of elements, a melange of the old and the new, the urban and the natural. It consists of dirt footpaths, an old railroad bed, sidewalks, a paved bike path, and wide open beaches. It rolls through varied surroundings, from rugged, dramatic cliffs above the ocean to clusters of condominium complexes along the highway. The only elements that remain consistent are the overall beauty of the route and the ease of taking a bike trip through it all.

If you have a mountain bike, you can start your ride at the northern edge of the Merrie Way parking lot, at the sign for the Coastal Trail. If you don't have a mountain bike, be sure to walk this short section of trail anyway—it shouldn't be missed. There are a couple of trail offshoots immediately, but those on the left go only a few hundred yards to the edge of the bluffs, overlooking the ocean. While these are all spectacular sunset-watching spots, they make for a short bike ride, so take the right fork to connect to the main trail, a wide, hard-packed trail, which is what remains of the roadbed for Adolph Sutro's 1888 steam train.

Sutro was a San Francisco entrepreneur who wanted to make his Cliff House Restaurant and adjoining bathhouse more accessible to working class folks. He built the railroad, then he only charged people a nickel to ride. Unfortunately, numerous landslides made maintaining the railway too expensive, and in 1925 it was closed down.

Today, Sutro's former rail trail offers postcard views of the Golden Gate Bridge, the Marin Headlands, Pacific Ocean, and San Francisco Bay. The trail is lined with windswept cypress trees, which can take on odd shapes, as if they've been hair-sprayed into permanent forms. One-half mile in is a right fork, with a gated dirt road that heads uphill to the Palace of Legion of Honor, a terrific art museum. You can ride up to it, or continue straight on the Coastal Trail, following the San Francisco shoreline on top of 300-foot cliffs.

Be wary of other trail users, as this section of the Coastal Trail gets a ton of foot traffic from tourists and locals alike. Many San Franciscans like to walk their dogs out here, or just show up and look at the ocean. In some places, the trail has become eroded and narrow.

You can only ride for about one mile on Sutro's rail trail, then you reach a fence and a section of trail that is for hikers only, leading uphill. Turn around and retrace your tire treads, but stay to the left on the trail (instead of taking the right cutoff to the Merrie Way parking area). Ride to the intersection of Point Lobos Avenue, El Camino del Mar, and 48th Avenue (about 200 yards uphill from Merrie Way). Use the crosswalk to cross the road, then continue on the rail trail into Sutro Heights Park, the remains of Sutro's estate. Ride the short

Golden Gate Bridge from the Coastal Trail

loop trail around the park, heading to the right as you enter. Be sure to stop at the far end of the loop, just below a rock parapet which was built in the 1880s as a viewing platform. From here, you are directly above the Cliff House (still a popular tourist destination), looking out toward the Farallon Islands.

From Sutro Park, walk your bike across Point Lobos Avenue again, then head downhill past the Merrie Way parking lot, Louis' Restaurant and the Cliff House. Although many people ride their bikes on the wide sidewalk, I'd recommend that you walk from Sutro Park to beyond the Cliff House, as the area is crowded with people and makes for a steep and fast downhill. When you get past the hill and the crowds, mount your bike and ride along Ocean Beach on the wide concrete path. At Lincoln Avenue, the concrete ends, so cross over to the inland side of the Great Highway (use the crosswalk and walk your bike), then cross Lincoln Avenue (using the crosswalk again). At the southeast corner of the intersection of Great Highway and Lincoln, you can pick up the paved Great Highway bike path.

Now you can follow the paved trail for two miles to its end at Sloat Boulevard. Although you are on the inland side of the highway, your ocean views are still good, and become progressively better as you ride south on the trail. (Do your best to ignore the cars that run between you and the beach.) When you reach Sloat Boulevard, the trail abruptly ends, so turn your wheels around and ride back to the Cliff House, then dismount your bike and walk uphill on the sidewalk to the Merrie Way parking area.

Make it easier: If you just want to ride along Ocean Beach and on the paved bike path, it's easier to park along Ocean Beach, in any of the areas south of the Cliff House. Start riding from there for a six-mile round-trip, completely on pavement.

Trip notes: There is no fee. A free map of Golden Gate National Recreation Area is available by contacting GGNRA, Fort Mason, Building 201, San Francisco, CA 94123; (415) 556-0560. For information about this trail, phone the Presidio Visitor Center at (415) 561-4323 or the Fort Funston Ranger Station at (415) 239-2366. Or phone the Cliff House Visitor Center at (415) 556-8642.

Directions: In San Francisco, head west on Geary Boulevard to 48th Avenue, where Geary becomes Point Lobos Avenue. Continue on Point Lobos Avenue for one-half block to the Merrie Way parking lot on the right, just above Louis' Restaurant. The trail leads from the north side of the parking lot. (See also "Make it easier," above.)

78. LAKE MERCED BIKE PATH
San Francisco Parks & Recreation
Off Highway 1 on the San Francisco coast
4.25 miles/1 hour — paved bike trail/RB or MB
steepness: ⬤   skill level: ⬤

Lake Merced is a city lake that feels like a small-town lake, with a variety of recreation options making a lot of people happy. It provides good fishing, boating in row boats and canoes, windsurfing, picnicking, and a par course and golf course along its edges. If that isn't enough, it also has a paved bike trail that runs around its perimeter, offering a great workout area and a place to unwind near the thousands of homes of San Francisco's Sunset District and San Francisco State University.

The trail sees plenty of use, from joggers, walkers, par-course exercisers, cyclists, people pushing baby strollers, and the like. That's because a trip to Lake Merced with its grass lawns, trees, birds, and water offers such a pleasant break from urban life. While the bike trail runs parallel to roads for its entire length, having the lake on the inside of its loop provides a calming influence, something pretty to look at all the way around. The trail is also wide enough and far enough away from the road that it is completely safe to ride on, even for families.

There are many possible places to park your car and start riding, but the biggest and most accessible parking lot is at the corner of Sunset Boulevard and Lake Merced Boulevard. From there you can ride the loop in either direction, but most people ride it clockwise. This means that the parallel roads are always on your left, the lake on your right.

Starting at Sunset and Lake Merced boulevards, you are on the northern edge of Merced's two main bodies of water: Lake Merced North, which is just over 100 surface acres and offers good fishing prospects for trout and bass; and larger Lake Merced South (203 acres), popular with rowers and windsurfers. You ride to Lake Merced South next as you head clockwise. Then there's the tiny Lake Merced Impoundment (17 acres), which is little more than a pond, but can offer decent trout fishing in heavy rain years.

There is a short stretch on Lake Merced Boulevard where you are in the void between the lakes and the trail's scenery becomes rather dull—apartment complexes and the back side of San Francisco State University—but soon you reach the edge of the southern lake. Then just a quarter-mile before the trail loops right and parallels John Muir Drive, you reach a big statue of a penguin in grey and pink granite. It's called Penguin's Prayer by Beniamino Bufano, and it's quite beautiful, although a statue of a pigeon or a mud hen may have been more appropriate for the surroundings. Nonetheless, make a stop here for the great lake views, walking your bike down to the picnic area below the statue, where you can get away from the noise of the road.

When you're ready, continue on the loop. Ride along the path as it parallels John Muir Drive and Skyline Boulevard (with its big stands of eucalyptus), and then crosses Harding Drive, where you'll find the main entrance to Harding Park and Lake Merced. If you want to fish the lake, you have to do it from here, not from anywhere else along the bike path, and you must pay for a Lake Merced fishing permit as well as have a state fishing license. Both can be purchased at the Boathouse at Lake Merced, just up Harding Drive. From Harding Drive, it's only another half-mile along Skyline Boulevard back to the parking area at Sunset and Lake Merced boulevards.

Make it more challenging: Ride the loop more than once. Or, if you don't mind riding with car traffic, ride from the Lake Merced bike path to where Skyline Boulevard meets Sloat Boulevard, then west along Sloat to the Great Highway bike path, and continue riding there.

Trip notes: There is no fee. For more information, contact the San Francisco Parks and Recreation Department at (415) 831-2700.

Directions: From Highway 1 (19th Avenue) in San Francisco, turn west on Sloat Boulevard and follow it for one-half mile to Highway 35. Turn left (south) on Highway 35 and then bear left again on Lake Merced Boulevard. Stay in the right lane and in less than a quarter-mile, turn right into the large parking area. The bike trail runs alongside the parking area.

---

79. SADDLE & OLD GUADALUPE TRAILS
San Bruno Mountain State & County Park
Off U.S. 101 near Brisbane
2.5 miles/1 hour — dirt double-track/MB
steepness: ✸ ✸   skill level: ✸

Everyone who works in an office in Brisbane, South San Francisco or Daly City should make a lunch-hour trip to San Bruno Mountain State and County Park. It's the kind of place where it only takes a ten-minute drive from the freeway to make you feel like you've gotten away from it all.

That's why the park is such a happy surprise to first-time visitors. You can drive up and down U.S. 101 all day long and never get an inkling that this terrific open-space area is so nearby. It's situated about 1,200 feet in elevation above the Cow Palace, that huge entertainment arena that houses everything from monster truck shows to well-bred cat competitions. It overlooks 3Com Park and the business complexes at Sierra Point and Oyster Point along U.S. 101. Seems like an unlikely place for a pretty park? You bet. But all of San Bruno Mountain's quirky surroundings simply add to its charm.

The Saddle and Old Guadalupe trails take you on an easy tour of the northeast side of the park, providing a mix of city and bay views and grassy hillsides brimming with wildflowers. The latter are particularly important here, because San Bruno Mountain is the habitat of the mission blue butterfly, which thrives on three kinds of native lupine. The mission blue is an endangered species that lives only on San Bruno Mountain and in the Golden Gate National Recreation Area.

San Bruno Mountain is also home to another endangered butterfly, the San Bruno elfin, as well as rare plants including Montara manzanita (found nowhere else in the world) and Franciscan wallflower. The 2,700-acre park is carefully managed with a habitat conservation plan to protect the precious species. It's basically a legal agreement between the public and local developers, who would prefer to grow

Saddle Trail, San Bruno Mountain State and County Park

housing tracts on the mountain's hillsides. Although developers have contested the conservation plan in court several times, it has always been upheld.

Meanwhile, bicyclists and walkers are allowed to share the hillsides with butterflies and wildflowers. Since the Saddle and Old Guadalupe trails make a 2.5-mile loop around the mountainside, your views change with almost every minute of your ride. The trail is hard-packed gravel, easy enough for even the most novice mountain biker, and well-marked with little jogger signs that note your mileage. Riding the loop counterclockwise, in the first half-mile you round a bend and see Oyster Point and Sierra Point far below you and to the south. Then you reach a strategically positioned bench with a wide-angle view (north to south) of Twin Peaks, San Francisco's downtown, the Cow Palace directly below, 3Com Park, the Bay Bridge and the East Bay hills, and Oyster and Sierra points. You can hear the freeway, but you feel oddly remote from it, perched high on this oasis.

As you continue riding northward, you lose your southern Bay vistas but the view of San Francisco gets clearer. A grassy knoll at about 1.3 miles offers a terrific view of the city, where you can even see the tip of the cross on Mount Davidson, a city landmark.

As the trail begins to loop back to your left, you pass a junction with an unmarked trail that leads to a day camp and group picnic area. (If anyone in your party wants to cut the trip short, this trail also leads back to the parking lot.) After a long spell of seeing only low coastal scrub, thorny yellow gorse bushes, and grasslands, trees are now visible on the trail, a mix of pines and eucalyptus, both nonnatives.

Keep riding straight to the junction with Old Guadalupe Trail, where you turn left to complete the loop (the right fork just deadends in a housing development). Old Guadalupe is a bumpy paved trail, shaded by eucalyptus.

When you close out your loop and return to the picnic area, you'll find plenty of bike posts for locking up your wheels, and other hiking trails to explore on foot. A park map, available at the entrance kiosk, details all the options.

Make it more challenging: This is a fun loop to ride twice, once in either direction, since the views are so stunning.

Trip notes: A $4 park entrance fee is charged per vehicle. Free maps are available at the entrance kiosk. For more information, contact San Bruno Mountain State and County Park, 555 Guadalupe Canyon Parkway, Brisbane, CA 94005; (650) 992-6770.

Directions: From U.S. 101 between San Francisco and South San Francisco, take the Brisbane/Cow Palace exit and drive for 1.8 miles on Bayshore Boulevard, past downtown Brisbane. Turn left on Guadalupe Canyon Parkway and drive 2.3 miles to the park entrance. Turn right and drive through the kiosk, then park in the first parking lot, near the picnic area. Follow the paved trail to the far side of the picnic area, on the right. The trail turns to gravel double-track and is signed as the Saddle Trail.

80. SWEEENEY RIDGE PAVED TRAIL
Golden Gate National Recreation Area
Off Interstate 280 near San Bruno
4.4 miles/2 hours — paved bike trail/RB or MB
steepness: ◉ ◉ ◉   skill level: ◉

Has the fog vanished from San Francisco? Good. Is it morning? Good. These are the two crucial elements for a trip to Sweeney Ridge and the San Francisco Bay Discovery Site. Why are they crucial? Zero fog is imperative in order to fully appreciate the stupendous views from the top of the ridge. And morning is the critical time to ride, because if the weather is clear, by midday the wind will probably howl. Pick a sunny, still morning (most likely to occur in spring or fall) and you're set for a great biking trip.

Oh yes, there is one more factor you should be aware of: The trail to Sweeney Ridge climbs like a son of a gun. It's paved, so the surface is smooth and easy to manage, but it has a few steep sections in its latter

On top of Sweeney Ridge

half that may make you stop to gasp for breath. No matter, though, there's plenty to look at while you wait for your heart rate to slow down. As you ascend up the trail your views keep expanding—first of the open space areas around San Andreas Lake, then of the prominent landmarks of South San Francisco and the northern peninsula, and finally culminating in the incredible 360-degree panorama from the top of Sweeney Ridge. This vista takes in the Pacific coastline and San Francisco Bay as well as the land mass to the east, north, and south.

It was here, at the 1,200-foot summit on top of Sweeney Ridge, that Gaspar de Portola and the Portola Expedition discovered San Francisco Bay on November 4, 1769. A stone monument has been erected to commemorate their discovery. A few feet from it is a second monument in memory of Carl Patrick McCarthy, who "personally brought 11,863 visitors to this discovery site" and was instrumental in obtaining protective status for Sweeney Ridge. Carved on the granite marker are all the major landmarks you can see from this spot, including Mount Tamalpais, Mount Diablo, Mount Hamilton, Montara Mountain, Point Reyes, Farallon Islands, and Point San Pedro. Yes, the view is spectacular.

The paved trail is simple to follow. It begins at a gate at the parking area and slowly winds its way uphill. About two thirds of the way up you'll see a yellow line painted on the trail; that's the "fog line" designed to aid bikers and hikers when visibility is bad. Once you reach the fog line, the trail enters into its steepest stretch. Just take your time, rest and catch your breath, and walk your bike if you need to. At the top of the ridge, you'll find a major junction of trails. This is where you gain wide westward views to add to your collection of eastern views. Straight ahead is a wooden bench that overlooks the Half Moon Bay coast. Go left for a few yards to see the Portola monument. Then take the paved ridge trail to the right, which stays nice and level for a quarter mile, passes a big water tower, and then ends at the abandoned buildings of an old Nike missile site. It's an interesting spot to explore around.

Another highlight on this trail is the amount of wildlife you are likely to see, especially on an early morning trip. On our way up the ridge, we see deer, hawks, and numerous bunnies. The terrain surrounding the trail is mostly coastal scrub and grasslands. In spring, the hillsides bloom with Douglas irises and purple nightshade.

Make it more challenging: From the junction of trails at the top of Sweeney Ridge, mountain bikers can take either of the dirt roads that lead south along the ridge or west toward Pacifica. Remember that it's all downhill from Sweeney Ridge, so unless you plan on making a loop, you'll have to climb back up to this junction to return on the paved trail to the parking area.

Trip notes: There is no fee. A free map of Golden Gate National Recreation Area is available by contacting GGNRA, Fort Mason, Building 201, San Francisco, CA 94123; (415) 556-0560. For information about this trail, phone the Presidio Visitor Center at (415) 561-4323 or the Fort Funston Ranger Station at (415) 239-2366.

Directions: From Interstate 280 south of San Francisco, take the Sneath Lane/San Bruno Avenue exit and bear right. At the stoplight, turn left on Sneath Lane. Drive 1.8 miles to the trailhead parking area.

81. SAWYER CAMP RECREATION TRAIL
San Mateo County Parks
Off Interstate 280 near Hillsborough
12 miles/2 hours — paved bike trail/RB or MB
steepness: ◉ ◉   skill level: ◉

I know it's crowded. I know that rollerbladers run rampant here. I know it's hard to find a parking place on Sundays. But hey, at least it's not without good reason. The Sawyer Camp Recreation Trail is a just plain perfect paved bike trail, long enough to make you feel like you really rode somewhere, diverse enough to provide both stunning scenery and some interesting history, and managed properly so that even with all the trail's varied and abundant users, everybody has fun.

And here's a tip: You, on your bike, can travel farther and faster than all the walkers, joggers, rollerbladers, and baby strollers, so you may even get a chance at a few miles of solitude. Especially if you make your trip on a weekday, or early in the morning on a weekend.

The trail travels the length of Lower Crystal Springs Reservoir, then leads through marshlands to southern San Andreas Lake, continuing to the dam at San Andreas and slightly beyond to Hillcrest Boulevard in Millbrae. There are several interpretive signs on the trail that explain everything from the rather unstable geology of the area (the trail parallels the nearby San Andreas Fault) to the history of the trail (a whole lot of politicians got together and actually agreed on something; the path was paved and opened in 1978 through the cooperation of the California Department of Parks and Recreation, the San Francisco Water Department, and the San Mateo County Board of Supervisors).

A highlight on the trail is the Jepson laurel tree at 3.5 miles, named after one of California's noted botanists, Willis Jepson. A sign at its base says it is the second largest laurel tree in California, but that was true in 1923 when the sign was posted. At about 600 years old and 55 feet tall, it is now the oldest and largest California laurel tree, as the previous title holder in Cloverdale was cut down by a farmer because— get this—it shaded too much of his hayfield. Don't stories like that make your skin crawl?

The ride is an easy cruise; you probably won't even shift gears until after mile marker 4.5, where there is the first small grade. The scenery is truly beautiful, with the summer fog often streaming in over the slopes of Montara Mountain across from the lakes. Parts of the trail are heavily shaded by Monterey cypress, Monterey pines, and various kinds of eucalyptus—all planted non-natives, but pretty nonetheless. The marshy area in between Lower Crystal Springs Reservoir and San Andreas Lake often has deer grazing in it; sometimes they come right up to the trail's edge. On one trip, I saw 15 deer, as well as numerous egrets and raptors.

The trail ends shortly after crossing San Andreas Dam (where you can stop and enjoy the view across the water), with a short but steep hill climb to trail's end. A plaque on a rock notes that this spot on the trail was Captain Gaspar de Portola's first camp after his discovery of San Francisco Bay on November 4th, 1769.

The Sawyer Camp Trail is simple to follow, with no intersections or turnoffs, but you must remember to keep your speed down. A posted 15-mile-per-hour speed limit is enforced, and at both ends of the trail it drops to five miles per hour to accommodate the many pedestrians.

Make it more challenging: Mountain bikers can connect this trail with the San Andreas Trail for another five miles of riding. Ride under the freeway at Hillcrest Boulevard, turn left and ride north on the frontage road, then turn left on Larkspur. Cross back under the freeway to pick up San Andreas.

Trip notes: There is no fee, but donations are accepted. For more information, contact San Mateo County Parks and Recreation, 455 County Center, Redwood City, CA 94063; (650) 363-4020.

Directions: From San Francisco, drive south on Interstate 280 for 19 miles to Highway 92. Take the Highway 92 exit west, but at the stop sign, turn right immediately on Skyline Boulevard instead of proceeding on Highway 92. Drive one-half mile to Crystal Springs Road, and park along the road near the intersection of Crystal Springs Road and Skyline Boulevard. The trail begins across from Crystal Springs Road.

82. CAÑADA ROAD BICYCLE SUNDAYS
San Mateo County Parks
Off Highway 92 near Woodside
8 miles/1.5 hours — paved road (closed to cars)/RB or MB
steepness: ● skill level: ●

Cañada Road Bicycle Sundays have become ritualized events on the San Francisco Peninsula. While Cañada Road is popular for bicycling year-round, weekdays and weekends alike, Bicycle Sundays are the days when the San Mateo County Parks Department closes off Cañada Road to cars, and the four miles from Edgewood Road to Highway 92 become a parade of bicyclists of all shapes and sizes.

It's a great ride even *with* cars, which makes it a stellar ride *without* cars. The road has a flat and smooth surface, great views of Upper Crystal Springs Reservoir and the eastern slopes of Montara Mountain, and just the right amount of mileage to give you that good feeling of having gotten some fresh air and exercise.

If you want to ride without motorized traffic, you've got to time it right. Cañada Road is closed to cars only on the 1st, 3rd and 4th Sundays of the month from March through October. Occasionally they don't close the entire four-mile section from Edgewood Road to Highway 92, instead only closing the two miles from Edgewood Road to Filoli Estate, but a phone call to the San Mateo County Parks Department can give you the updated scoop.

The route traverses typical Palo Alto area foothill country, with lots of grasslands, low oak trees, and thistles, but its best feature is that it provides views of Upper Crystal Springs Reservoir, the hidden paradise of the San Francisco watershed that you don't get to see from the Sawyer Camp Trail (see story on page 186). It's a beautiful body of water, but public access is strictly forbidden, for reasons that only a bureaucrat could understand.

Pulgas Water Temple along Cañada Road

The ride also takes you past the Pulgas Water Temple, where the San Francisco Water District celebrates the terminus of the Hetch Hetchy aqueduct, bringing water over 200 miles by canal from Yosemite. Good for San Francisco, bad for Yosemite. The concept is weird, but the temple is pretty and worth seeing. Although the gate to the parking area is closed to cars on weekends, bicyclists can enter just to the left of the gate, then ride the short trail to the temple, which looks like a big swimming pool with some Roman pillars and a lot of expensive landscaping. To reach it, take the narrow gravel trail marked with two posts, just to the right of the parking area. It's about 100 yards to the water temple.

Less than a half-mile from the Pulgas Water Temple is the Filoli Estate, a historic 1917 mansion and 16 acres of spectacular formal gardens, open to the public from mid-February through early November. Tours are available by reservation only on Sundays, but if you phone them in advance at (650) 364-2880, you could add on a walk through Filoli's gardens to your trip.

Make it more challenging: A dirt trail parallels Edgewood Road from the parking area. It leads to Edgewood Park for more riding and hiking possibilities.

Trip notes: There is no fee. For more information, contact San Mateo County Parks and Recreation, 455 County Center, Redwood City, CA 94063; (650) 363-4020.

Directions: From San Francisco, drive south on Interstate 280, past Highway 92 in Woodside, and take the Edgewood Road exit. At the stop sign, turn right and drive one-half mile to the intersection of Edgewood Road and Cañada Road. There is a dirt parking area off Edgewood Road by the intersection.

---

83. RANCH TRAIL
Burleigh Murray Ranch State Park
Off Highway 1 near Half Moon Bay
4 miles/1 hour — dirt double-track/MB
steepness: ◉   skill level: ◉

This easy bike trip is a ride through Half Moon Bay history. Burleigh Murray Ranch State Park may be one of California's newest state parks, but more than 100 years ago its land was home to a bustling dairy farm, owned by an artisan named Robert Mills. Mills leased the land to recently immigrated English, Irish, Italian, and Portuguese farmers, who ran successful dairy businesses. Mills built a giant dairy barn on the property, plus a ranch house and other outbuildings.

Mills' still standing barn is the showpiece of this park. It is an English bank barn, one of only two that exist in the United States. Built in 1889, the barn was two stories high and 200 feet long. Because it was built into the hillside, the upper story could easily be loaded by wagon. The barn could hold 100 cows. Today the barn is a favorite spot for photographers, who like to shoot its rustic weathered wood and the rusted farm implements found around its foundation. A beautiful old stone wall lines the barn's southern side.

Mills and his heirs leased the property to immigrant farmers for more than a century. In 1979 it was donated to the state to preserve its natural and cultural heritage. The park's 1,300 acres are bisected by Mills Creek and contain three major habitats: The alder shaded stream canyon, north-facing canyon slopes blanketed with dense coastal scrub, and south-facing canyon slopes covered with coastal grasses. In early and mid spring, ceanothus bushes bloom with fragrant white and blue flowers. In late spring and summer, orange sticky monkeyflower is in display.

Mountain bikers will find the riding blessedly easy, with only a 200 foot elevation gain over the entire course of the trip. The trail is short—only four miles round-trip—so you might as well bring your binoculars, camera, and a picnic, and take your time. Perhaps the best thing about this park is not the historical interest or the easy biking trail, but rather the promise of near solitude in this coastal canyon.

The trail runs right alongside Mills Creek, which is bordered by a dense mass of black-berry, poison oak, willows, and alders. It passes a few of the old ranch buildings, crosses the stream twice, and then reaches the remark-ably large barn at one mile out. The trail ends at a set of wooden water tanks at two miles out. Along the way you'll pass a couple of picnic areas—one by the barn

English bank barn, Burleigh Murray Ranch

and one in a stand of eucalyptus trees along the trail.

One further note of historical interest: As you drive in or out of the park on Higgins Purisima Road, be sure to check out the historic James Johnston House, a huge white farmhouse that is plainly visible on the hillside. It was built in 1853 and was the center of cultural and social life in Half Moon Bay in the late nineteenth century. The Johnston House is considered to be the earliest American home still standing along the coast of San Mateo County. It is often open for tours on Sunday afternoons.

Make it more challenging: You can combine this ride with the following ride on the Half Moon Bay Bike Path. Or, if you don't mind some car traffic, you can ride out and back as far as you wish on Higgins Purisima Road.

Trip notes: There is no fee. For more information, contact California State Parks Bay Area District, 250 Executive Park Boulevard, Suite 4900, San Francisco, CA 94134; (415) 330-6300.

Directions: From Highway 1 in Half Moon Bay, turn east on Higgins Purisima Road and drive 1.6 miles to the state park entrance on the left.

84. HALF MOON BAY BIKE PATH
Half Moon Bay State Beach
Off Highway 1 in Half Moon Bay
5 miles/1 hour — paved bike trail/RB or MB
steepness: ◉   skill level: ◉

Ask anybody who lives anywhere near the San Francisco coast when is the best season to go to the beach, and they will answer unanimously that it sure isn't summer. From June to August, the coast here is often fogged-in day after endless day, so there is little need to search through your glove compartment for the #30 sunscreen. But come in winter or spring, and instead of being gray, the sky is often crystal clear and blue, mirroring the sea's sparkling waves. Add in a paved bike trail along the coast, and you have the ingredients for a first-rate bike ride.

November through April is the time to go, when the RVs aren't crowding the parking lots at the beach, the coastal wind is milder than the rest of the year, and the sun shines. The trail is short, but you can combine it with a day at the beach, so who's complaining? The route starts at the parking lot at Francis Beach, which on a weekend morning is bustling with surfers, campers, picnickers, and beachgoers. It runs about 2.5 miles along the coast until it deadends at Mirada Road in Miramar Beach, where there are several popular eateries if you're in the mood for brunch.

The first mile of the trail runs parallel to an equestrian trail (the routes are divided by a fence), so you often have the good company of happy riders on horseback. After crossing two wooden bridges across a coastal marsh, the horse trail and paved bike trail suddenly merge for a brief moment; here you must make a hard left turn and stay along the coast or you will end up on the dirt equestrian trail leading inland.

If you like ocean views, the Half Moon Bay Bike Path is your trail. Aside from the back sides of some pretty coastside homes, all you see are waves and seagulls, plus maybe a kayaker gliding by on the water or a surf fisherman poised on the sand. The ride is perfect for little kids, since it's short and completely flat, and you'll see plenty of them on tricycles and training wheels.

The trail passes by three state park beach areas: Francis, Venice and Dunes beaches, each with a parking lot and public access. Although swimming is not recommended at Half Moon Bay because of cold water and rip currents, hiking and picnicking on the beach are great year-round activities.

One important note about timing: Remember to avoid visiting Half Moon Bay on weekends during the month of October, when the annual town pumpkin festival takes place. The event turns the town streets into a traffic nightmare.

Make it more challenging: You can lock up your bike at either end of the trail and walk on Francis Beach or Miramar Beach.

Trip notes: A $3 state park entrance fee is charged per vehicle. For more information, contact Half Moon Bay State Beach c/o California State Parks Bay Area District, 250 Executive Park Boulevard, Suite 4900, San Francisco, CA 94134; (415) 330-6300.

Directions: From San Francisco, drive south on Highway 1 for about 20 miles to Half Moon Bay. In Half Moon Bay, turn right (west) on Kelly Avenue and drive one-half mile to the beach park on the right. Drive through the kiosk; you will see the bike trail on your right.

85. CORTE MADERA TRAIL
Arastradero Preserve
Off Interstate 280 near Palo Alto
5 miles/2 hours — dirt double-track/MB
steepness: ✹ ✹   skill level: ✹

Arastradero Preserve is a Palo Alto city park, a favorite of locals but little-known outside of the immediate area. Unlike Foothills Park in Palo Alto, which has the ludicrous rule that only people with Palo Alto driver's licenses can enter it, Arastradero Preserve accepts all comers, including plenty of dog-walkers and mountain bike riders.

Because of the pedestrians, we bikers must mind our manners on the trails, and take care not to run over anybody or scare them as we ride up behind. A ranger here told me that this park has few conflicts between bikers and hikers, because the place has a great neighborhood-like atmosphere and most visitors stay aware and tolerant.

Start riding out of the east side of the parking lot, paralleling Arastradero Road for a few hundred yards, then crossing the road and picking up Corte Madera Trail, the main access trail into the park. As you ride through grassy foothills, heading toward Arastradero Lake, consider your options: For the easiest ride, you can head out-and-back on Corte Madera Trail, riding around the west side of the lake to the southern border of the park. For a tougher climb but a killer view, you can veer to the right on the wide unmarked trail at the lake's northwest-

Corte Madera Trail, Arastradero Preserve

ern border, then connect with Meadowlark Trail and follow it to the left all the way to the highest point in the park, at 700 feet in elevation. There you'll find a horse paddock and the Casa de Martinez, a ranch house, but note that all buildings on the preserve are closed to the public. Nonetheless, from this high point you can see parts of the Stanford University campus, San Francisco and its bay, and many upper-class Palo Alto hillside homes. It's quite a pretty sight, especially when the park's rolling hills are green and the sky is filled with puffy white clouds. Hawks continually soar overhead, always looking for an updraft or an easy meal.

To return from the top of Meadowlark, your best bet is just to turn around and ride *slowly* back downhill (it's quite steep, so take it easy). Experienced riders like to ride the single-track on Acorn Trail back down to Corte Madera Trail, making a loop out of the trip.

Get a park map at the parking lot to help plan your ride, but keep in mind that neither the hill on Meadowlark nor the single-track on Acorn Trail are for the faint of heart. Parents riding with children and novice riders should stick to the out-and-back on Corte Madera Trail, then take a break on the return trip at pretty Arastradero Lake, a big pond circled by tules.

Make it easier: A five-mile trip is possible by riding both Corte Madera Trail and Meadowlark Trail, but if you ride only Corte Madera Trail, your trip will be 2.5 flat miles.

Trip notes: There is no fee. A free map of Arastradero Preserve is available at the trailhead. For more information, contact Arastradero Preserve and Foothills Park, City of Palo Alto, (650) 329-2423.

Directions: From Interstate 280 in Palo Alto, take the Page Mill Road exit and head west for one-quarter mile to Arastradero Road. Turn right on Arastradero Road and drive one-half mile to the parking area on the right.

86. DUMBARTON BRIDGE RIDE
San Francisco Bay National Wildlife Refuge
Off Highway 84 near Menlo Park
4 miles/1 hour — paved bike trail/RB or MB
steepness: ⊛ ⊛   skill level: ⊛

When you first drive to the area surrounding the Dumbarton Bridge, you may wonder why on earth its bike trail was selected for this book. Traffic is heavy. Concrete surrounds you. Suburban sprawl is the accepted architectural norm. You may wonder, is this a bike path, or is it hell?

Well, time your ride for a sparkling clear day, and you'll soon understand why you made the trip. The view from the highest point on the span of the Dumbarton Bridge is spectacular, and you'll realize that you could never see the vista this way just by driving your car. You are surrounded by the Bay Area's highest peaks—Mount Hamilton (4,062 feet), Mount Diablo (3,849 feet), Mount Tamalpais (2,571 feet), and Montara Mountain (1,930 feet). The tidelands below you can be either high water or mudflats, but are great for viewing either way. Bicycling on the Dumbarton Bridge bike path, comfortably separated from auto traffic by a concrete barrier, brings the entire South Bay into reach.

At the site where Dumbarton Bridge crosses the bay, the west and east shores are only one mile apart, making your ride over water fairly short. You'll see another bridge just to the south of Dumbarton, which was the first bridge built across the bay in 1908. It was called the Dumbarton Cutoff and carried Southern Pacific freight trains across the water until 1982.

Two piers alongside the Dumbarton Bridge are also a part of history; both the Ravenswood Pier on the west side (where you parked your car) and the Dumbarton Pier on the east side were parts of the first Dumbarton Bridge built for auto traffic in 1927. The present-day Dumbarton Bridge was constructed right alongside the remains of the old bridge.

Your riding options are wide open. The trail along the south side of Dumbarton accommodates riders traveling in either direction, and on both sides of the bay the trail connects to an array of other trails. If you want to explore the East Bay side, you have the choice of riding in the San Francisco Bay National Wildlife Refuge or Coyote Hills Regional Park (although getting to Coyote Hills requires some travel on bike lanes along busy roads). Many people coming from the East Bay prefer to park at the wildlife refuge's visitor center, ride out and back along the bridge, then continue riding or hiking in the refuge.

If you want to explore the Palo Alto/Menlo Park side, a paved bike trail leads north to Bayfront Park, completely separate from car traffic. Dirt trails lead to the southern portion of Ravenswood Preserve and beyond to Palo Alto Baylands. To ride from the Palo Alto side without confronting any auto traffic, it's best to drive on Highway 84 to the entrance of the bridge, then take the side road on the right that is signed for Ravenswood Pier. There are numerous parking spots there.

Make it more challenging: Add on a trip on the paved recreation trail to Bayfront Park, or ride the three-mile-long pier on the East Bay side of the bridge. After exiting Dumbarton Bridge, the bike trail joins with the pier, which gets some car traffic but has a wide bike lane. The path leads along the bay to San Francisco Bay National Wildlife Refuge headquarters.

Trip notes: There is no fee. A free map of the San Francisco Bay National Wildlife Refuge is available by contacting the refuge at P.O. Box 524, Newark, CA 94560; (510) 792-4275 or (510) 792-0222.

Directions: From U.S. 101 near Palo Alto, take the Willow Road exit (Highway 84 east). In just under one mile, turn right at the stoplight to continue to the Dumbarton Bridge entrance. Look for the signs for Ravenswood/San Francisco Bay National Wildlife Refuge on the right, and just before getting on the bridge, bear right into the parking area for the Ravenswood Pier. Drive two-tenths of a mile, paralleling the bridge approach, then park in the parking area. Ride your bike back along the access road and pick up the trail signed "Dumbarton Bridge to Fremont."

87. MOUNTAIN VIEW to PALO ALTO BAYLANDS
Mountain View Shoreline Park
Off U.S. 101 near Mountain View
8 miles/2 hours — dirt double-track & paved bike trail/RB or MB
steepness: ⬤ skill level: ⬤

Okay everybody, let's saddle up and go ride our bikes on top of a garbage dump. It doesn't sound appealing? I didn't think so either, until the first time I made the trip down the peninsula and gave the

Mountain View Shoreline Park a try. This place is a whole lot better than it sounds.

At Shoreline Park, there are trails all over the place. My favorite route starts by the Lakeside Cafe, where mountain bikers can get off pavement quickly and be separated from most of the recreational walkers. Those with skinny tires can ride here too, even though much of the trail is dirt, because it's completely smooth and hard-packed. I saw several skinny-tire bikers on the trail, most of them on longer trips, connecting to the Stevens Creek Trail and beyond (see "Make it more challenging").

As you ride, try to keep in mind that this well-groomed park was built on domestic garbage landfill, which raised the height of the land about 15 feet, just enough to avoid bayside high tide and flooding problems. From 1970 to 1983, the city of San Francisco dumped its garbage here at Shoreline, while engineers figured out how to use its byproduct, methane gas, to generate electricity. The power generated every day at Shoreline supports the park's maintenance and operation.

Meanwhile, bikers and other trail users cruise around on the surface of that landfill, following trails that lead from the park along the bay's edge, catching glimpses of the many birds and mammals who make their home here.

From the cafe parking lot, ride around the back side of Shoreline Lake and then to the left, heading north along the bay. Shoreline Lake is a 50-acre artificial salt lake, often crowded with small craft sailers and windsurfers on summer afternoons. The bike trail runs on a bluff above it (don't ride on the trail right next to the lake, where bikes are forbidden), between the lake and the bay's edge. The trail is paved for the first quarter-mile, then turns into a very wide dirt path as it curves around Charleston Slough, with plenty of room for all kinds of users.

Although you will see many trail offshoots, stay on the wide main path and remain as close to the bay as possible. You'll start seeing signs for Palo Alto Baylands within the first mile on this trail, and after three miles you'll cross a bridge, walk your bike through a turnstile, and see the Palo Alto Baylands Interpretive Center about a half-mile ahead of you, across a marsh.

To get to the interpretive center, stay on the wide dirt trail which leads away from the bay, heading past Bixby Landfill Park and its interesting sculptures (on your left—they look like odd-sized telephone poles, but trust me, they're sculptures). The trail dumps you out on a road, where you ride the bike lane to your right for 100 yards to the access road for Palo Alto Baylands, then turn right again. Technically

Egrets and coots at the Palo Alto Baylands

you can ride the Baylands Trail that starts from the interpretive center, but it's better to lock up your bike and walk because there are so many neat things to see, including tons of bird life and jackrabbits, and small planes taking off and landing at Palo Alto Airport.

Riding back to Shoreline Park from Palo Alto Baylands, you get a nice long-distance view of Moffett Field Air Station and the Shoreline Amphitheatre with its two architectural peaks. When you return to the parking area, you can buy a snack at the cafe, hang out on the patio, and watch windsurfers on the lake practice their waterstarts, while pelicans dive in between them.

Make it more challenging: You can ride from Shoreline Park southward for three-plus more miles on the perfectly paved Stevens Creek Trail, although the scenery leaves something to be desired. The first mile is pretty, riding past a golf course and along the Mountain View marshlands, but soon you turn inland on the unbelievably straight and monotonous Stevens Creek Trail, eventually crossing under U.S. 101 into Mountain View.

Trip notes: There is no fee. A free map of Shoreline Park is available at the entrance gate. For more information, contact Shoreline Park, City of Mountain View, 3070 North Shoreline Boulevard, Mountain View, CA 94043; (650) 903-6392.

Directions: From U.S. 101 in Mountain View, take the Shoreline Boulevard exit and turn left at the stoplight. Drive 1.2 miles on Shoreline Boulevard to the entrance gate for Shoreline Park. Continue past the entrance gate and you will see a sign for "Bicycle Use Parking." Turn right and park there, or continue on the park road to Lakeside Cafe, which is located next to the sailing lake. Park in the Lakeside Cafe parking lot.

---

88. ALVISO SLOUGH TRAIL
San Francisco Bay National Wildlife Refuge
Off Highway 237 near Sunnyvale
8.5 miles/2 hours — dirt double-track/MB
steepness: ◉   skill level: ◉

The first time I tried to ride at Alviso Slough was just after a few days of rain, on a gorgeous sunny day when the bay was sparkling in all its majesty. I headed out from the dirt trail, happy to be outside and riding, ready for a good eight-mile loop trip. The trail looked damp, but firmly packed, with no visible puddles or soft spots. But after riding only a quarter-mile, so much mud caked up underneath my front fork that the wheel wouldn't turn. I scraped the mud off, walked my bike to what looked like firmer ground, and tried again. One hundred yards later — same problem.

And so it went. This was some kind of super-mud, more powerful and more sticky than ordinary mud. I wound up walking my bike back to my car, with the stuff caking up on my shoes as well as my wheels. Then I rode all around the parking lot, trying to get some of the ick off before I loaded my bike back in my car. This is supposed to be easy?

Well, let's all learn from my experience. Ride the Alviso Slough Trail after a period of dry weather and you'll have a great time. Ride it after a rain, and you'll have mud pies for dinner. It's the clingiest, stickiest, worst mud known to man (or woman). Don't let it happen to you.

So, assuming it's been dry for a while, drive over to the Alviso marina at the very southern tip of San Francisco Bay, the place where the East Bay and the South Bay meet and shake hands. Alviso Slough is part of the San Francisco Bay National Wildlife Refuge, which means there are all kinds of critters to be seen here, particularly wetlands birds like egrets and herons, and lots of ground squirrels darting about. Still waters, salt marshes, rich mud flats and the slough itself border the trail, which is built on a levee. Much of the land is leased to Cargill Salt Company, which uses the salt marshes to manufacture—you guessed it—salt.

It's an easy-to-follow loop, leading along Alviso Slough to the edge of the bay and Coyote Creek, then cutting across the salt marsh to loop back to the parking area. A 1.5-mile trail offshoot leads across railroad tracks to the Environmental Education Center, which is open on weekends from 10 A.M. to 5 P.M.

By the way, if you're wondering about the worn-down boats that are slowly decomposing in the marsh by the Alviso parking lot, they're a few remainders from the days when Alviso was a working marina, before it completely silted up. Alviso, a 130-year-old town, was once one of the busiest ports on the bay.

Make it easier: Just ride out-and-back for a few miles along Alviso Slough.

Trip notes: There is no fee. A free map of Alviso Slough/San Francisco Bay National Wildlife Refuge is available by contacting San Francisco Bay National Wildlife Refuge, P.O. Box 524, Newark, CA 94560; (510) 792-4275 or (510) 792-0222. Or contact the Alviso Environmental Education Center at (408) 262-5513.

Directions: From U.S. 101 in Sunnyvale, take the Highway 237 exit east. Follow Highway 237 for 4.5 miles to the Gold Street exit. Take Gold Street all the way toward the bay, then turn left on Elizabeth Street. Drive two blocks on Elizabeth, then turn right on Hope Street, which will lead you into the Alviso parking lot. (The parking lot is at the intersection of Hope and Elizabeth Streets.) The trail leads from the right (south) side of the parking lot.

89. PENITENCIA CREEK TRAIL
Alum Rock Park
Off U.S. 101 near San Jose
4 miles/1 hour — dirt double-track & paved trail/MB
steepness: ● skill level: ●

For those who regularly commute down U.S. 101 in the South Bay, San Jose can seem like just another series of off-ramps and on-ramps, another place where the traffic may come to a dead halt as too many people try to merge and exit the freeway. But if all the gray concrete, metal bumpers, and highway dividers are making you nuts, a trip to Alum Rock Park can be just the antidote you need, offering a visit to a shady, tree-filled canyon nestled within the lower mountains of the Diablo range.

Alum Rock's claim to fame is that it is California's first and oldest park. From 1890 to 1932, the area was a health resort, offering visitors a dip in its 27 separate mineral springs. Even today, the smell of sulphur is present in the park, and you can see the rock pools where bathers once lolled in the waters. A steam railroad was built in 1890 to take visitors from downtown San Jose uphill to the park.

Bridge over Penitencia Creek, Alum Rock Park

The abandoned rail bed is the basis for the Penitencia Creek Trail, which travels along year-round Penitencia Creek, its edges lined with ferns in winter and wildflowers in spring. The creek is shaded by big-leaf maples, alders, oaks and bays, making riding here possible even in the heat of summer. Late fall and winter is still the best time to visit, however, when the park is uncrowded and the deciduous trees put on a nice display of color.

The easiest parking is at the end of the park road, across the creek from the park visitor center. From there, you can ride to the east (left), crossing Penitencia Creek and heading deeper into its canyon. Then turn around at the bike trail's end and ride in the opposite direction. The first mile is perhaps the most interesting, as you ride past the mineral springs and beautiful old rock bridges and structures along Penitencia Creek. The park *looks* old, as few places do in California. It isn't hard to imagine turn-of-the-century ladies and gentlemen strolling through these grounds, taking their "cures" in the magic waters.

Continue riding past the picnic areas (the trail turns from pavement to dirt) to the place where Penitencia Creek joins with Aguague Creek and only hikers may continue on the route. Be sure to walk across the bridge and take a peek at the creek intersection, which can be full of miniature waterfalls after winter rains. Then ride back along the creek trail, keeping the stream on your right, heading past the visitor center and other park facilities to a bridge that crosses over the main park road. After the bridge, a trail branches off to the left, then shortly thereafter another trail branches off to the right, leading uphill toward Eagle Rock and connecting to the North Rim Trail, which loops back to the parking area in 1.5 miles. Riders who don't want to do any climbing can just turn around at the North Rim Trail intersection and ride back along the creek for a four-mile round-trip.

Make it more challenging: Instead of riding out-and-back along the flat creek trail, add on the return loop on the North Rim Trail, which proceeds along the higher north side of the canyon.

Trip notes: A $3 entrance fee is charged per vehicle. A free map of Alum Rock Park is available at the visitor center. For more information, contact Alum Rock Park, 16240 Alum Rock Avenue, San Jose, CA 95127; (408) 259-5477 or (408) 27-PARKS.

Directions: From U.S. 101 in San Jose, take the Alum Rock exit east for 4.2 miles to the park entrance. (The entrance is at the intersection of Alum Rock Avenue and Canon Vista Avenue.) From the entrance sign, continue 1.2 miles to the end of the road and the parking area.

---

90. LOS GATOS CREEK TRAIL
Vasona Lake County Park
Off Highway 17 near Los Gatos
9 miles/1.5 hours — dirt double-track & paved bike trail/RB or MB
steepness: ◉ ◉   skill level: ◉

Now here's a perfect family trip, with plenty to offer your kids besides a little fresh air and a bike ride. Although anyone who likes to have a good time will enjoy it here, Vasona Lake County Park is perfectly set up for families, with a section of the 14-mile long Los Gatos Creek Trail running through it and a miniature train, carousel, and children's play area besides. It's the kind of place you could take your kids to every weekend all summer long, and nobody would get bored.

The Los Gatos Creek Trail is the main attraction for bike riders, and the section that runs from Vasona Lake County Park to Lexington Reservoir is one of the prettiest stretches of the route, which currently runs from Campbell to the reservoir, but may someday extend all the way to San Francisco Bay. The problem with the trail is that its northern section runs parallel to Highway 17, completely exposed to the busy freeway and the backs of hundreds of housing tracts. But from Vasona Lake to Lexington Reservoir, the trail is largely shaded by trees and protected from the sounds and sights of the highway, offering an escape from the urbanization of the South Bay.

If you park by the children's playground, you can ride out of the parking lot in either direction and pick up the bike trail on the far side of the playground. Right away you'll notice the plethora of birds—and people who come to feed them—including ducks, geese, coots, and in winter, even some Canada geese, just down from Quebec or Toronto. You can ride to the right first, for a quick tour around the edge of Vasona Lake, but turn around when you reach the dam, because the real fun is in the other direction, heading southward.

Riding south out of the park, you'll parallel the narrow-gauge railroad tracks (narrow as in *real* narrow). Be sure to cross over the creek at the railroad crossing and check out the depot for the Billy Jones Wildcat Railroad (remember, you have to be 38 inches tall to ride) and the carousel (on summer weekends, you are likely to hear its nostalgic music from the trail).

Back on the main trail, ride with the creek on your right and Highway 17 on your left, for just over a mile until the trail becomes wooden planks instead of pavement and you reach the Forbes Mill Footbridge, where you must walk your bike on the Highway 17 overpass. The trail turns right and deposits you at the former Forbes Flour Mill. It is now a museum of local history, located in the beautiful old stone building built in 1854 by James Forbes.

Skinny-tire riders will have to turn around here for a six-mile round-trip, as the trail turns to dirt and becomes a bit more rugged as it climbs to the dam at Lexington Reservoir. Fat-tire riders can ride up

Los Gatos Creek Trail

the left or right side of the spillway to get to the top of the dam, but either way, you gotta climb. You can then ride across the dam and back down the other side, but first stop and gaze at the 450-acre reservoir, popular with sailboaters, anglers, and rowing teams, and quite pretty when filled with water, which is not all that often.

On your ride back, make a stop in Old Town Los Gatos, walking through the big wooden doors on the western side of the Forbes Mill Footbridge. It's little more than a shopping district, but it has a candy store that comes highly recommended by several bikers I know.

Make it more challenging: If you want more miles, help yourself. The Los Gatos Creek Trail continues as a paved, separate-from-cars trail for 4.6 more miles from Vasona Lake to Campbell, heading northward, so you could add on up to nine miles more round-trip.

Trip notes: A $4 entrance fee is charged per vehicle. A free map of Vasona Lake County Park is available by contacting Santa Clara County Parks and Recreation Department, 298 Garden Hill Drive, Los Gatos, CA 95030; (408) 356-2729 or (408) 358-3741.

Directions: From U.S. 101 in San Jose, take Interstate 880 south toward Santa Cruz. Interstate 880 becomes Highway 17; continue on Highway 17 to Los Gatos. Take the Lark Avenue exit and travel east, then turn right on Los Gatos Boulevard and right again on Blossom Hill Road. Continue to the park entrance on the right side of the road. Park in the lot nearest the children's play area, and locate the bike trail on the far side of the play area. (You can ride your bike out either end of the parking lot to connect to the bike trail.)

91. COYOTE CREEK TRAIL
Coyote Hellyer County Park
Off U.S. 101 near San Jose
14 miles/2 hours — paved bike trail/RB or MB
steepness: ◉ skill level: ◉

Think San Jose and you probably think "industrial parks." It's true, San Jose has its share of these mammoth concrete complexes, but it also has peaceful farmlands, orchards, and gurgling creeks. The Coyote Creek Trail passes by all of these along its seven-mile length from Coyote Hellyer County Park south to Metcalf Road. Cyclists looking for a longer trip can continue another seven miles from Metcalf Road south to the ranger station at Anderson Reservoir. This makes a nearly level 28-mile round-trip!

The trail begins at Coyote Hellyer County Park, home of the only bicycle racing track in Northern California. Races are usually held on

Cottonwood Lake along the Coyote Creek Trail

Friday nights in summer. You can begin riding right at the velodrome, or pick up the bike trail from the parking lots just before it.

In the first half-mile of trail, you'll ride past the park's small Cottonwood Lake on the left, a popular spot with shore fishermen. The lake is stocked with rainbow trout. Shortly past Cottonwood Lake, you'll cross underneath U.S. 101 to the east side.

As you ride, ignore the numerous side bridges that cross the creek and provide access to San Jose neighborhoods. Stay on the main path, which for a paved trail is a bit rough in places. (Make sure your tires are in good shape if you're on a road bike.) You'll hear some road noise from U.S. 101, which is never far away from this trail, but you'll see little of the freeway. Mostly you'll have the fine companionship of sycamores and cottonwoods along Coyote Creek, plus occasional blue jays and squirrels.

Watch for one tricky intersection that occurs at three miles out. Look to your left as you cross a bridge. Straight ahead the trail seems to end at a road, but you'll see the path continuing to the left. Make a tight left turn on the far side of the bridge to regain the trail.

At 5.8 miles out, you'll cross U.S. 101 again, now back on the west side. Shortly thereafter the trail reaches a levee along a dam on Coyote Creek. This makes a good turnaround spot, although an option is to continue riding to Metcalf Road and beyond for as far as you please. (See the "Make it more challenging" option that follows.)

Make it more challenging: Continue riding further south for up to seven miles. The paved bike trail ends at the ranger station at Anderson Reservoir in Morgan Hill.

Trip notes: A $3 entrance fee is charged per vehicle. For more information, contact Santa Clara County Parks and Recreation Department, 298 Garden Hill Drive, Los Gatos, CA 95030; (408) 356-2729 or (408) 358-3741.

Directions: From U.S. 101 in San Jose, drive south for four miles and take the Hellyer Avenue exit. Drive a quarter mile to the Coyote Hellyer County Park entrance. Just beyond the entrance kiosk, bear left at the fork and park at one of the picnic areas or at the velodrome parking lot.

92. RUSSIAN RIDGE LOOP
Russian Ridge Open Space Preserve
Off Highway 35 near Palo Alto
8.8 miles/2 hours — dirt double-track/MB
steepness: ◉ ◉   skill level: ◉ ◉

Russian Ridge Open Space Preserve is more than 1,500 acres of paradise. First, we're talking location, location, location, as in directly off Skyline Boulevard (Highway 35), near the well-to-do town of Woodside. The first time I visited the weather was foggy along the coast, but the sun was shining brightly on Skyline. From the preserve's 2,300-foot elevation, I could look out and over the blanket of fog that covered the ocean. From this perspective, the fog looks absolutely gorgeous—like layers of white cotton candy. You get to appreciate the beauty of it without being stuck in the middle of it.

As you admire the vistas, you ride on a wide, easy path through rolling hills that will make you want to sing songs from *Brigadoon*. But unlike that legendary place, Russian Ridge doesn't just appear once every 100 years. Thanks to some smart buying on the part of the Midpeninsula Regional Open Space District, this preserve is a permanent fixture.

If it's spring, you'll be charmed by colorful wildflowers and verdant grasslands. If it's summer or fall, you'll see the hillsides turned to gold, and watch the grasses sway in unison to the ridgetop winds.

Although many people visit this preserve for the views, Russian Ridge offers plenty more. Its acreage combines several plant environments, including lush grasslands, creeks, springs, and oak-shaded canyons. The area is ideal for wildlife, including a variety of raptors, coyotes, and mountain lions. What impressed me most here one April day were the wildflowers—I had never seen such an explosion of natural color, particularly poppies, lupine, goldfields, and blue-eyed grass. Later on I found out that this preserve is considered to be one of the five best places to see wildflowers in the entire Bay Area.

The route described here is a 4.2-mile loop plus an out-and-back of an additional 2.3 miles, making your total trip just shy of nine miles. If you want the easiest ride possible, stick to the loop trail and skip the out-and-back on Mindego Trail, which has a sizeable elevation gain on the return trip.

Begin riding at the trailhead parking area near the junction of Alpine Road and Highway 35. You'll start with a good climb up the Bay Area Ridge Trail to the top of Borel Hill, the highest named point in San Mateo County. (Stay to the right at two junctions.) Borel Hill is at 2,572 feet, just high enough to provide a 360-degree view of the South Bay, Skyline Ridge, and all the way west to the Pacific.

From there, you'll descend gently for a half-mile to a major junction of trails near Skyline Boulevard. Take the Ridge Trail, continuing northwest (and basically straight) for another half-mile to its junction with Hawk Hill Trail. Turn left on Hawk Hill, starting to loop back. Descend to the junction of Mindego Trail and Ancient Oaks Trail. Those opting for the longer trip will turn right here and ride out and back on Mindego Trail, dropping 400 feet in elevation and then turning around and climbing back up. The thickly forested trail is worth the extra effort required.

Back at the junction of Mindego Trail and Ancient Oaks Trail, proceed southeast on Ancient Oaks Trail, riding through a remarkable forest of gnarled oak trees interspersed with equally gnarled spruce trees, plus some madrones and ferns. Then cruise back out into the sunshine to join the Bay Area Ridge Trail again. (Watch for a wooden bench along this stretch that is surrounded by California poppies in springtime. A plaque on the side of the bench states: "There is great peace in this natural beauty. We must all help to preserve it.")

Make it easier: Just ride the 4.2-mile loop on the Ridge Trail, Hawk Trail, and Ancient Oaks Trail. Skip the out-and-back on Mindego Trail.

Trip notes: There is no fee. The preserve is open from dawn until sunset. Free trail maps are available at the trailhead. For more information, contact the Midpeninsula Regional Open Space District, 330 Distel Circle, Los Altos, CA 94022; (650) 691-1200.

Directions: From Interstate 280 or U.S. 101 on the San Francisco Peninsula, take Highway 84 west through the mountains to Skyline Boulevard (Highway 35). Turn left on Highway 35 and drive 6.7 miles south to the junction of Alpine Road, Page Mill Road, and Highway 35. Turn right on Alpine Road. In about 200 feet, turn right into the Russian Ridge entrance.

93. OLD HAUL ROAD
Pescadero Creek County Park
Off Highway 1 near Pescadero
10 miles/2.5 hours — dirt road/MB
steepness: ◉ ◉   skill level: ◉ ◉

The Old Haul Road is a logging route that runs for five miles between Pescadero Creek County Park and Portola State Park. It tunnels through a thick forest of second-growth redwoods, providing a smooth dirt route that is ideal for beginning mountain bike riders. Built on an old railroad bed, it never gains more than 400 feet in elevation and has an easy grade in both directions.

Given these facts, the uninitiated (okay, we're talking about me) might think you could start at either park, ride the trail back and forth, and have a perfectly good time. The uninformed (me again) would probably believe that it didn't matter which park you started from. Wrong on both counts.

I decided to set out on the Old Haul Road from Portola State Park (for reasons which seemed perfectly logical at the time, but now escape me). The following obstacles presented themselves: 1) Driving to Portola requires a circuitous, seemingly endless drive on a series of narrow, winding roads. 2) You have to pay a $5 state park access fee, even though all you are doing in the state park is parking your car. 3) Once you're in Portola, accessing the Old Haul Road requires riding your bike up a steep, paved park road for nearly a mile. 4) By the time you finally make it to the Old Haul Road, you're tired, hungry, and irritable.

Okay, take two. On the next trip, I started from Pescadero Creek County Park. Driving to Pescadero Creek requires a pleasant, 11-mile drive on Pescadero Road from Highway 1. There is no fee to park at the trailhead for the Old Haul Road, and the trail begins about 50 feet from where you park your car. You drive in, you unload your bike, you ride. You retain your sense of humor.

Then you can actually enjoy the Old Haul Road, which is a pretty, meandering cruise through the forest. On the Pescadero Creek County Park side, the trail starts by a small picnic area near the rushing creek gorge, then heads east to Portola State Park and slightly beyond. The forest is somewhat drier on the western side of the trail, with California laurel and bays mixed in among Douglas firs and second-growth redwoods. You'll see plenty of big stumps along the route, reminders of this forest's earlier state, and many tiny streams which run down the hillsides to empty into Pescadero Creek.

Equestrians like to use the Old Haul Road as well, so be on the alert for them, and for bicyclists speeding around the curves. Most people take their time, though, enjoying the diversity of the forest and the pleasant up-and-down of the ride. Since this is an old railroad route, the few steep sections are very brief. The hard-packed dirt and gravel road rarely gets muddy except after the hardest rains, and it is well signed the whole way.

If you ride all five miles to Portola State Park, lock up your bike near where the Old Haul Road meets the state park service road. Walk about a tenth of a mile up the paved road to where the Iverson Trail cuts off on your left. Follow Iverson Trail, crossing a bridge over Iverson Creek. In less than a mile, you will come to tiny Tiptoe Falls, a pretty little waterfall in a canyon along Fall Creek. Even if the waterfall is running low, it's worth the trip just for the walk through the ferns and the forest.

Make it more challenging: The trail continues for another mile beyond Portola State Park, so you can add on two more miles to your trip by riding out-and-back on the whole length of it.

Trip notes: There is no fee for parking at the Wurr Road trailhead for the Old Haul Road. A Pescadero Creek County Park map is available for $1 at Memorial Park, one quarter mile west on Pescadero Road. For more information, contact Memorial Park/Pescadero Creek County Park, San Mateo County Parks and Recreation, 455 County Center, Redwood City, CA 94063; (650) 363-4020.

Directions: From Highway 1 at Pescadero on the San Mateo County coast, drive east on Pescadero Road for 10 miles. Turn right at the second entrance to Wurr Road, a quarter-mile beyond the entrance to Memorial Park. (Look for the sign for Redwood Glen Baptist Camp). Drive a short distance to the parking area on the left that is signed as Pescadero Creek County Park. Adjacent to the parking area is the Hoffman Creek Trailhead, where the Old Haul Road begins.

---

94. SKYLINE-TO-THE-SEA TRAIL
Big Basin Redwoods State Park
Off Highway 1 near Davenport
10.5 miles/2.5 hours — dirt double-track/MB
steepness: ◉ ◉   skill level: ◉

Ah, bliss. The Skyline-to-the-Sea Trail to Berry Creek Falls is so superb, so much the embodiment of a perfect easy bike trail, that there's no way to describe it adequately. You'll run out of adjectives before you even get to the waterfall, and none of your friends will believe you, anyway.

So don't talk about it, just come to Big Basin State Park and ride the trail, making the trip down Highway 1 to the Waddell Beach/Rancho del Oso section of huge, 19,000-acre Big Basin Redwoods State Park. While 70-foot Berry Creek Falls is unquestionably the highlight of the ride, the entire trail is marked by beautiful scenery, including flowing Waddell Creek, ferns galore, alders, Douglas firs, and of course, big redwoods.

If you've ever made the nine-mile hiking trip to Berry Creek Falls from Big Basin's visitor center, you won't believe how quick and easy the bike trip is. Starting from Highway 1 and traveling north to the falls, rather than starting at park headquarters and heading west, makes all the difference. (Oh yeah, plus you're on a bike, which cuts the time required in half.)

The Skyline-to-the-Sea Trail winds through the flat Waddell Creek Canyon, making a very gradual ascent to 450 feet in elevation over five miles. It will take you about an hour to get to the point where the trail is closed to bikes; a bike rack is conveniently located there, and you can lock up your bike and continue on foot to the falls. The hike is very short—less than a mile—putting you at the waterfall in about 20 minutes. After getting an eyeful, your trip back to your car is an easy downhill cruise, with a lot of time spent just sitting in your saddle, looking around at all the gorgeous streamside scenery, rather than huffing and puffing.

The trail starts as pavement at the highway, but turns to dirt after passing the small Rancho del Oso visitor center. You pass a few homes and small farms on the border of park land, then quickly head deeper into the canyon, with woods and shade enveloping you. Waddell Creek accompanies the trail the whole way, with one creek crossing that is signed: "Equestrians, use the bridge when the creek is too high to ford." This means you, too, so if the creek is high, dismount your bike and walk it through the single-track trail in the forest for about 25 yards, then cross the creek on a long and narrow footbridge.

The trail then slowly climbs for another half-mile, depositing you at the bike rack. After locking up, cross the creek on the small footbridge, then follow the footpath through the woods to just beyond the intersection of Berry Creek and Waddell Creek, where Berry Creek Falls tumbles down. A wooden viewing platform is positioned directly in front of the falls, a good spot for a picnic or just watching water drip off the five-finger ferns growing around the waterfall. Berry Creek Falls can create a strong wind in winter, and on sunny days year-round, you can watch as light filters through the redwoods and makes beautiful patterns on the streams of water.

The final hike to the falls is not as well-signed as the bike trail, so make sure you stay along Waddell Creek and ignore any off-shoot trails. Just before the falls, the Skyline-to-the-Sea Trail veers to the right, heading to a little viewing bench about 100 yards from the falls, then beyond to park headquarters. Stay to the left to go directly to the falls (on the Berry Creek Falls Trail).

Skyline-to-the-Sea Trail

One final caveat for the best possible trip: The Skyline-to-the-Sea Trail is quite popular with local riders, so arrive early in the morning for the best chance of peace and quiet (or ride on a weekday). At any time, watch out for equestrians and hikers, who share the trail.

Make it more challenging: If you want to hike further, you can see two more waterfalls—Silver Falls and Golden Falls, just upstream from Berry Creek Falls. Continue uphill on Berry Creek Falls Trail, heading to the left of Berry Creek Falls, for just under two miles to the two cascades, one right after the other.

Trip notes: There is no fee. A map of Big Basin Redwoods State Park is available at the Rancho del Oso visitor center for $1. For more information, contact Big Basin Redwoods State Park, 21600 Big Basin Way, Boulder Creek, CA 95006; (831) 338-8860 or (831) 429-2851.

Directions: From Santa Cruz, travel north on Highway 1 for 18 miles to Waddell Beach (on the west side of the highway) and Big Basin Redwoods State Park/Rancho del Oso (on the east side of the highway). They are exactly 7.5 miles north of the town of Davenport on Highway 1. Park in either parking area and start riding from the Rancho del Oso trailhead.

95. WILDER RIDGE & ZANE GRAY LOOP
Wilder Ranch State Park
Off Highway 1 near Santa Cruz
6 miles/2 hours — dirt double-track/MB
steepness: ⊛ ⊛ ⊛   skill level: ⊛ ⊛

Wilder Ranch is a state park whose 3,000-acre north side is almost completely the domain of mountain bikers. The first time you ride here, you may think you are visiting a mountain bike park, like those in the ski areas of Tahoe and Mammoth. Bikers are everywhere. From the bottom of the hill looking up, the effect is much the same as standing at a ski lodge and watching the field of skiers *schussing* down the mountain. It seems as if there's a million of them, each making perfect S-turns on the hill.

But there's no reason to be intimidated by the crowds, because the park is big enough to accommodate everybody. While dedicated hill-haters should stick to the Old Landing Cove Trail on the west side of the park (see the following story), those who are willing to make a 500-foot climb can ride the Wilder Ridge Loop for a good taste of the park's backcountry offerings. Despite the hill, the trails are well-signed, hard-packed, and fairly smooth, with great views of Monterey Bay and the Pacific Ocean, making them excellent candidates for an easy bike trip.

From the parking lot, ride your bike to the left (east), following the path past the restrooms, then the park road to the right. Turn left and walk your bike through the cultural preserve/ranch buildings, around the back and past the picnic tables and chicken coops, to a tunnel that leads underneath Highway 1. (You must walk your bike through the preserve because there are so many visitors there.) After the tunnel, ride straight for a short distance, past a horse riding ring, then make a sharp left turn and head uphill. Congratulations—you are now on the Wilder Ridge Loop Trail.

Don't pat yourself on the back for too long, because now you've got some serious climbing to do. Pass a small pond on your left, then shortly after it, you'll see a trail marker for the Wilder Ridge Loop leading either left or right. Stay to the right on the double-track trail, saving the single-track fork for your return trip. It's a heck of a climb from here, and the trail can get somewhat eroded and bumpy, but at least you'll head in to the trees for a little shade.

Overlook of Monterey Bay from Wilder Ridge Loop

You can walk the steepest section of the hill, which only lasts for about a quarter-mile, and if you do, you'll probably have some company. Lots of folks walk a section of this trail, pushing their bikes and muttering, "This better be good." Well, it is good, as you'll discover as you reach the top and take the unmarked fork to the left, which in about 40 feet brings you to an incredible lookout over Monterey Bay. *Now* you can pat yourself on the back, and maybe have a Power Bar, too. Looking down at the valley below you, you'll be amazed at how high you've climbed.

Get back on the loop when you're ready, continuing along the ridge for about a half-mile to the Zane Gray Cutoff on the left, then ride down its single-track till it meets up with the Wilder Ridge Loop again—the single-track fork of it that you passed on the way in. Head left to close off the loop. While Zane Gray is a rather straight and practical trail, the single-track section of Wilder Ridge Loop has about a million curves and turns, making you wonder if you will ever get back to the main double-track part of the trail. Luckily, it's almost all downhill, but watch your speed or you can take a spill. When you finally meet the double-track section of Wilder Ridge Loop, turn right for an easy downhill back to the cultural preserve and the parking lot.

Make it easier: Just ride up to the lookout, then turn around and ride back the way you came. Also, be sure to ride these trails after a period of dry weather, as rain and mud can make them far more difficult—especially the single-track sections.

Trip notes: A $6 day-use fee is charged per vehicle. A map is available for free from the entrance kiosk. For more information, contact Wilder Ranch State Park, 1401 Old Coast Road, Santa Cruz, CA 95060; (831) 423-9703 or (831) 429-2851.

Directions: From Santa Cruz, travel north on Highway 1 for four miles. Turn left into the entrance for Wilder Ranch State Park, then follow the park road to its end at the main parking area. Walk your bike on the paved trail from the parking lot to the cultural preserve/ranch buildings. (You may ride on the road that leads to the buildings, but when you are inside the ranch's grounds, you must walk your bike.) Walk through the cultural preserve, past the buildings, picnic area, and chicken coop, then ride your bike through the tunnel to the other side of the freeway and the bike trail.

---

96. OLD LANDING COVE TRAIL
Wilder Ranch State Park
Off Highway 1 near Santa Cruz
2.5 miles/1 hour — dirt double-track/MB
steepness: ◉   skill level: ◉

The Old Landing Cove Trail is just the opposite of all the other trails at Wilder Ranch State Park. The Old Landing Cove Trail is coastal, while the other trails are inland. The Old Landing Cove Trail is completely flat, while the other trails are rollercoaster climbs and descents. The Old Landing Cove Trail is a short out-and-back, while the other trails are long loops. The Old Landing Cove Trail is perfect for people who like to see things close up, while the other trails offer stunning vistas from far away.

If the shoe fits, wear it. For those who don't have a lot of time, or don't want to do any climbing, or just like to be near the ocean, the Old Landing Cove Trail is a great way to spend a morning or an afternoon at Wilder Ranch State Park. It's a true gem of a coastal trail which offers several great surprises, including a seal rookery, some spectacular beaches, and a hidden fern cave.

You'll want to get off your bike and wander a bit in order to best explore this area, so be sure to bring a bike lock. (Unfortunately, there isn't much to lock your bike *to* out here, so you'll have to be creative— use a signpost or lock your bike to your riding partner's bike.) The Old Landing Cove Trail begins from the parking lot, at the rather nebulous sign that simply reads "Nature Trail." Begin riding on a flat ranch road through the park's agricultural preserve of brussels sprouts fields. Yup, it's true, Wilder Ranch's biggest claim to fame is not its historic ranch buildings, nor its excellent mountain biking trail system, nor its beautiful beaches and coastal vistas, but rather the fact that 12 percent of our national brussels sprouts production happens right here within park boundaries. One question: Who's eating all of them, anyway?

Ride toward the coast, then turn right and ride along the sandstone and mudstone bluffs. The first beach you see, Wilder Beach off to your left, is a critical habitat area for the endangered snowy plover and is fenced off and protected as a natural preserve.

There are plenty of other beaches left to explore. A quarter-mile further you'll come to the trail's namesake, the old landing cove, a remarkably narrow inlet where small schooners pulled in and anchored to load lumber in the late 1800s.

Just off Old Landing Cove is a huge flat rock where harbor seals hang out, laying around in the sun all day to warm their flippers. You can't really see the seals on the rock until you ride past the Old Landing Cove and look back, which means your best view of the seals comes on your return trip.

For now, continue riding. The highlight of this trip is coming up shortly, following the wooden post that is marked as number 8. Just beyond that trail marker is Fern Grotto Beach, a small sandy cove with a fern cave tucked into its back wall. A narrow offshoot trail leads down to the cove from the main trail; lock up your bike and explore. When you stand inside the cave, sword ferns and bracken ferns hanging down from the ceiling will tickle your head. The ferns manage to thrive in the harsh, salty environment because an underground spring keeps them moist.

Harbor seals on the rocks at Wilder Ranch State Park

You can ride only a quarter-mile further on the Old Landing Cove Trail, as the trail is usually closed to visitors beyond this point. There is one more beach to visit, though, which has a wider and more visible trail leading down to it. You can explore or picnic there, then turn around and ride back.

Make it easier: You can cut this trip short anywhere you like, as the views of the jagged coastline are excellent from all points on the trail.

Trip notes: A $6 day-use fee is charged per vehicle. A map is available for free from the entrance kiosk. For more information, contact Wilder Ranch State Park, 1401 Old Coast Road, Santa Cruz, CA 95060; (831) 423-9703 or (831) 429-2851.

Directions: From Santa Cruz, travel north on Highway 1 for four miles. Turn left into the entrance for Wilder Ranch State Park, then follow the park road to its end at the main parking area. Take the trail that is marked "Nature Trail" from the southwest side of the parking lot.

97. PIPELINE ROAD
Henry Cowell Redwoods State Park
Off Highway 9 near Santa Cruz
6 miles/1.5 hours — paved bike trail/RB or MB
steepness: ◉ ◉ ◉   skill level: ◉

Henry Cowell Redwoods State Park is celebrated for its ancient groves of coast redwoods. It's famous for its Roaring Camp Railroad steam trains, whose whistles' blow as they roar through tracks that carve through the center of the park. And it's well known for the San Lorenzo River, which offers good swimming and wading to park visitors in summer, and rushing waters for runs of salmon and steelhead in winter.

But while bicyclists may enjoy all these aspects of Henry Cowell Redwoods State Park, what they'll really like is Pipeline Road, a three-mile paved service road that is closed to cars but open to bikers, hikers, and dogs on leash. The road has a few steep pitches, but much of it just rolls gently beside the San Lorenzo River, or cruises along a ridgeline in a dense forest of redwoods, laurels, and Douglas firs. If you carry a bike lock on your Pipeline Road ride, you can visit another of the park's highlights—the Observation Platform on Ridge Fire Road, where you'll find a fine view of Monterey Bay and some unusual flora.

The paved road begins behind the nature center, not far from the park's Redwood Trail Loop. (Make sure you walk this quarter-mile trail through the redwoods before or after your bike ride.) Follow Pipeline Road on your bike, paralleling the San Lorenzo River and the hikers-

Pipeline Road, Henry Cowell Redwoods State Park

only River Trail. You're in a forest of second- and third-growth red-woods; if you look carefully among them you'll see giant stumps that belonged to the first growth of trees. In short order you'll pass under a railroad trestle that crosses the San Lorenzo River, where you'll find a signboard with a park map. Although the river is only a few inches deep in summer, it can be 20 or 30 feet deep during winter rains. Chances are good that as you ride along the river, you'll hear the wail of a train screeching around a curve in the canyon. The privately oper-ated Roaring Camp Railroad runs through the park (the ticket office and station are located near the parking lot where you left your car). When you hear one of its trains, you may think it sounds more like the "Wailing" Camp Railroad.

The first stretch of trail is pretty mellow, with many small ups and downs. The middle stretch is the harder, steeper part, with one half-mile section that may force you to stop and walk your bike. Fortu-nately, the road is shaded by redwoods and Douglas firs, so at least you won't be overheated. The final stretch of road is easy again, and features a nice level stint along the ridgeline. On this last stretch you reach an overlook point with a bench, from which you can see all the way down the San Lorenzo River canyon to Monterey Bay and the Pacific Ocean. There are many, many conifers between you and the beach.

Keep riding beyond the overlook to a major junction of trails at three miles out, where Huckleberry Trail goes right, Pipeline Road continues straight ahead, and Powder Mill Fire Road and Graham Hill Trail head left. There's a picnic table at this junction, on the left side of

Pipeline Road. (Pipeline Road continues from here for another half-mile, but it's unwise to ride it. The trail makes a serious descent and then ends abruptly at Graham Hill Road, at which point you would simply have to turn around and climb back up.)

This junction is your turnaround point, but before you make the fast and furious descent back to the trailhead, you might want to lock up your bike and take a walk to the park's Observation Platform. (Technically, you're allowed to ride there, but the road is ridiculously sandy. You might as well leave your bike and walk.) Follow Powder Mill Fire Road gently uphill for a half mile to the concrete observation deck, where you'll find a picnic table, hitching post, and water fountain, plus two surprising types of trees—knobcone pines and ponderosa pines. The latter, with its distinctive jigsaw puzzle bark, usually is found at much higher elevations in places like the Sierra Nevada. Here at 800 feet in elevation in the Santa Cruz Mountains, the ponderosa pine grows only in this strange "sand hill chaparral" community. This region's sandy soil is the remains of an ancient ocean floor. Four million years ago a shallow sea completely covered the area.

Walk up the observation platform's stairs and you'll get a somewhat obstructed view of Monterey Bay. (The forest has grown up around the observation platform since it was built.) Even if the view is only fair, the sunny platform is a fine place to lay down and take a nap.

When you return to your bike and Pipeline Road, remember that your downhill return is going to be fast. Be sure to keep your speed down and watch for hikers, bikers, and dogs coming uphill.

Make it easier: Just cut your trip short, riding out and back as far as you please along Pipeline Road.

Trip notes: A $6 day-use fee is charged per vehicle. A park map is available from the visitor center for $1.50. For more information, contact Henry Cowell Redwoods State Park, 101 North Big Trees Park Road, Felton, CA 95018; (831) 335-4598 or (831) 429-2851.

Directions: From the junction of Interstate 280 and Highway 17 near San Jose, take Highway 17 south for 24 miles to Scotts Valley. Take the Mount Hermon Road exit. At the stoplight, turn right. Drive 3.5 miles west, turn right on Graham Hill Road, then turn left immediately on Highway 9. Drive six-tenths of a mile on Highway 9 to Henry Cowell Redwoods State Park on the left. Continue past the entrance kiosk to the visitor center and main parking lot. Follow the signs to the Redwood Grove and the Nature Center, then take the paved road that leads to the right of the Nature Center. Pipeline Road begins behind the Nature Center.

Alternatively, from Highway 1 in Santa Cruz, take Highway 9 and drive north six miles to the right turnoff for the park.

98. APTOS CREEK FIRE ROAD

Forest of Nisene Marks State Park

Off Highway 1 near Aptos
5 miles/1.5 hours — dirt double-track/MB
steepness: ⊛   skill level: ⊛

The Forest of Nisene Marks State Park is one of those not-too-developed, lower-priced state parks, the kind that doesn't have a campground or a visitor center or even paved parking lots. Sounds good already, right? It gets better. In terms of scenery, the park looks like the young cousin of Big Basin Redwoods State Park, with second-growth redwoods, more ferns than you can shake a stick at, and a wide and smooth trail that parallels Aptos Creek much the same as the Skyline-to-the-Sea Trail parallels Waddell Creek (see story on page 209).

Two major forces have shaped the land here: the railroad and unstable geology. Although old-growth redwoods remained untouched in this steep and winding canyon for hundreds of years, the Loma Prieta Lumber Company got ownership of the valley in 1881 and teamed up with Southern Pacific Railroad to destroy it—oops, I mean log it. They built a railroad along Aptos Creek and worked the land with trains, oxen, skid roads, inclines, horses, and as many men as they could get, removing 140 million board feet of lumber over the course of 40 years. In 1922, when they put their saws down, there were no trees left.

Luckily, since 1922, Mother Nature has been busy. The forest is now filled with second-growth redwoods and Douglas firs, and the higher ridges have eucalyptus and madrones. Still, every now and then you come across a magnificent old stump, and you gotta think those lumber barons must be sitting it out in purgatory.

Mother Nature was really busy on October 17, 1989, when the park was the epicenter of the famous Loma Prieta earthquake, which forcefully shook the entire San Francisco Bay Area, nearly destroying much of Santa Cruz. The easiest bike ride in the park is along Aptos Creek Fire Road to the earthquake epicenter, requiring a five-mile bike ride and a one-mile hike.

Park at George's Picnic Area and ride along the creek for 2.5 miles, past two other picnic areas and several cutoffs for hikers-only trails. The trail is wide, hard-packed and smooth the whole way, with an almost imperceptible climb until you near the epicenter. There you head downhill and cross a steel bridge, then come to a large sign that reads: "Epicenter Area, 7.1 Earthquake, 5:04 P.M., October 17, 1989. You are in the vicinity of the earthquake's epicenter. Though there is little evidence here, slides and fissures occurred in more remote areas of the park."

A hiking trail leads to the exact epicenter from the left side of the earthquake sign. You must cross Aptos Creek and walk a half-mile, and although there is little to see of the earthquake, hike it anyway just to enjoy the forest. (There is a bike rack near the earthquake sign, so bring a lock.)

Aptos Creek Fire Road continues for four more miles to Sand Point Overlook at 1,500 feet in elevation, but it's a very intense climb, so unless you're up for it you should turn around and head back for a five-mile round-trip ride.

Make it easier: If you visit the park in summer, you can park at the Porter Picnic Area, which brings you one mile closer to the earthquake epicenter, shortening your ride to a three-mile round-trip. In winter, the road is gated off at George's Picnic Area, so you must start riding from there, requiring a five-mile round-trip ride.

Trip notes: A $3 day-use fee is charged per vehicle. A free map is available at the entrance kiosk. For more information, contact Sunset State Beach/Forest of Nisene Marks State Park, 201 Sunset Beach Road, Watsonville, CA 95076; (831) 763-7063 or (831) 429-2851.

Directions: From Santa Cruz, travel south on Highway 1 for six miles to the Aptos exit. Go left at the exit, then turn right on Soquel Drive and drive one-half mile to Aptos, then turn left on Aptos Creek Road. Stop and pay at the park entrance kiosk, then continue up the road and park at George's Picnic Area (the only choice in winter, for a five-mile round-trip) or Porter Picnic Area (an option in summer, for a three-mile round-trip).

99. MONTEREY PENINSULA RECREATIONAL TRAIL
Monterey & Pacific Grove
Off Highway 1 in Monterey
10 miles/2 hours — paved bike trail/RB or MB
steepness: ◉   skill level: ◉

If you ever make the trip to Monterey to visit its famous aquarium or Steinbeck's Cannery Row, or just to hang out by the ocean and eat seafood for a while, be absolutely certain to bring your bike. There's so much action in Monterey, so much to see and do, that many people forget about the paved Monterey Peninsula Recreational Trail until they arrive at the coast and see it. You don't want to be in Monterey wishing you had your wheels; pack them along and make this bike path a part of your trip.

The easiest and cheapest parking is in the Monterey Harbor parking lot, at the corner of Del Monte Avenue and Washington Street. The trail leads in both directions from the lot, and the mileage above reflects riding both ends. However, the eastern route, which leads to the town of Seaside, is commonplace at best and dreary at worst, particularly after it leaves the beach and heads inland along Del Monte Avenue. After about two miles, the trail ends abruptly at an intersection and a shopping center.

That's the bad news; now for the good news. The trail heading west, leading to the town of Pacific Grove, is stellar all the way. All your senses get involved in the experience of this ride, particularly your olfactory sense. It takes a while to get accustomed to how wonderfully fishy it smells in Monterey, and the scent is very evocative—it can make you want to stow away on a freighter and live a life at sea.

Stick to your two wheels for now, though, and pedal toward Cannery Row and the Monterey Bay Aquarium. Go very slowly and watch out for walkers and especially kids, particularly near the aquarium. Also try to avoid the four wheeled rental bikes with canopies over them that take up more than half of the trail.

In between all the bustle and the tourism are marvelous stretches consisting of only you, the trail, and the sea. We watched some scuba divers coming up out of the water, saw the sun starting to set over the harbor, and witnessed a sea lion trying with all his might to clamber up

Monterey Peninsula Recreational Trail

on a rock. Kayakers paddled by us and waved, and a pelican dove into the waves 50 feet away.

After the busiest section right by the Cannery's shops, the trail gets quieter as it leads into the wealthy neighborhood of Pacific Grove, with its bed-and-breakfast hotels and restaurants. The views of the rugged, rocky coastline and the white sand beaches, get even better. Pacific Grove also happens to be an over-wintering spot for monarch butterflies, which can sometimes be seen hanging in clusters in the tree tops from October to January.

The trail ends near a seaside park at 17th Street, and if you turn right and ride or walk down the road for about 100 yards, you can enter the park, explore around its incredible lawns and look out over the marine refuge below. There are some wonderful rounded rock formations right by the water's edge, which children love to climb on, and plenty of windswept Monterey pines. Two interesting sculptures are also on display in the park, one of a butterfly and one of a child pointing to the sea.

Make it easier: Skip the ride to Seaside, and just ride out-and-back to Pacific Grove for a six-mile round-trip and the prettiest scenery.

Trip notes: There is no fee. For more information, contact Monterey Parks Department, 23 Ryan Ranch Road, Monterey, CA 93940; (831) 646-3860 or Pacific Grove Recreation Department, 515 Junipero Avenue, Pacific Grove, CA 93950; (831) 648-3130.

Directions: From U.S. 101 in Salinas, take Highway 68 southwest to Highway 1. Take the Monterey Peninsula exit, which puts you on Camino Aguajito. Follow Camino Aguajito to Del Monte Avenue along the bay. Turn left on Del Monte and park in the Monterey Harbor parking lot, at the corner of Del Monte Avenue and Washington Street. (Parking costs $1 per hour.) Ride your bike back out of the parking lot to pick up the bike trail, which runs parallel to Del Monte Avenue.

Yosemite & Mammoth Lakes

100—Merced River Railroad Grade, *BLM Folsom Resource Area* 224
101– Yosemite Valley Bike Path, *Yosemite National Park* 226
102—Bodie Ghost Town Ride, *Bodie State Historic Park* 229
103—Mono Lake South Tufa Area Trails, *Mono Lake Tufa
    State Reserve* 230
104—Inyo Craters Loop, *Inyo National Forest* 233
105—Shady Rest Trail, *Shady Rest Town Park* 235
106—Paper Route & Juniper Trails, *Mammoth Mountain Bike Park* . 236
107—Beach Cruiser Trail, *Mammoth Mountain Bike Park* 239
108—Horseshoe Lake Loop, *Inyo National Forest* 240
109 –Twin Lakes Route, *Inyo National Forest* 243
110—Hot Creek Fish Hatchery & Geothermal Area, *Inyo
    National Forest* 245

⚙ For locations of trails, see map on page 8. ⚙

100. MERCED RIVER RAILROAD GRADE
BLM Folsom Resource Area
Off Highway 140 near Mariposa
6 miles/2 hours — dirt double-track/MB
steepness: ⊛   skill level: ⊛ ⊛

The Merced River Railroad Grade is a mountain biker's dream trail. Take a sunny May or June day, when the Merced River is running strong and the grassland wildflowers are blooming. Cruise along the wide, level path, enjoying nonstop river views and the continual entertainment of whitewater rafters floating by. Feel the smooth gravel and dirt surface under your wheels and the wind in your hair.

Honestly, does it get any better than this?

Not that I know of. The Merced River Railroad Grade begins at the Bureau of Land Management's Railroad Flat Campground along the Merced River, only a few miles from the entrance to Yosemite National Park and Yosemite Valley. It takes a nearly five-mile drive on a dirt road to reach the camp and trailhead, but it's manageable in a passenger car (even my low-slung Toyota Celica.) The first stretch of the railroad grade is rideable year-round, although it can be quite hot in summer. After the first couple of miles, the trail can become impassable in winter and early spring, due to side streams pouring across that have no bridges. For scenery, the best season to ride here is late spring and early summer, when the foothill wildflowers are in bloom. If you want to be assured of the longest possible ride, the best season to ride is autumn, when the trail will be dry.

Because it's an old railroad grade along the river, the trail is as flat as a pancake. You'll drive the first 4.8 miles of the grade to reach the trailhead, then leave your vehicle at Railroad Flat Campground. Walk your bike around the white metal gate signed "Do not block." One hundred yards beyond the white gate is a second, more formal gate. Shoulder your bike to heft it over the top, then enjoy the scene on the gate's far side where Halls Gulch cascades down the hillside to join the Merced River. A bench is situated here, at the official start of the trail.

Begin your ride. Everything should go smoothly in the first stretch. About a half-mile in, you'll pass the remains of an old diversion dam that was removed from the river. In the next mile, the canyon gets narrower and the river gets more ferocious as it builds up power for North Fork Falls. Between the second and third mile, the trail starts to get more rutted and rocky. Washouts sometimes here occur during heavy rain years. (The quality of this part of the trail varies greatly from

Merced River Railroad Grade

season to season; if you're concerned about the possibility of facing some rough trail, call the Bureau of Land Management for updated trail conditions.) At three miles out, you reach the point where the North Fork converges with the main fork of the Merced River. There is no bridge across the North Fork, and in spring, you will be forced to turn back. (You may be joined by rafters on the trail here, who must make a mandatory portage at this stretch of river.) No matter; this makes an excellent turnaround spot. Just wheel your bike around, start pedaling, and watch the river roll by from the opposite perspective.

Make it more challenging: If you ride this trail in late summer or autumn, you will probably be able to cross the North Fork of the Merced River and keep riding along the railroad grade. The trail continues beyond the North Fork for another six miles to Bagby.

Trip notes: There is no fee. For more information, contact Bureau of Land Management, Folsom Resource Area, 63 Natoma Street, Folsom, CA 95630; (916) 985-4474.

Directions: From Merced, drive 45 miles northeast on Highway 140 to Mariposa. Continue east on Highway 140 to the Briceburg Visitor Center on the left. Turn left at the visitor center, and continue past it for 100 yards to the suspension bridge over the Merced River. Drive across the bridge and turn left, paralleling the river. (The road is dirt but passable in a passenger car.) Drive 4.8 miles to Railroad Flat Campground, where the road is gated off and the rail trail begins.

101. YOSEMITE VALLEY BIKE PATH
Yosemite National Park
Off Highway 120 in Yosemite Valley
5 miles/1.5 hours — paved bike trail/RB or MB
steepness: ⊛　skill level: ⊛

It's congested, it's crowded, and it can be a zoo on summer week-ends, but hey, Yosemite Valley is still one of the greatest shows on earth. If you see it from your bicycle seat rather than your car window, you'll see it in the best possible way.

Now listen carefully, because there is one critical tip for having the best possible experience: Ride this trail as early in the morning as you possibly can, and get out of the valley before 10 A.M. when the day-users arrive *en masse*. If you can't bear to get up early, here's another option: Ride this trail pre-season (in April or May) or post-season (in October or November). Even then, try to do it on a weekday, not a weekend.

The best place to start your bike trip is at the picnic area along Southside Drive, located just east of the trailhead for the Four-Mile Trail. This gives you the chance to get out of your car and on your bike before you've driven all the way into the valley; you'll avoid the crowds at the parking lots in Yosemite Village. The paved bike trail starts just beyond the picnic area. Head straight for the wooden bridge across the Merced River, then ride through the big meadow that faces Yosemite Falls. The drama begins immediately with the sight of this stunning waterfall and the immense granite walls that surround it.

Ride over to the Lower Yosemite Falls trailhead, where you'll find a bike rack. Lock up your bike and take the quarter-mile hike on a paved trail to the falls. When Yosemite Falls is running (usually from about March to early July), it's a sight to behold. In early spring, the waterfall flows with such force that onlookers get showered with spray, even while standing 50 yards away at the falls' overlook. Some people come prepared with their raingear.

Now steel yourself for the ride through Yosemite Village and past the Visitor Center, where the path can get really congested. Pay close attention to stop signs on the trail and the intersections you must cross. Cars are plentiful on these cross-streets, and they don't necessarily stop for bicyclists, even at crosswalks. Also, watch out for other trail users, who can be completely oblivious. Follow the trail, now paralleling Northside Drive, until you see the turnoff for Curry Village. Ignore this turnoff and head left instead. You'll move away from the road and things will start to quiet down. Be grateful to the biking gods—there are no more road intersections from here on.

Now you can relax and cruise through the forest, crossing the Merced River again and going past Upper River, Lower Pines and North Pines campgrounds. At a signed junction, the trail turns to dirt and heads to Mirror Lake in six-tenths of a mile, or curves right (still paved) to go to Happy Isles and Curry Village. Take the smooth dirt cutoff for about 30 yards until it joins with pavement again. This

Yosemite Valley Bike Path

puts you on the paved two-lane road (with no cars) that leads to Mirror Lake. Be on the lookout for walkers, bikers, and rollerbladers who share the trail.

On the road to Mirror Lake, you meet the only hill of your whole ride. If you've rented your bike in Yosemite Village, you aren't allowed to ride up the hill; there is a bike rack where you should park your bike and walk. (The park service is trying to control the number of people racing back down the hill, bowling over international tourists.) If you're on your own bike, pedal away, but remember to watch for human obstacles on the return trip.

At the top of the hill, park your bike and walk around Mirror Lake. In spring, it is a lovely sight, but by late summer, the lake has mostly disappeared. Mirror Lake is not a true lake; it's a large, shallow pool in Tenaya Creek, which varies in size from season to season. Over the years, the pool has undergone the process of sedimentation—it has

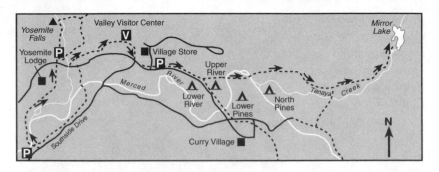

filled with sand and gravel from Tenaya Creek. Today, even in spring the lake is quite shallow. Still, when Tenaya Creek is full of water, Mirror Lake is a sight to see. The view of Half Dome's 4,700-foot perpendicular face, seen from its base, is awe-inspiring. Directly in front of Half Dome is Ahwiyah Point; Mount Watkins is the prominent rounded peak on the left.

Most visitors mill around on the road side of the lake, swimming and sunning, but if you walk to the north side, you will find a lovely hiking trail where you can get a little solitude.

When it's time to mount your wheels to make the return trip, don't go so fast that you miss the awesome view of Half Dome. About halfway down the hill is an incredible spot to look up and admire that huge piece of granite.

Make it easier: If you drive further into the valley and park near the Village Store, you can ride from there to Mirror Lake and back for a round-trip of three miles.

Trip notes: There is a $20 fee per vehicle for entrance into Yosemite National Park. Keep your receipt because the fee is good for seven days. Bike rentals are available in Yosemite Village. Park maps are available for free at the entrance kiosk. For more information, contact Yosemite National Park Public Information Office, P.O. Box 577, Yosemite National Park, CA 95389; (209) 372-0200.

Directions: From Merced, drive 70 miles northeast on Highway 140 to Yosemite National Park. Follow the signs toward Yosemite Valley, entering through the Arch Rock entrance station and continuing on El Portal Road, which becomes Southside Drive. Park alongside the road near the trailhead for the Four-Mile Trail (on the right), or at the picnic area just past this trailhead (on the left). The bike trail begins at the picnic area. You can also pick up the bike trail from several other points in the valley, including the parking area near Yosemite Falls or by the Village Store.

102. BODIE GHOST TOWN RIDE
Bodie State Historic Park
Off U.S. 395 near Bridgeport
2.5 miles/1.5 hours — dirt roads/MB
steepness: ● skill level: ●

"Are you *sure* we can ride in the ghost town?" We asked the park rangers on the phone before we made the long drive. "Absolutely," they said.

"Are you *sure* it's okay that we brought our bikes?" We asked at the kiosk as we paid our entrance fee. "Sure, just keep your speed down and be courteous," the ranger said.

Still, we felt like criminals as we saddled up in the parking lot of Bodie State Historic Park, a fascinating and well-preserved Old West ghost town located way out in the desert near Bridgeport. Bike riding in a state historic park is usually forbidden, banned, nixed, taboo. But sure enough, they let us ride.

Bodie is just a little too big for families to walk the entire route, especially if it's hot weather. Cruising around Bodie on a bike, however, is a great way to see the old town. You won't be riding for any long stretches, though, which is why I list the mileage as only 2.5 miles but the time required as an hour and a half. At Bodie, there is so much to see and wonder at that you will be constantly getting off your bike to look in the windows of the old buildings, maybe even explore inside. If you have children with you, you'll be even slower, because kids have a natural fascination with this stuff.

Bodie, or what remains of it, is a California gold-mining ghost town which had its heyday in the 1870s, when it boasted more than 30 operating mines, 65 saloons, and a population of more than 10,000 people. It later suffered a steady and complete decline. The last folks moved out in the early 1930s, and the town became a state historic park in 1962. The park system maintains Bodie in a state of "arrested decay," which means they don't fix it up, they just keep it from collapsing. Roofs are repaired, but floors are not, for example, which means this place does not look like Disneyland's version of the Old West, it looks like the real Old West. A true ghost town.

From the parking lot, you can ride straight down Green Street and start peeking in the windows of homes that belonged to Bodie families. Many of them left Bodie in a hurry after the gold rush ended, often leaving their furniture and sometimes even their dishes on the table. Pass the intersection with Main Street and ride up to the Wheaton

& Hollis Hotel on your left, which also housed the Bodie Store, and its neighbor, the old schoolhouse, with its chalkboard still hanging and books open on the desks. Ride as far as you like up Green Street, then head back and explore Main Street in both directions, making sure you look in the windows of the saloon and general store. A highlight of the trip is a visit to the Bodie Museum, right on Main Street, where you can view all kinds of paraphernalia left over from Bodie's lively past—old photographs, personal items left by local families, and even the town hearse.

Saving the best for last, take a ride out of town from the west end of Green Street, and cross over the park access road to the Bodie Cemetery. Here you'll find the gravestones of those who were deemed "respectable" in the community, while those who were not so respectable, like the town madam, Rosa Mae, are buried on the hill outside the cemetery's fence. The epitaphs on the gravestones give you a good sense of the town's bawdy history.

Make it more challenging: Bodie Road (Highway 270) and Cottonwood Canyon Road provide fun riding for mountain bikers who are prepared for occasional car traffic and extreme weather conditions. Carry water and food with you if you ride here. Remember that if you start from the state park, you will be heading downhill and will have to regain the elevation on your return.

Trip notes: A $2 per person entrance fee is charged by Bodie State Historic Park. A map/brochure is available for $1 at the entrance kiosk. The park is open year-round, but reaching it can be extremely difficult in winter. The best months to visit are from June to October, depending on snow conditions. For more information, contact Bodie State Historic Park, P.O. Box 515, Bridgeport, CA 93517; (760) 647-6445.

Directions: From Lee Vining, drive north on U.S. 395 for 18 miles. Turn east on Highway 270 and drive 13 miles to Bodie State Historic Park. (The last three miles are very rough dirt road.)

103. MONO LAKE SOUTH TUFA AREA TRAILS
Mono Lake Tufa State Reserve
Off U.S. 395 at Mono Lake
4 miles/1.5 hours — dirt roads/MB
steepness: ◉ ◉   skill level: ◉

In an area rife with geologic oddities and dramatic and fascinating natural phenomena, Mono Lake is hands-down the most unusual place to visit in the entire Mammoth basin. With 60,000 surface acres of water and 16,000 acres of exposed shoreline, Mono Lake is bigger than you might expect, and being three times as salty as the ocean and 80 times more alkaline, it's weirder than you can imagine.

Surrounded by the snow-capped Sierras to the west and sagebrush desert to the east, and edged with strange coral-like structures called "tufa," Mono Lake is also very beautiful, which is why you should bring your bike here and take a ride. Although the lake is ringed by many dirt roads suitable for riding, the best place to start is from the parking lot at the South Tufa Area of Mono Lake Tufa State Reserve. If you park there and ride on the four-wheel drive road that leads to the northwest, past the Overflow Parking Area, you get the best and most close-up views of the lake, with little or no chance of cars kicking up dust in your face. Then when you return, you can lock up your bike and walk the Mark Twain Scenic Tufa Trail (no bikes allowed) which leads from the South Tufa Area parking lot. (This interpretive trail gives you an intimate look at the tufa spires, and a chemistry lesson about how they are formed when springs containing calcium rise up through the lake's alkaline water.)

Start by riding one-tenth of a mile from the South Tufa Area parking lot, back up the access road, then turning right and traveling nine-tenths of a mile (heading north) until you come to a little cutoff on your right that is a four-wheel-drive road only. This is the first cutoff you will come to after the turnoff for the overflow parking area, and if you take it you will ride down to a small parking area for four-wheel-drive vehicles. From this parking area, you are only about 50 yards from the lake and you can look back at the tufas to the south. Unlike at the South Tufa Area, here you probably will not have to share the spectacular view with anyone else.

From this point, ride back past the South Tufa Area again, this time heading toward Navy Beach. The four-wheel-drive road you're on will meet up with the improved dirt road to Navy Beach, which will have some car traffic for one-half mile as it descends to the beach, where car-top boaters launch their boats. Navy Beach Road is somewhat deceiving—it actually winds farther east, taking you past the boat ramp, then loops back. Return to the South Tufa

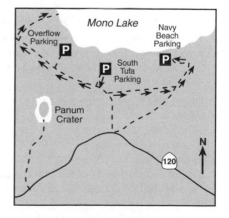

Mono Lake South Tufa Area

Area parking when you are ready, for a four-mile round-trip.

You will see more sea gulls on this ride than you can count, since Mono Lake is the breeding ground for 85 percent of all California gulls. You'll also see desert wildflowers and sagebrush, which turns bright yellow in the late summer and fall. At any time of year, you'll have stellar views of snow-capped mountains to the west and wide-open desert to the east. The best time to ride is just before sunset, when you can watch the surrounding hills turn astounding shades of pink and red, a sight you will never forget.

Make it easier: You can just take the two-mile round-trip ride back and forth from the South Tufa Area parking lot to the four-wheel-drive parking area, skipping the ride to Navy Beach.

Trip notes: There is no fee. Park maps are available at the South Tufa Area parking lot for $1. For more information, contact Mono Lake Tufa State Reserve, P.O. Box 99 (Highway 395), Lee Vining, CA 93541; (760) 647-6331.

Directions: From the town of Mammoth Lakes, travel three miles east on Highway 203 to its junction with U.S. 395. Take U.S. 395 north for 20 miles to the Mono Lake South Tufa exit, which is also Highway 120 east. (If you're traveling south on U.S. 395, the Mono Lake South Tufa exit is five miles south of Lee Vining.) Turn east and drive 4.6 miles until you reach a dirt road on your left that is signed for South Tufa Area parking. Turn left and drive one mile to the parking area and trailhead.

104. INYO CRATERS LOOP
Inyo National Forest

Off Highway 203 near Mammoth Lakes
10 miles/2.5 hours — dirt and gravel roads/MB
steepness: ⊛ ⊛ ⊛   skill level: ⊛ ⊛

If you don't know what to expect when you first ride Inyo Craters, you'll spend all 10 miles of the loop wondering where the craters are. Guess how I know?

I'll spare you a lot of conjecturing and tell you that you can't see the craters from the bike trail. The trail circumnavigates the craters in a large loop, but never goes very near them. You have to take a short hike from the trailhead parking lot to visit the twin craters and their tiny lakes, either before or after your ride.

That said, you can relax and enjoy the ride. Inyo Craters Loop is a classic Mammoth bike trip through cool pine forest and dusty desert flats. Although it is 10 miles in length and will take a couple of hours to complete, the ride is still relatively easy, due to an elevation gain of less than 500 feet and smooth riding on firmly packed pumice logging roads. The key is to bring plenty of water and maybe a snack with you, especially if the day is hot. Also, don't forget your bike lock, so you can secure your bike (or load it back in your car) and take the short, half-mile hike to Inyo Craters when you're finished riding.

Make sure you know where you are going on this loop, since like most of Mammoth, numerous logging roads crisscross the area. The trail is fairly well signed by the Forest Service, although as always, signs can get knocked down. Carry a Forest Service map for extra security.

Start by riding one-quarter mile back down the access road for the parking lot, then turning left at the intersection of three dirt roads, which you passed as you drove in. Check for signs—you want to be heading west and then north on Forest Service Road 3S22. In a half mile, you reach and ride through Crater Flat, a wide-open desert meadow with spectacularly open, almost Arctic-looking Sierra Crest panoramas. The mountains seem to rise straight up from the dry desert floor.

Cross a small creek after about 40 minutes of riding, 3.5 miles in, then half a mile further, cross the larger Deadman Creek. The first creek can be crossed either by riding through the water or by dismounting and walking your bike to the right of the trail, where the stream is narrower and shallower and you can rock-hop across, walking your bike alongside you. At Deadman Creek, walk to the left of the trail about

100 feet and find a small bridge over the water. Take a moment to notice all the flowers and greenery growing along Deadman Creek, a major contrast to the dry sagebrush country you've been riding through. There are some picnic tables here, and this might be a good time for a rest break, because you're almost halfway through the loop.

Continue to your right, paralleling the creek as it heads downstream, and turn right on Deadman Creek Road. What's that giant pile of rubble on your left? It's a glass flow, a heap of rocky leftovers formed from viscous lava. If you look closely, you may see shiny black rock in the pile; this is obsidian, which some rockhounds collect.

Ride east for two miles (the road gets wider and smoother as you go, and it becomes very flat and easy riding), passing the signs for Deadman Campground and Obsidian Flats, until you reach Road 2S29, where you head southeast (a right turn). This leads all the way back to the paved Mammoth Scenic Loop in 2.5 miles, but you want to turn right onto 2S29D (about a mile before the pavement) which becomes 3S22 and leads you back to the parking area. Save a little energy for the last two miles of the loop, as the trail can get a little soft and sandy and you may face a headwind.

Okay, now that you've had a great ride and you're back at the parking area, it's time to see the craters. There is a single-track bike trail that leads to them from the far end of the parking lot, but it's a brute of a climb, especially if you've just ridden 10 miles. Better to walk up the separate hiking trail to Inyo Craters, which starts from the middle of the parking lot. The hiking trail is uphill as well, but at least you're not toting a 30-pound bike.

Inyo Craters are evidence of the Mammoth area's fiery past, remains of a volcanic explosion that occurred a mere 600 years ago. They are part of a chain of craters and other volcanic formations that reaches from Mammoth to Mono Lake. Both of the craters have tiny lakes inside of them, an unusual feature in this barren land. Check them out (the lower one is neater and more forested), read the interpretive signs, learn your geology lesson, and then head back downhill.

Make it easier: Don't ride the whole loop—just ride out and back through Crater Flat, turning around at the first stream crossing, for a seven-mile round-trip. Then walk the trail to the craters.

Trip notes: There is no fee. For more information and a map, contact Inyo National Forest, Mammoth Ranger District, P.O. Box 148, Mammoth Lakes, CA 93546; (760) 924-5500.

Directions: From U.S. 395 in Lee Vining, travel 25 miles south to the Mammoth Lakes/Highway 203 cutoff. Take Highway 203 west for four miles, through the town of Mammoth Lakes, then turn right at Minaret Road (which is still Highway 203) and drive for one mile to the Mammoth Lakes Scenic Loop. Turn right on the Scenic Loop, then drive for 2.7 miles to the turnoff for Inyo Craters. Turn left on to Inyo Craters Road and drive for one mile until you come to an intersection of three dirt roads. Bear right (on the main, middle road) and drive one-quarter mile to the Inyo Craters parking area. Ride your bike back out of the parking lot for one-quarter mile, returning to the intersection of three dirt roads. Make a hard left on to the Inyo Craters Loop Trail.

105. SHADY REST TRAIL
Shady Rest Town Park
Off Highway 203 in Mammoth Lakes
5 miles/1 hour — paved bike trail and dirt roads/RB or MB
steepness: ◉ ◉   skill level: ◉

Here's a trail that is perfect for families, located in a town park that has all the great stuff that parks had when you were a kid: soccer fields, a baseball diamond, a playground and acres and acres of trees. The trail has a one-mile paved portion and a five-mile dirt-and-gravel portion, so everybody can ride at least a part of it, fat tires and skinny tires alike. Shady Rest Park is the kind of place to go with your kids when they're tired of hiking and fishing and having outdoor adventures in Mammoth and they want something more like home. But at the same time, the five-mile mountain bike loop around the outside of the park takes you away from the developed areas and into a thick pine forest, so you can get the best of two worlds in one trip.

Most people start their ride by parking at Shady Rest Campground and taking the paved trail first, then connecting to the dirt loop trail and riding around it, then returning on the paved trail. If you're on a mountain bike, I'd recommend doing the opposite: Drive and park all the way at the end of the paved trail, past the soccer fields in the park, and ride the dirt loop trail first. There is more parking near the soccer fields, and the loop trail is more appealing to ride, taking you right into the woods. Then you can ride the paved trail at the end of your trip, out of the park and into the campground and back, just for fun. (If you're on a road bike, you can only ride the short paved trail, so start at either end.)

The paved trail frequently has packs of six-year-olds flying by on their bikes, so keep your eyes open for them. The dirt trail, in comparison, frequently has no one on it, although you may see people on the adjacent Knolls Trail, which connects with Shady Rest for a short portion. (While adding on the Knolls Trail to your trip may seem tempting, don't do it unless you are physically prepared—it's a 10-mile loop with some strenuous climbs.)

The dirt portion of the Shady Rest Loop is fairly well signed, but when we rode it some signs had been knocked over by errant riders. Since several other dirt roads intersect with this loop, watch carefully for trail signs and always keep in mind that you should be riding in a clockwise loop. Follow the majority of the tire treads and you should have no problem, and remember to stop every once in a while to listen to the wind in the pines—one of the most pleasing sounds on earth.

When you return to where you've left your car, there are picnic sites as well as water and restrooms available at Shady Rest Park.

Make it easier: Younger riders who can't complete a five-mile trip can just ride out-and-back on the one-mile paved trail from the campground to the playing fields.

Trip notes: There is no fee. For more information and a map, contact Inyo National Forest, Mammoth Ranger District, P.O. Box 148, Mammoth Lakes, CA 93546; (760) 924-5500.

Directions: From U.S. 395 in Lee Vining, travel 25 miles south to the Mammoth Lakes/Highway 203 cutoff. Take Highway 203 west for 2.5 miles into the town of Mammoth Lakes, then turn right into the access road for Shady Rest Campground (just past the Forest Service Visitors Center sign). Drive down this access road, past the campground, following the signs for Shady Rest Town Park. Drive past the soccer fields and park at the very end of the road, where dirt roads lead off from the paved road and parking area. The Shady Rest Trail begins to the right of the end of the road (across from the paved bike trail that leads behind the soccer fields). Look for the Forest Service trail marker, which is a green circle on a post.

106. PAPER ROUTE & JUNIPER TRAILS
Mammoth Mountain Bike Park
Off Highway 203 in Mammoth Lakes
6.5 miles/1.5 hours — dirt single-track/MB
steepness: ◉ ◉   skill level: ◉ ◉

When I first heard about the Mammoth Mountain Bike Park, I was skeptical. It sounded like some ridiculous scheme by the folks who own Mammoth Ski Resort to keep raking in more money in the off-season. But now that I've ridden a few of their trails, I'm a believer, and you will be, too.

The best thing about the bike park is that it gives mountain bike

Paper Route Trail, Mammoth Mountain Bike Park

riders the precious opportunity to ride single-track trails that wind through thick forest, often breaking out into stunning ridgetop views. These well-designed trails are a far cry from the usual two-lane dirt-and-gravel fire roads that we're often relegated to. The price for admission is a little steep—$23 for adults and $12 for children aged 12 and under—but it includes all-day trail access and unlimited gondola rides up the mountain and shuttle bus service to and from town. For bikers on a budget, a discounted ticket gives you limited gondola rides and shuttle services, plus all the trails you can reach under your own pedal power.

Being something of a cheapskate in addition to a skeptic, I sprung for the discounted ticket and headed for a trail called Paper Route, which leads from the east (left) side of the main lodge and bike park entrance. Paper Route bears no resemblance to the suburban blocks many of us traveled as kids, tossing newspapers to supplement our meager allowances. Instead it is a narrow, winding stretch of single-track, with a few tree roots and rocks underfoot to keep things interesting, full of tight turns with big tree trunks right at your elbows. It's challenging, but not too much, so even novice mountain bikers can have a good time. Just take it at your own pace. The trickiest obstacles are the cute ground squirrels who shuttle across the trail, always just ahead of your front tire, and occasional deer in the forest, especially on the upper reaches of trail.

You take the right side of the Paper Route loop, heading uphill through Jeffrey pines till you cross an intersection with a trail called Follow Me. You end up right underneath the ski lift; suddenly the views open up and you're out of the woods. You can see all the way to Crowley Lake from several vantage points. The surrounding mountains are crowned with snow even late in the summer. Climb some more until you reach the Twin Lakes Lookout, where there is a convenient bench for resting and admiring the pretty double lakes. If you look closely, you can even make out the waterfall on their far side.

The Paper Route loop circles back down the mountain and then connects with Juniper Trail, a short but slightly more technical down-hill trail that drops you off at the edge of the bike park at Lake Mary Road. From there, you turn left on the road and ride a half mile into town. (Turn left again at the stoplight.) Pick up the park shuttle bus which runs every half-hour from Wilderness Outfitters, the outdoors store just past the stoplight. It's a 10-minute van ride back to the bike park. Then off you go again on your next ride, by which time you, too, will be a believer.

Make it easier: For a shorter route with less climbing, you can ride Paper Route to its intersection with Downtown, then ride Downtown all the way to—you guessed it—downtown, where you pick up the shuttle bus to return. This ride is almost all downhill, but it does not have the spectacular views of upper Paper Route.

Trip notes: Mammoth Mountain Bike Park is open from July 1 to early October, weather permitting. Call for updates on season opening and closing dates. Remember that trail conditions change with the seasons. For the easiest riding, wait till after Labor Day to visit the bike park, when crowds are lessened and the dirt trails are hard-packed. Ticket prices are $23 for trail use and unlimited gondola rides and shuttle van rides; $18 for trail use and limited gondola/van rides; and half-price for children under 12. Park maps are available for free at the bike park headquarters. Helmets are required to ride at the park. Bike rentals are available. For more information, contact Mammoth Mountain Bike Park, Box 353, Mammoth Lakes, CA 93546; (760) 934-0706.

Directions: From U.S. 395 in Lee Vining, travel 25 miles south to the Mammoth Lakes/Highway 203 cutoff. Take Highway 203 west for four miles, through the town of Mammoth Lakes, then turn right at Minaret Road (which is still Highway 203) and drive for four miles to the Mammoth Mountain Bike Park, located at the ski lodge. Park in the large lot on the right side of the road and enter the bike park store on the left, where you purchase your bike park ticket and get a trail map. Affix the self-stick ticket to your front brake cable. Start riding on the Paper Route Trail from the east (left) side of the building.

107. BEACH CRUISER TRAIL

Mammoth Mountain Bike Park

Off Highway 203 in Mammoth Lakes
6 miles/1.5 hours — dirt single-track/MB
steepness: ⊛ ⊛ ⊛   skill level: ⊛ ⊛

The big draw at Mammoth Mountain Bike Park is that you get to ride downhill to your heart's content without having to pay the price of grinding your way back uphill. The place is set up so that you (with your bike) can ride the skiers' gondola uphill, get off at the top, put on your helmet and race downhill on lots of different and exciting trails. You zip along down the mountain, hardly ever having to pedal, then jump on a shuttle bus to be driven back to the gondola to start all over again. It's basically the same principle as downhill skiing, but with a van and a gondola substituting for the chair lift.

Hey, call me old-fashioned, but I believe I should have to pedal once in a while. Taking a bus ride as part of my bike ride seems just a little bit over the top. Riding in a gondola seems almost like heresy.

If you, too, believe that your bike pedals should not be used as foot pegs only, the Beach Cruiser Trail gives you the opportunity to go up *and* down on a loop trail, returning to your starting point under your own power. There's something very simple and appealing about that, plus it saves you eight bucks on your admission.

It's not without a physical price, of course. Beach Cruiser requires an uphill climb lasting 30 to 40 minutes, working steadily and gradually with lots of switchbacks. But it's smooth—it's a smartly built trail of fine pumice, free of ruts, tree roots and rocks, and without any sand traps. It's a favorite trail of local riders at the Bike Park, because it offers a workout with many rewards.

Anyone can make the climb just by taking their time, gearing down and spinning away, taking a rest break at any point. The trail is almost completely forested, which keeps you cool, and there are plenty of ground squirrels squirreling about, running right across your path at the critical moment.

Get on your bike and start climbing on the trail just to the west (right) of the bike park/ski lodge building, just underneath chairlift number 11. I rode this trail one early autumn when there was serious construction going on at the base of the lifts, so the first hundred yards were a bit of a mess. But things got better fast, and the gorgeous single-track trail through the forest made the climb seem painless.

The trail goes up and up and up through a thick stand of Jeffrey pines, sometimes so gradually that it feels like you are just lateraling the mountain, not climbing it, and you start to wonder if you will ever come out of the trees. But all at once, you come to an open ski run and an intersection with a trail called Off The Top, and suddenly the trail goes flat as you head around Red's Lake, elevation 9,300 feet, the perfect place to stop for a picnic or just lay around in the sun.

Now don't be deceived here—just because the trail has flattened out doesn't mean you are about to descend and fly downhill on your return loop. Shortly after Red's Lake, there is one more climb to make, and this one is a steeper grade than what you've been facing, but stick it out because it's all over in about 10 minutes.

Finally you get your long-awaited downhill run all the way back to the bike park headquarters, a long bout of pure fun which you've truly earned by climbing your way up. Be sure to apply the brakes once in a while, though, because the downhill side of the loop is more rutted and has some soft, sandy patches which can take you by surprise.

And when you get to the bottom, you can cast a superior glance at all those folks getting on the gondola, about to head to the top without making any effort.

Make it more challenging: You can ride the bike park's gondola to mid-chalet (halfway up), get off and ride Trail Home and River Crossing, connecting to this Beach Cruiser loop and adding four more miles to your ride.

Trip notes: See the trip notes on page 238. For more information, contact Mammoth Mountain Bike Park, Box 353, Mammoth Lakes, CA 93546; (760) 934-0706.

Directions: See the directions on page 238. Start riding on the Beach Cruiser Trail from the west (right) side of the building.

108. HORSESHOE LAKE LOOP
Inyo National Forest
Off Highway 203 in Mammoth Lakes
1.6 miles/30 minutes — dirt single-track/MB
steepness: ●   skill level: ● ●

A biking trail that is also a first-rate hiking trail is a rare find indeed. Because trail builders often like to keep bikers and hikers separate, hikers often get all the delicious single-track trails that roam through pretty forests and across gurgling streams, and bikers are left with two-lane gravel roads in the middle of the wide-open desert. But not at Horseshoe Lake, where the loop trail around the perimeter of the

Horseshoe Lake Loop, Inyo National Forest

lake is so pretty, and so surprising, that its only drawback is that it ends too soon. The mileage rating for this trail really could be doubled, because there's a near-certain guarantee that you will ride the loop twice. It's that good.

When I first came to Horseshoe Lake, I took one look at the parking lot and almost turned around. The lake was surrounded by a rather barren-looking, pumice-lined Jeffrey pine forest, and many of the trees were dead, giving an eerie feel to the place.

Turns out first appearances are deceiving, because the trail looks nothing like the barren trailhead. It also turns out that it isn't fire or disease that caused all the dead trees, but rather carbon dioxide gas venting up through the soil, probably linked to some seismic action that occurred at Mammoth in 1989. The trees started to die in 1990, and since then more than 30 acres have perished. The USGS and Forest Service have been collecting air samples and say the area is perfectly safe for humans (although unsafe for tree roots), since the carbon dioxide dilutes quickly once it hits the air.

Still, many visitors have stayed away from Horseshoe Lake, and that's good news for bike riders. The Forest Service calls the lakeside trail the Waterwheel Trail, but everyone else calls it the Horseshoe Lake Loop. The Waterwheel designation quickly becomes apparent, though, when right from the start you have four bridge crossings and four unbridged stream crossings to negotiate. The first eighth of a mile is the trickiest part of the whole trail, and unless you have great technical riding skills, you should dismount and walk across the narrow bridges and streams. What the heck, there's no reason to hurry—Horseshoe Lake, at elevation 8,950 feet, is just plain gorgeous. With its sandy shores, deep blue water, and a backdrop of snow-crested, craggy mountains, it's a perfect example of what makes Mammoth a prime summer destination.

After you've crossed the series of creeks at the beginning of the loop, you can start riding without interruption, but go slowly and take a look at your surroundings. While most of what you are riding through is classic high alpine stuff—Jeffrey pines in sand and pumice, with very little undergrowth—the many small ravines that flow into the lake provide a lush green contrast. One small stream in particular, about halfway around the loop, is particularly stunning with wildflowers and lots of greenery in summer. It is as if Mother Nature is spending her whole production budget on what she knows is a very short growing season.

Shortly past this stream, you pass a couple of burned-down house foundations. The lake views vanish as you ride through forest for the rest of the trip. When you come out near Lake Mary Road, you have the choice of riding back on the road or on the parallel gravel trail for the last half-mile.

When you're done, well, the only logical thing to do is to ride the loop again, or lock up your bike and walk it. This is definitely the kind of trip that you'll want to make twice.

Make it easier: Anyone unsure of their riding skills should walk the first short section of trail, as the narrow bridges and stream crossings can be tricky to negotiate. After these first stream crossings, this ride is perfect for riders of any ability.

Trip notes: There is no fee. For more information and a map, contact Inyo National Forest, Mammoth Ranger District, P.O. Box 148, Mammoth Lakes, CA 93546; (760) 924-5500.

Directions: From U.S. 395 in Lee Vining, travel 25 miles south to the Mammoth Lakes/Highway 203 cutoff. Take Highway 203 west for four miles, through the town of Mammoth Lakes, to the intersection of Highway 203/Minaret Road and Lake Mary Road. Drive straight at this intersection (do not continue on Highway 203 which heads to the right), following Lake Mary Road for five miles until it ends at Horseshoe Lake. Drive to the day-use parking lot that is closest to the water's edge, then look for the dirt road that leads off to the right to the campground. Ride your bike down this dirt road, through the group campsites, until you see the Forest Service trail marker for Waterwheel Trail.

109. TWIN LAKES ROUTE
Inyo National Forest

Off Highway 203 in Mammoth Lakes
3 miles/30 minutes — paved road and bike trail/RB or MB
steepness: 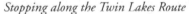 skill level: ⬤

Twin Lakes is the initial set of lakes you come to as you head out on Lake Mary Road, the first of the more than 20 lakes in the Mammoth Lakes area. Maybe that's why they've always had such a strong effect on me—I see Twin Lakes and I know I've arrived in Mammoth. That means I'm about to have a really good time, whether I'm biking, hiking, camping, fishing, cross-country skiing, or just reading a good book in a cabin somewhere.

If you like sweeping views of granite crags, scenic glacial valleys, clear lakes with silvery streams and maybe a waterfall flowing into them, as well as plenty of wildlife and wildflowers, you've come to the right place. Might as well bring your bike, too.

The ride around Twin Lakes is a bit informal; there is a short paved bike trail but mostly you ride on campground roads and the dead-end access road to Twin Lakes. You may have to deal with a car or two, but since the speed limit is only five miles per hour on the camp roads and Twin Lakes Road has a huge shoulder, this ride is safe even for families with small children. Here's a tip: If you come after Labor Day, the campgrounds and the roads are often deserted, and the weather is usually spectacular. In October, the colors of the deciduous trees are so stunning, they can make you weep.

Stopping along the Twin Lakes Route

Start by riding across the Twin Lakes bridge (which separates the lakes and the two campgrounds) heading into the farthest campground. Cruise around, take your time—the views of the lakes and the mountains from the bridge will seriously slow you down—and then when you reach campsites 36 and 37, look for the gravel road between them. Ride down it and you'll find a trail marked "private road, public trail." The private road to the right goes to some homes, so follow the single-track trail to the left. If you're on a mountain bike, you could ride, but there are obstacles and the trail is only a few hundred yards long, so you might as well walk your bike. The route tunnels through a very lush mixed forest, not the usual high-alpine Jeffrey pine forest but a much greener one, filled with oaks, bays, maples, aspens, and dense undergrowth including columbine and corn lilies. The trail takes you right to the base of Twin Falls, where the water comes down the mountain and pours into Upper Twin Lake. Late in the season, you can cross the stream (by rockhopping) at the base of the waterfall, getting a perfect view of the falls on one side and the lakes and their bridge on the other.

Return the way you came, back through the campground and over the Twin Lakes bridge, and pick up the short paved bike trail from where you parked your car. You'll see plenty of anglers fishing Twin Lakes, and tons of ducks bobbing around on the lake's surface, floating with the breeze. You may even see a bear—they've gotten in the habit of raiding the two campgrounds, and one had just passed through when I rode the route. Continue alongside the lakes till the bike trail ends, then ride on Twin Lakes Road, still bordering the lakes, till you reach its intersection with Lake Mary Road. I'd turn around there, since Lake Mary Road gets substantial traffic, and reverse your route back to your car.

Make it more challenging: Many other road rides are possible beginning from Twin Lakes, the most popular of which is riding out to Lake Mary Road, then turning south (right) and riding the loop around Lake Mary, or continuing on Lake Mary Road to its end at Horseshoe Lake. Watch for traffic on Lake Mary Road.

Trip notes: There is no fee. For more information and a map, contact Inyo National Forest, Mammoth Ranger District, P.O. Box 148, Mammoth Lakes, CA 93546; (760) 924-5500.

Directions: From U.S. 395 in Lee Vining, travel 25 miles south to the Mammoth Lakes/Highway 203 cutoff. Take Highway 203 west for four miles, through the town of Mammoth Lakes, to the intersection of Highway 203/Minaret Road and Lake Mary Road. Drive straight at this intersection (do not continue on Highway 203 which heads to the right), following Lake Mary Road for 2.2 miles, then bear right on Twin Lakes Road and follow it for one-half mile, past the camp store. About 50 yards past the camp store, bear right, heading for the small parking area located adjacent to the start of the paved bike trail, by the campground manager's site. If you drive across the bridge between the lakes, you've gone too far.

110. HOT CREEK FISH HATCHERY & GEOTHERMAL AREA
Inyo National Forest
Off U.S. 395 near Mammoth Lakes
4 miles/1 hour — gravel and paved road/MB
steepness: ⊛ ⊛   skill level: ⊛ ⊛

There aren't many places in California where you can end your bike ride with a dip in some hot springs, but at Hot Creek you can. Not only that, but you start your ride at the Hot Creek Fish Hatchery, where you are likely to see more trout swimming around than you've ever seen in your life. You can even bring your catch-and-release equipment with you on your bike trip; not for use at the hatchery, of course, but for casting into Hot Creek.

Yup, this ride offers something for everyone. When I parked my car at the fish hatchery parking lot, a group of parents had brought their kids to look at the thousands of growing trout swimming around in holding troughs. Then when I rode the gravel road from the hatchery to Hot Creek, I saw dozens of anglers catch-and-release fishing. Along the route, several bicyclists happily rode by me, spinning their wheels in the warm sun. And further downstream at the geothermal area, there were all these smiling hot-springs-lovers, floating in Hot Creek.

Start riding from the fish hatchery day-use parking lot, heading back out to Fish Hatchery Road, the road you drove in on. Ride east (left), toward the geothermal area, on an alternately paved and gravel road. The paved sections will feel blissfully smooth in comparison to the bumpy gravel, which can be especially rough if the road was recently graded. If the bumps bother you, remember to stand up on your pedals as you ride and let your arms and legs take the jolting instead of your spine and brains.

The ride takes you through sagebrush country, past some anglers' cabins at Hot Creek Ranch and several stream-access parking areas. You get stunning mountain vistas the whole way, with sporadic rock formations in the sagebrush. Cars are permitted on Fish Hatchery Road,

Hot Creek

although they are rare, since the only visitors are those heading to the hot springs. The route is minimally uphill on the way out, which means a nice easy cruise on the way back.

At two miles in, you reach the parking area for Hot Creek Geothermal Area. Peek over the parking lot's overlook wall for a preview of your destination: A deep canyon with narrow Hot Creek winding through, and three bright turquoise, boiling hot pools separate from the creek, fenced off to protect visitors from falling in. These pools are not where you can take a dip; their water is so hot that they could fatally burn you. Rather, the usable hot pool is right in the middle of the flow of Hot Creek; visitors clamber off a small footbridge and into the stream, where geothermally heated water rises up from under the ground and is cooled to manageable temperatures by the creek's flow. Exactly how hot the spring water is changes according to how low the river is and how much water is flowing through to cool it.

You can ride your bike down the paved trail to the creek and hot springs, but then you must lock it and walk. (There are better places to lock your bike at the top of the paved trail, by the parking area.) As you explore, to keep from burning your buns, or worse, be sure to stay away from the fenced and signed areas that are marked as "geologically unstable." They're not kidding. After exploring around the hot pools and bathing in the river, you can add on to your trip by walking the creekside trail that heads west, passing through the narrow and dramatic rocky canyon.

Make it easier: You can drive you car further, past the fish hatchery, and park in any of the anglers' parking areas along Hot Creek, then ride to the geothermal area from there.

Trip notes: There is no fee. For more information and a map, contact Inyo National Forest, Mammoth Ranger District, P.O. Box 148, Mammoth Lakes, CA 93546; (760) 924-5500.

Directions: From U.S. 395 in Lee Vining, travel 28 miles south, 2.8 miles past the Mammoth Lakes/Highway 203 cutoff, to the Hot Creek Fish Hatchery exit, where you turn left (northeast). Drive nine-tenths of a mile on Hot Creek Hatchery Road (following the signs and turning right at the hatchery residences) to the hatchery parking area driveway, where you turn left and drive to the parking lot. Start your trip by riding from the parking area back to Hot Creek Hatchery Road. Turn left (east) to reach the geothermal area.

INDEX

A

Abbott's Lagoon Trail 101
Abbott's Lagoon Trailhead 103
Acorn Trail 194
Aguague Creek 201
Ahwiyah Point 228
Alameda Creek Ponding Area 174
Alameda Creek Trail 163, 174
Alamo Square 164
Alcatraz 139
Alpine Lake 126, 128
Alum Rock Park 200, 202
Alviso 200
Alviso Environmental Education
    Center 200
Alviso Slough 199, 200
Alviso Slough Trail 199
American River 73, 74, 75, 76
American River Parkway 75
Ancient Oaks Trail 207
Angel Island 137, 138, 139, 140,
    146, 157
Angel Island Fire Station 140
Angel Island State Park 138, 140
Angora Fire Lookout 98
Angora Lakes 96-98
Angora Lakes Resort 96, 97
Annadel State Park 61, 62, 63
Anthony Chabot Regional Park 171,
    172
Antioch 166
Antone Meadows 83
Apay Way Trail 174
Aptos 219, 220
Aptos Creek 219, 220
Aptos Creek Fire Road 219, 220
Arastradero Lake 193, 194
Arastradero Preserve 193, 195
Arcata 30, 31, 32, 33
Arcata Bottoms 31
Arcata Environmental Services
    Department, City of 33

Arcata Marsh 32, 33
Arcata Marsh and Wildlife Sanctuary
    Trail 32, 33
Arch Rock 114, 115, 228
Auburn 73, 75, 80
Auburn State Recreation Area 73, 75
Ayala Cove 138, 139

B

Back Ranch Meadows Campground
    134, 136
Bagby 225
Baldwin Beach 93, 94, 96, 98
Baldy Trail 115
Barker Peak 89
Barnaby Peak 124, 125
Barries Bay 104
Barth's Retreat 141
Bass Cove Trail 172
Bay Area Ridge Trail 207
Bay Bridge 139, 142, 143, 183
Bay Tree Junction 129
Bay View Trail 152, 154, 173, 174
Bayfront Park 196
Baylands Trail 198
Beach Cruiser Trail 239, 240
Beal's Point 75, 76
Bear Valley Trail 114, 115
Bear Valley Visitor Center 101, 103,
    105, 108, 110, 111, 113, 114,
    115, 117, 119, 121
Belgum Trail 158
Benton Ranch 46
Berkeley 139, 153, 156
Berry Creek Falls 209, 210, 211
Berry Creek Falls Trail 211
Bicycle Sundays 188
Bidwell Park 68, 69
Big Basin Redwoods State Park 209,
    210, 211, 219
Big Break Regional Trail 165
Billy Jones Wildcat Railroad 203

Bixby Landfill Park 197
Blackie 136, 137
Blackie's Pasture 136, 137
Blackwood Canyon 88, 89, 90
Blackwood Creek 89
Blackwood Middle Fork Trail 88, 89
BLM Folsom Resource Area 224
Blue Oak Trail 169, 170
Boathouse, The 181
Bodie 229, 230
Bodie Ghost Town Ride 229
Bodie Museum 230
Bodie State Historic Park 229, 230
Bolema Trail 116
Bolinas 142, 145
Bolinas Ridge Trail 119, 120, 121
Bon Tempe Lake 141
Borel Hill 207
Bothin Marsh 149
Boulder Creek 211
Boy Scout Tree Trail 23
Brandon Trail 172
Brentwood 165, 166
Briceburg Visitor Center 225
Bridgeport 229, 230
Bridgeway 150
Briones Reservoir 157
Brisbane 182, 184
Brothers Islands, East and West 153, 157
Brushy Peaks Trail 63
Bufano, Beniamino 181
Bull Creek 34
Bull Creek Road to Gould Barn 33, 34
Bull Creek Trail Camp 34
Bull Point 103, 105
Bull Point Trail 103, 105
Bullhead Flat 136
Bureau of Land Management, Folsom Resource Area 225
Burleigh Murray Ranch State Park 190
Burma Trail 61, 62
Burton Creek 83
Burton Creek State Park 83, 85

Butler Creek 25
Butte County 70
Butte County Department of Public Works 71

C

Cal Trans 48
Caldecott Tunnel 158, 160, 162
Caldwell Park 46
California Department of Parks and Recreation 187
California State Parks Bay Area District 191, 193
Camden, Charles 41, 42
Camden House 42
Camden Water Ditch Trail 42
Cameron Loop 172
Camp Richardson 96, 98
Campbell 202, 204
Cañada Road Bicycle Sundays 188
Cannery Row 220, 221, 222
Canyon Trail 64
Cargill Salt Company 199
Carquinez 157
Carquinez Bridge 153
Carr, Feely & Island Lakes Trail 78
Carr Lake 78, 80
Carr Powerhouse 43
Casa de Martinez 194
Caspian Bicycle Camp/Blackwood Canyon 90
Cataract Trail 141
Chabot, Lake 171, 172
Chabot Marina, Lake 172
Chabot Regional Park, Anthony 171, 172
Chabot West & East Shore Trails, Lake 171
Charleston Slough 197
Cherokee Bar 75
Chico 68, 69, 70, 71
Chico Creek 69
Chico Municipal Airport 70
Chico to Durham Bike Path 70
China Camp State Park 134-136
China Camp Village 134, 135

Clayton 170
Clear Creek 42
Cleone, Lake 48, 50
Cliff House 179, 180
Cliff House Restaurant 178
Clikapudi Creek Trail 39, 40, 41
Clikapudi Creek Trail to Jones Valley
    Camp 39
Clikapudi Trailhead 40, 41
Coast Camp 112, 113
Coast Creek 115
Coast Trail (Point Reyes National
    Seashore) 112, 113, 115
Coastal Trail (Mount Tamalpais) 142
Coastal Trail (Redwood National
    Park) 24, 25, 27
Coastal Trail/Great Highway Bike
    Path (Golden Gate National
    Recreation Area) 178
Concrete Pipe 131
Conlon Trail 156, 158
Contra Costa Canal Trail 163
Contra Costa County 163, 165, 168
Cook's Point Trail 154
Cool, CA 75
Corte Madera 127, 129, 132, 137,
    141, 148, 149
Corte Madera Trail 193, 194
Cottonwood Lake 205
Cow Palace 182, 183, 184
Coyote Creek 199, 205
Coyote Creek Trail 204
Coyote Hellyer County Park 204,
    206
Coyote Hills 173, 174
Coyote Hills Regional Park 173, 196
Crater Flat 233, 234
Creamery Bay 104
Creekside Park 165
Crescent City 20, 22, 23, 30
Crooked Lakes Trail 79
Crookedest Railroad in the World
    145
Cross Marin Trail 122, 124
Cross Marin Trail/Sir Francis Drake
    Bikeway 120, 121, 122

Crowley Lake 238
Crystal Springs Reservoir 187-189
Curry Village 226, 227

D
Dairy Glen Trail 174, 175
Daly City 182
Danville 163, 164
Davenport 209, 212
Davidson, Mount 183
Davison Trail 26-28
de Portola, Captain Gaspar 185, 187
Deadman Campground 234
Deadman Creek 233, 234
Delta De Anza Regional Trail 165
Department of Public Works, City of
    Tiburon 137
Devil's Gulch 124, 125
Devil's Gulch Horse Camp 124, 125
Devil's Gulch Trail 124
Diablo, Mount 152, 157, 195
Diablo range 200
Diestleherst Bridge 45, 46
Discovery Park 75
Divide Meadow 114, 115
Dogtown 117
Downtown Trail 238
Drake, Sir Francis 104
Drake's Beach 103
Drake's Estero 103, 104, 107, 108,
    109, 110
Drake's Head 106, 110
Drake's Head Trail 108, 109, 110
Dumbarton Bridge 173, 175, 176,
    195, 196
Dumbarton Cutoff 195
Dumbarton Pier 195
Dunes Beach 192
Durham 70, 71

E
Eagle Falls 94, 96, 98
Eagle Rock 202
Earl, Lake 20, 22
Earl State Park, Lake 20, 22
Earl Wildlife Area, Lake 20

East Bay Municipal Utility District 158, 162
East Bay Regional Park District 154, 156, 158, 161, 162, 163, 164, 166, 167, 168, 170, 172, 175
East Peak 142, 143, 144, 145, 146
Eastern Contra Costa Regional Trails 164-166
El Dorado Mine 41, 42, 43
Elk Prairie Campground/Visitors Center 28
Emerald Bay 94, 96, 98
Emigrant Gap 80
Empire Mine State Historic Park 71, 73
Environmental Education Center 200
Estero Trail 105, 106, 107, 108, 109, 110
Estero Trail to Drake's Head 108
Estero Trail to Sunset Beach 105
Estero Trailhead 105, 108, 110
Eureka 26, 28, 30, 31, 33

F

Fairfax 126, 128, 130, 141
Fall Creek 209
Fallen Bridge Trail 66
Fallen Leaf Campground 94
Fallen Leaf Lake 94, 95, 96, 98
Fallen Leaf Lake Trails 94, 96
Farallon Islands 179, 185
Feely Lake 78, 80
Feely Lake Dam 78
Felton 218
Fern Canyon (Prairie Creek Redwoods State Park) 24, 25, 26
Fern Canyon (Van Damme State Park) 52, 53
Fern Canyon Trail (Van Damme State Park) 50, 52, 53
Fern Canyon & Falls Loop Trails (Russian Gulch State Park) 50
Fern Grotto Beach 215
Fibreboard Freeway 80-82

Filoli Estate 188, 189
Fish Loop Trail 37, 38, 39
Five Brooks Trailhead 116, 117
Five Corners 131
Five Mile Recreation Area 68
Follow Me Trail 238
Folsom 76, 225
Folsom Lake 75, 76
Folsom Lake State Recreation Area 75, 76
Folsom State prison 76
Foothills Park 193, 195
Forbes Flour Mill 203
Forbes, James 203
Forbes Mill Footbridge 203, 204
Forest of Nisene Marks State Park 219, 220
Fort Bragg 48, 49
Fort Cronkite 148
Fort Funston Ranger Station 186
Fort Mason 180, 186
Founder's Grove 34
Four-Mile Trail 226, 228
Fox Trail 168
Francis Beach 192, 193
Franklin R. Klopp Recreation Lake 33
Fremont 175

G

Garberville 33, 34
Gaspar de Portola, Captain 185, 187
General Creek Campground 91, 92
General Creek Loop 90-92
George's Picnic Area 219, 220
Georgia-Pacific Lumber Company 49
Gerstle Cove 55, 56, 57
Gerstle Cove Marine Reserve 56
Gerstle Cove to Stump Beach Cove Trail 56
Giant Powder Company 153
Glen Ellen 65, 66
Glen Trail 115
Gold Coast 157

Golden Falls 211
Golden Gate Bridge 101, 121, 123,
    125, 128, 129, 132, 134, 136,
    137, 138, 139, 142, 144, 146,
    148, 150, 157, 178
Golden Gate National Recreation
    Area 116, 117, 119, 121, 122,
    123, 146, 148, 178, 180, 182,
    184, 186
Goldenrod Trail 172
Gould Barn 33
Gould Road 34
Graham Hill Trail 217
Grass Valley 71, 73
Gray Pine Trail 63
Great Highway bike path 182
Greene Park, Natalie Coffin 130,
    132
Grouse Ridge Campground 79
Guerneville 55, 57

H

Half Dome 228
Half Moon Bay 186, 190, 191, 192,
    193
Half Moon Bay Bike Path 191, 192
Half Moon Bay State Beach 192,
    193
Hamilton, Mount 195
Hammond Trail 30, 31
Happy Isles 227
Harding Park 181
Hardrock Trail 71, 72, 73
Havey Canyon Trail 156
Hawk Hill Trail 207
Henry Cowell Redwoods State Park
    216, 218
Hetch Hetchy aqueduct 189
Hiller Park 31
Hillsborough 186
Hillside Trail 63, 64
Hoffman Creek Trailhead 209
Holter Ridge 28, 30
Home Bay 104, 107, 108
Horseshoe Lake 240, 241, 242, 244
Horseshoe Lake Loop 240, 241

Hot Creek 245, 246
Hot Creek Fish Hatchery 245, 246
Hot Creek Geothermal Area 245,
    246
Hot Creek Ranch 245
Howarth Park 59, 60, 61
Howarth Park/Spring Lake Park Bike
    Trail 59
Howland Hill Outdoors School 23
Howland Hill Road 22, 23
Howland Summit 23
Huckleberry Trail 217
Humboldt Bay 33
Humboldt County Parks 30, 31
Humboldt Redwoods State Park 33,
    34

I

Ilsanjo, Lake 61
Ilsanjo Trail Loop, Lake 61
Inspiration Point 157, 158
Inverness 118
Inverness Ridge 100
Inyo Craters 233, 234, 235
Inyo Craters Loop 233-235
Inyo National Forest 233, 234, 236,
    240, 242, 243, 244, 245, 246
Iron Horse Regional Trail to Danville
    163
Iron Horse Trail 163, 164
Island Lake 78, 79
Island Lake Trail 78
Iverson Creek 209
Iverson Trail 209

J

Jack London Museum 65
Jack London State Historic Park 63,
    65, 66
Jackrabbit Parcourse/Picnic Area 60
Jake's Island 135
Jedediah Smith Redwoods State Park
    22, 23
Jenner 53, 55, 56, 57
Jepson, Willis 187
Jewell Trail 120, 122

Jogging Trail 26, 28
John F. McInnis Park and Golf
    Course 134
Johnson's Oyster Farm 105
Johnston House, James 191
Jones Valley 40, 41
Jones Valley Campground 39, 40
Juniper Trail 238

K

K Land 60
Kelham Beach 115
Kent Lake 123, 126, 127
Kent Pump Road 126, 127
Kenwood 63, 65
Keswick Dam 45
Keswick Reservoir 45
Kilner Park 88
Klopp Recreation Lake, Franklin R.
    33
Knolls Trail 235, 236

L

Lafayette 158, 161, 162
Lafayette Community Center 161,
    162
Lafayette Reservoir 158, 159, 160
Lafayette Reservoir Trail 158
Lafayette-Moraga Regional Trail
    161, 162
Laguna Point 48, 49, 50
Lagunitas 121, 123, 124, 125
Lagunitas Country Club 132
Lagunitas Creek 122, 129
Lagunitas, Lake 128, 129, 130
Lagunitas/Rock Springs Fire Road
    141
Lake Chabot, Lake 171, 172
Lake Chabot Marina, Lake 172
Lake Chabot West & East Shore
    Trails, Lake 171
Lake Cleone 48, 50
Lake Earl State Park 20-22
Lake Earl Wildlife Area 20
Lake Earl/Yontocket Indian Village
    Trail 20

Lake Ilsanjo Trail Loop 61
Lake Lagunitas 128-130
Lake Merced Bike Path 180
Lake Natoma 76
Lake Ralphine 60, 61
Lake Shasta 36-41
Lake Siskiyou 36
Lake Tahoe Basin Management Unit
    88, 90, 92, 94, 95, 98
Lake Tahoe 80, 84, 85, 92, 93, 94,
    96
Lake Talawa 20
Lake Trail 65, 66
Lakeside Cafe 197, 199
Larkspur 148, 149
Larkspur Landing 104, 143
Las Gallinas Valley Sanitary District
    132, 134
Las Gallinas Wildlife Ponds 132
Laurel Dell 140, 141, 142
Laurel Dell Fire Road 140, 141
Lee Vining 230, 232, 234, 236, 238,
    242, 244, 246
Levee Trail 133
Lexington Reservoir 202, 203
Lily Lake 91, 92
Limantour Beach 111, 113
Limantour Estero 108, 109, 110,
    111
Limantour Spit 109
Lindsey Lake 80
Little River 52
Live Oak Trail 61, 172
Livermore 168, 169, 170
Loma Prieta earthquake 219
Loma Prieta Lumber Company 219
London, Jack 65, 66
London Museum, Jack 65
London State Historic Park, Jack 65,
    66
Long Loop Trail 72, 73
Los Altos 207
Los Gatos 202, 204, 206
Los Gatos Creek Trail 202, 204
Lost Man Creek 29
Lost Man Creek Trail 28, 29

Lost Man Road 29, 30
Louis' Restaurant 179, 180
Lower Gould Barn 34
Lower Pines Campground 227

M

MacKerricher State Park 48, 49, 50
Mad River 31
Mad River County Park 31
Mammoth Lakes 212, 232, 233,
        234, 235, 236, 238, 239, 240,
        241, 242, 243, 244, 245, 246
Mammoth Lakes Scenic Loop 234,
        235
Mammoth Mountain Bike Park 236,
        238, 239, 240
Mammoth Ranger District 234,
        236, 242, 244, 246
Mammoth Ski Resort 236
Manzanita Junction 149
Marin Art and Garden Center 132
Marin Audubon Society 133
Marin City 149
Marin Civic Center 150
Marin County 103, 105, 108, 110,
        111, 113, 115, 117, 119, 122,
        125, 128, 130, 144, 147, 148
Marin County Department of Parks
        148, 150
Marin Headlands 178
Marin Municipal Water District
        126, 127, 128, 129, 130, 132,
        140, 141, 143, 146
Mariposa 224
Market Street bridge 46
Marsh Creek 165, 166, 167
Marsh Creek Regional Trail 165,
        266
Marsh Creek Staging Area 166
Marsh Trail 153, 154
Marshall 100
Marshall Beach Trail 100, 101, 103
Matt Davis Trail 143
May's Clearing 66
McCarthy, Carl Patrick 185

McInnis Park 132, 134
McKinleyville 30, 31
Meadow Trail 63, 65
Meadow & Hillside Trail Loop 63
Meadowlark Trail 174, 194
Memorial Park 209
Mendocino 49, 50, 51, 52, 53
Menlo Park 195, 196
Merced 225, 228
Merced Bike Path, Lake 180, 181
Merced, Lake 180, 181
Merced River 224, 225, 227
Merced River Railroad Grade 224-
        225
Merrie Way 178, 179, 180
Middle Fork Trail 90
Midpeninsula Regional Open Space
        District 206, 207
Milk Lake 79, 80
Mill Creek Trail 42
Mill Valley 140, 142, 144, 146, 148,
        150
Mill Valley/Sausalito Bike Path 148
Millbrae 187
Millerton Point 119
Mills Creek 191
Mills, Robert 190
Mindego Trail 207
Miramar Beach 192, 193
Mirror Lake 227, 228
Miwok Stables 147
Miwok Trail 135, 167, 168
Moffett Field Air Station 198
Mono Lake 230, 231, 232, 234
Mono Lake Tufa State Reserve 230,
        231, 232
Montara Mountain 185, 187, 188,
        195
Monterey 220, 221, 222
Monterey Bay 212, 216, 217, 218
Monterey Bay Aquarium 221
Monterey Harbor 221, 222
Monterey Parks Department 222
Monterey Peninsula Recreational
        Trail 220

Moraga 161
Moraga Commons 162
Morgan Horse Ranch 114
Morgan Territory Regional Preserve
    168-170
Mount Diablo 132, 152, 157, 166,
    169, 185, 195
Mount Hamilton 185, 195
Mount Shasta 36, 37
Mount Shasta Ranger District 37
Mount Saint Helena 141
Mount Tamalpais 119, 129, 132,
    137, 140, 141, 142, 144, 147,
    149, 152, 153, 185, 195
Mount Tamalpais State Park 141,
    142, 144, 146
Mount Tamalpais Scenic Railway
    142, 145
Mount Watkins 228
Mountain Home Inn 143
Mountain Summit 66
Mountain Trail 66
Mountain View 196, 198
Mountain View Shoreline Park 196,
    197
Mt. Shasta (town of) 37
Muddy Hollow Trail 110, 111, 112
Muddy Hollow Trailhead 111
Murphy's Meadow Trail 168

N
Napa 141, 153, 157
Natalie Coffin Greene Park 130, 132
Natoma, Lake 76
Nature Trail 214
Navy Beach 231
Negro Bar 75, 76
Nevada City 80
Nevada City Ranger District 80
Newark 173, 175, 176, 196, 200
Newark Slough Trail 175, 176
Nike Trail 174
Nimbus Dam 76
Nimitz Way 156, 158
Nimitz Way Bike Trail 156, 157

Nisene Marks State Park, Forest of
    219, 220
Nora Trail 143
North Fork Trail 90
North Pacific Coast Railroad 118,
    122
North Pines Campground 227
North Rim Trail 69, 202
North Tahoe Trail Dusters 88
Northstar at Tahoe 80, 82
Northstar at Tahoe Mountain
    Adventure Shop 82
Northstar Reservoir 82
Northwestern Pacific Railroad 137

O
Oak Bottom campground 43
Oak Bottom marina 44
Oakland 156, 158, 160, 162, 164,
    166, 168, 170, 172, 175
Oakley 165, 166
Observation Platform 216, 218
Obsidian Flats 234
Ocean Beach 179, 180
Off The Top Trail 240
Ohlone Indians 173
Old Guadalupe Trail 182, 183, 184
Old Haul Road 48, 49, 208, 209
Old Landing Cove Trail 214, 215,
    216
Old Railroad Grade 142, 143, 144,
    145, 146
Old Railroad Grade: East Peak to
    West Point Inn 144
Old Stage Road 142, 143, 144
Old Stage Road: Pantoll to West
    Point Inn 142
Old Town Los Gatos 204
Old Vee Road 127
Olema 100, 101, 103, 105, 108,
    110, 111, 112, 113, 114, 115,
    116, 117, 119, 121, 123
Olema Valley Trail 116, 117
One Mile Recreation Area 68
Orick 24, 26, 28, 30

Orinda 158
Orleans mine 72
Orleans stamp mill 72
Oroville 71
Osborn Hill 72
Osborn Loop Trail 72, 73
Ossagon Trail 24, 25, 27
Oyster Point 182, 183

P

Pacific Grove 220, 221, 222
Pacific Grove Recreation Department
    222
Packers Bay 38, 39
Palace of Legion of Honor 178
Palo Alto 189, 193, 194, 195, 196,
    206
Palo Alto Airport 198
Palo Alto Baylands 196, 197, 198
Pantoll Ranger Station 142, 143,
    144, 146
Paper Route Trail 236, 237, 238
Papermill Creek 122
Penguin's Prayer 181
Penitencia Creek 201
Penitencia Creek Trail 200, 201
Penner Lake 79
Perimeter Trail 137, 138, 139, 140,
    146
Pescadero 208, 209
Pescadero Creek 208, 209
Pescadero Creek County Park 208,
    209
Phoenix Junction 131
Phoenix Lake 130, 131, 132
Phoenix Log Cabin 131
Pine Mountain 126
Pioneer Cemetery 34
Pipeline Road 216, 217, 218
Pit River 39
Pleasanton 163
Pluto, Mount 81
Point Pinole 152, 153, 154
Point Pinole Regional Shoreline 152
Point Reyes Beach 101, 102, 103

Point Reyes Lighthouse 103
Point Reyes National Seashore 100-
    123, 147
Point Reyes Station (town of) 117,
    119
Point Reyes Youth Hostel 112, 113
Point San Pedro 185
Pope Beach 93
Pope-Baldwin Bike Path 92, 95
Porter Picnic Area 220
Portola Expedition 185
Portola State Park 208, 209
Potrero Camp 141
Potrero Meadows 129, 141
Powder Mill Fire Road 217, 218
Prairie Creek Redwoods State Park
    24, 26, 28
Preacher Gulch Road 34
Presidio Visitor Center 186
Pudding Creek 49
Pulgas Water Temple 189
Pygmy Forest 54, 55
Pygmy Forest Trail 53-56

Q

Quarry Road Trail 73-75
Quarry/Dairy Glen Trail 174, 175
Quebec 203

R

Railroad Flat Campground 224, 225
Ralphine, Lake 60, 61
Ranch Trail 190
Rancho del Oso 210, 211, 212
Randall Trail 116, 117
Rat Rock 135
Ravenswood Pier 195, 196
Ravenswood Preserve 196
Reading, Pearson B. 42
Red & White Fleet 140
Red Hill Trail 174
Redding 37, 39, 41, 43, 44, 45, 46
Redding Parks and Recreation, City
    of 46
Red's Lake 240

Redwood City 188, 190, 209
Redwood National Park 28-30
Redwood National Park Headquarters 30
Redwood Trail Loop 216
Repack Trail 126
Richardson Bay 149
Richardson Bay Sanitary District 137
Richardson Bay Wildlife Ponds 137
Richardson Trail, Warren P. 61, 62
Richardson's Resort 93
Richmond 152, 154, 156
Richmond Bridge 138, 143, 153, 157
Ridge Trail 207
Rifle Camp 141
Rifle Range Road 155
River Crossing 240
River Trail 217
Roaring Camp Railroad 216, 217
Rock Springs Fire Road 141
Rockefeller Forest 33, 34
Ross 130
Rough Go Trail 61
Round Lake 79, 80
Round Valley Creek 167, 168
Round Valley Regional Preserve 166, 167
Russian Gulch Falls 50
Russian Gulch State Park 50, 51, 52
Russian Ridge Loop 206-207
Russian Ridge Open Space Preserve 206-207

S

Sacramento 69, 71, 73, 75, 76
Sacramento Railroad 70
Sacramento River 36, 43, 45, 46
Sacramento River Trail 45
Saddle Trail 182, 183, 184
Saint Helena, Mount 141
Salinas 222
Salt Point State Park 53, 55, 56, 57
Salt Point Trail 56

Samuel P. Taylor Bike Path 122-123
Samuel P. Taylor State Park 122, 123, 124, 125
San Andreas Fault 187
San Andreas Lake 185, 187
San Andreas Trail 188
San Anselmo 101, 121, 123, 125, 128, 130, 132
San Bruno 184, 186
San Bruno Mountain State & County Park 182-184
San Francisco 76, 101, 112, 121, 123, 125, 128, 129, 132, 134, 136, 137, 138, 140, 142, 143, 144, 146, 147, 148, 150, 153, 157, 173, 178-197
San Francisco Bay Discovery Site 184
San Francisco Bay National Wildlife Refuge 174, 175, 176, 195, 196, 199, 200
San Francisco Parks and Recreation Department 180, 182
San Francisco State University 180, 181
San Francisco Water Department 187, 189
San Francisco-Sacramento Railroad 161
San Joaquin Delta 165
San Joaquin Valley 167, 169, 170
San Jose 200, 202, 204, 205, 206, 218
San Leandro 171, 172
San Lorenzo River 216, 217
San Mateo County 191, 209
San Mateo County Board of Supervisors 187
San Mateo County Parks 186, 188, 190, 209
San Pablo Bay 132, 133, 134, 153
San Pablo Reservoir 157, 158
San Pablo Ridge 156, 158, 159
San Rafael 121, 128, 129, 132, 134, 136, 138, 150

San Ramon 163, 164
San Ramon Valley Iron Horse Trail 163
Sand Point Overlook 220
Santa Clara County Parks and Recreation Department 204, 206
Santa Cruz 204, 211, 212, 214, 216, 218, 219, 220
Santa Cruz Mountains 218
Santa Rosa 55, 57, 58, 59, 60, 61, 63, 65
Sausalito 137, 139, 148, 149, 150
Sausalito Bike Path 148
Sawmill Flat 82
Sawyer Camp Recreation Trail 186-189
Schooner Bay 104, 105
Schwarzenegger, Arnold 120
Scotts Valley 218
Sculptured Beach 113
Sea View Trail 55
Seaside 221, 222
Sebastopol 55, 57, 58, 59
Sebastopol-Santa Rosa Multi-Use Trail 58
Shady Rest Campground 235, 236
Shady Rest Town Park 235, 236
Shady Rest Trail 235, 236
Shafter Bridge 123
Shafter Trail 121
Shasta Lake 36-41
Shasta Lake Ranger District 39, 41
Shasta, Mount 36, 37
Shasta Ranger District, Mount 37
Shasta-Trinity National Forest 36, 37, 39, 41, 44
Shaver Grade 131
Shoreline Amphitheatre 198
Shoreline Lake 197
Shoreline Park 197, 198
Shoreline Trail (China Camp State Park) 134, 135, 136
Short Loop Trail 72, 73
Sierra Point 182, 183

Silver Falls 211
Sir Francis Drake Bikeway 120, 121, 122
Siskiyou, Lake 36
Sky Oaks Ranger Station 127, 129, 132, 141
Skyline-to-the-Sea Trail 210, 211, 219
Skyline-to-the-Sea Trail to Berry Creek Falls 209
Smith River 20, 21
Sonoma 58, 59, 61, 63, 64, 66
Sonoma County Regional Parks 58, 59, 60
Sonoma Creek 64
Sonoma Mountain 65
South Lake Tahoe (town of) 88, 90, 93, 94, 95, 98
South San Francisco 182, 185
South Tufa Area 231, 232
Southern Pacific Railroad 163, 195, 219
Spring Lake Park 59, 60
Spring Lake Park Bike Trail 59, 60
Squaw Valley 86
Stairstep Falls 124, 125
Stanford University 194
Steep Ravine 142
Steinbeck, John 220
Stevens Creek Trail 197, 198
Steve's S Trail 62
Stinson Beach 142, 144, 145, 146, 148
Stout Grove 23
Stout Tree 23
Stump Beach Cove 56, 57
Stump Beach Cove Trail 56
Sugar Pine Point State Park 90, 92
Sugarloaf Ridge State Park 63, 65
Suisun Bay 163
Sunnyvale 199, 200
Sunset Beach 106, 107, 108, 109
Sunset Beach Trail 107, 108
Sutro, Adolph 178, 179
Sutro Heights Park 179

Sweeney Ridge 184, 185, 186
Sweeney Ridge Paved Trail 184
Sycamore Park 148, 149

T

Tahoe (area) 77-98, 212
Tahoe Basin Management Unit, Lake
    88, 90, 92, 94, 95, 98
Tahoe City 82, 83, 85, 86, 87, 88,
    90, 92, 94, 96, 98
Tahoe City Public Utility District 87
Tahoe, Lake 80, 84, 85, 92, 93, 94,
    96
Tahoe National Forest 78, 80, 81,
    87, 88, 94, 96
Tahoe State Recreation Area 83, 85
Tahoma 92
Talawa, Lake 20
Tallac Historic Site 93, 94
Tamalpais, Mount 119, 129, 132,
    137, 140, 141, 142, 144, 147,
    149, 152, 153, 185, 195
Tamalpais Scenic Railway, Mount
    142, 145
Tamalpais State Park, Mount 141,
    142, 144, 146
Tamalpais Watershed, Mount 128
Taylor Creek 93, 95
Taylor, Samuel 122
Teixeira Trail 117
Ten Mile River 49
Tenaya Creek 227, 228
Tennessee steamship 147
Tennessee Valley Beach 146-147
Tennessee Valley Trail 146-147
Tiburon 136, 137, 138, 140
Tiburon Bike Path 136, 137, 148
Tiburon Ferry 140
Tidelands Trail 175, 176
Tilden Nature Area 156
Tilden Regional Park 156
Tiptoe Falls 209
Tomales Bay 100, 118, 119, 121
Tomales Bay State Park 100, 101
Tomales Bay Trail 117, 119

Tower House Historic District 41,
    43, 44
Tower House Hotel 42
Tower, Levi 41, 42, 43
Towhee Trail 172
Trail Home 240
Trinity Lake 43
Trinity River 43
Truckee 80
Truckee River Recreation Trail 85,
    92
Try-umph 81
Tufa Area, South 231, 232
Turtle Back 135
Twain Scenic Tufa Trail, Mark 231
Twin Falls 244
Twin Lakes 243, 244
Twin Lakes Lookout 238
Twin Lakes Route 243
Twin Peaks 183
Two Quarry Trail 62

U

Upper River Campground 227

V

Valle Vista Staging Area 162
Vallejo 138
Valley View Trail 170
Van Damme State Park 50, 52, 53,
    55
Vasona Lake 202, 203, 204
Vasona Lake County Park 202, 204
Venice Beach 192
Verna Dunshee Trail 144
Village Run 82
Village Store, The 228
Vision, Mount 106
Volvon Trail 169, 170

W

W.Y.O.D. mine 72, 73
Waddell Beach 210, 211
Waddell Creek 210, 211, 219
Waldo Point Harbor 150
Walnut Creek 163, 164, 168, 170

Ward Creek 87, 88
Ward Creek Trail 87
Warren P. Richardson Trail 61, 62
Water Ditch Trail 41, 43
Waters Gulch 38, 39
Waters Gulch Trail 37, 38, 39
Waterwheel Trail 241, 242
Watson Lake 81, 82
Weott 34
West Point Inn 142, 143, 145, 146
West Shore Trail 85
Western States Trail 74, 86
Wheaton & Hollis Hotel 229
Whiskeytown Lake 41-43
Whiskeytown Lake Visitor Informa-
    tion Center 44
Whiskeytown National Recreation
    Area 41-44
Whittell Marsh 154
Wildcat Canyon Regional Park 154,
    156, 158
Wildcat Creek Trail 155, 156, 158
Wildcat Creek Trail to Tilden Nature
    Area 154
Wilder Beach 215
Wilder Ranch State Park 212, 214,
    216
Wilder Ridge Loop 212, 213
Wilderness Outfitters 238
Willow Creek 42
Willows 71
Wolf Creek, Little 72
Woodside 190, 206
Woodside Campground 55
Wurr Road trailhead 209

Y

Yolanda Trail 131
Yontocket Indian Memorial Cem-
    etery 20, 21
Yontocket Indian Village Trail
    (Lake Earl) 20
Yosemite Falls 226
Yosemite National Park 189, 224,
    225, 226, 228

Yosemite Valley 224, 226, 228
Yosemite Valley Bike Path 226
Yosemite Village 226, 227, 228

Z

Zane Gray Cutoff 213

APPENDIX: PAVED TRAILS FOR ROAD BIKES

North Coast & The Redwoods
Hammond Trail, p. 30

Redding & Shasta
Sacramento River Trail, p. 45

Napa, Sonoma, & Mendocino
Old Haul Road, p. 48
Fern Canyon & Falls Loop Trails, p. 50
Fern Canyon Trail, p. 52
Sebastopol-Santa Rosa Multi-Use Trail, p. 58
Howarth Park & Spring Lake Park Trails, p. 59

Sierra Foothills & Central Valley
Bidwell Park Ride, p. 68
Chico to Durham Bike Path, p. 70
American River Parkway, p. 75

Tahoe
Truckee River Recreation Trail, p. 85
Pope-Baldwin Bike Path, p. 92

North San Francisco Bay Area
Cross Marin Trail & Sir Francis Drake Bikeway, p. 121
Tiburon Bike Path, p. 136
Perimeter Trail, p. 138
Mill Valley & Sausalito Bike Path, p. 148

East San Francisco Bay Area
Point Pinole Road & Bay View Trail, p. 152
Nimitz Way Bike Trail, p. 156
Lafayette Reservoir Trail, p. 158
Lafayette-Moraga Regional Trail, p. 161
Iron Horse Regional Trail to Danville, p. 163
Eastern Contra Costa Regional Trails, p. 164
Lake Chabot West & East Shore Trails, p. 171
Bay View Trail, p. 173

San Francisco & South Bay Area
Coastal Trail & Great Highway Bike Path, p. 178
Lake Merced Bike Path, p. 180
Sweeney Ridge Paved Trail, p. 184
Sawyer Camp Recreation Trail, p. 186
Cañada Road Bicycle Sundays, p. 188
Half Moon Bay Bike Path, p. 192
Dumbarton Bridge Ride, p. 195
Mountain View to Palo Alto Baylands, p. 196
Los Gatos Creek Trail, p. 202
Coyote Creek Trail, p. 204
Pipeline Road, p. 216
Monterey Peninsula Recreational Trail, p. 220

Yosemite & Mammoth Lakes
Yosemite Valley Bike Path, p. 226
Shady Rest Trail, p. 235
Twin Lakes Route, p. 243

ABOUT THE AUTHOR

Ann Marie Brown is an outdoors writer who lives in Northern California. She is the author of nine Foghorn Outdoors books:

California Hiking (with Tom Stienstra)
California Waterfalls
Day-Hiking California's National Parks
Easy Hiking in Northern California
Easy Hiking in Southern California
Easy Biking in Northern California
Easy Camping in Southern California
101 Great Hikes of the San Francisco Bay Area
Southern California Cabins & Cottages

FOGHORN ✹ OUTDOORS

Founded in 1985, Foghorn Outdoors has become one of the country's premier series of outdoor recreation guidebooks. Foghorn Outdoors books are available throughout the United States in bookstores and some outdoor retailers.

The Complete Guide Series

- *Easy Hiking in Northern California*—(256 pp) $ 12.95—2nd Edition
- *Easy Hiking in Southern California*—(256 pp) $ 12.95—1st Edition
- *Easy Camping in Northern California*—(256 pp) $ 12.95—2nd Edition
- *Easy Camping in Southern California*—(256 pp) $ 12.95—1st Edition
- *Tom Stienstra's Outdoor Getaway Guide for Northern California* (448 pp) $ 18.95—5th Edition
- *The Outdoor Getaway Guide for Southern California* (344 pp) $14.95—1st ed.
- *California Hiking* (720 pp) $20.95—4th edition
- *California Waterfalls* (408 pp) $17.95—1st edition
- *California Camping* (776 pp) $20.95—11th edition
- *California Fishing* (768 pp) $20.95—5th edition
- *California Recreational Lakes and Rivers* (600 pp) $19.95—3rd edition
- *California Beaches* (640 pp) $19.95—2nd edition
- *Pacific Northwest Camping* (656 pp) $20.95—6th edition
- *Pacific Northwest Hiking* (648 pp) $20.95—3rd edition
- *Tahoe* (678 pp) $20.95—2nd edition
- *Utah and Nevada Camping* (384 pp) $18.95—1st edition
- *Utah Hiking* (320 pp) $15.95—1st edition
- *Arizona/New Mexico Camping* (500 pp) $18.95—3rd edition
- *Colorado Camping* (480 pp) $16.95—1st edition
- *Baja Camping* (288 pp) $14.95—2nd edition
- *Florida Camping* (672 pp) $20.95—1st edition
- *Florida Beaches* (792pp) $19.95—1st edition
- *New England Hiking* (448 pp) $18.95—2nd edition
- *New England Camping* (520 pp) $19.95—2nd edition

The National Outdoors Series

- *The Camper's Companion—The Pack-Along Guide for Better Outdoor Trips* (458 pp) $15.95
- *Wild Places: 20 Journeys Into the North American Outdoors* (320 pp) $15.95

For more information, visit our websites at:
www.foghorn.com
or
www.travelmatters.com